Conversations with Mormon Authors

Conversations with Mormon Authors

Compiled and edited by Christopher Kimball Bigelow

MORMON ARTS AND LETTERS •

New York • 2007

CONVERSATIONS WITH MORMON AUTHORS

For information address:

Mormon Arts and Letters, an imprint of
Nauvoo Books
809 West 181st St, Suite 222
New York, NY 10033

Order toll-free: 800-796-9721

Website: www.MormonArtsandLetters.com
E-mail: info@MormonArtsandLetters.com

PB   ISBN+10: 0-85051-108-9
        ISBN+13: 978-0-85051-108-6
HC   ISBN+10: 0-85051-111-9
        ISBN+13: 978-0-85051-111-6

Library of Congress Cataloging in Publication Data

Conversations with Mormon authors / compiled and edited by Christopher Kimball Bigelow.
  -- Mormon arts and letters ed.
      p. cm.
  ISBN-13: 978-0-85051-108-6 (pbk.)
  ISBN-10: 0-85051-108-9 (pbk.)
  ISBN-13: 978-0-85051-111-6
  ISBN-10: 0-85051-111-9
1. Mormon authors--Interviews. 2. Authors, American--20th century--Interviews. 3. Authors, American--21st century--Interviews. 4. Authorship. I. Bigelow, Christopher Kimball.
PS129.C68 2006
808'.9212893--dc22
[B]
                          2006032850

Further information about this book can be found at:
                 www.MormonArtsandLetters.com

Cover Design: Kent Larsen

              1 3 5 7 9 8 6 4 2

TABLE OF CONTENTS

Introduction

After returning from my LDS mission to Australia, I attended Emerson College in Boston, where I worked as a cashier at the Harvard Bookstore Café on Newbury Street. Puttering around the store one evening, I stumbled across Walter Kirn's debut story collection *My Hard Bargain* (Knopf, 1990). To my shock, this writer of prestigious, nationally published fiction included Mormon themes and characters in some of his stories. This seemed as strange and unexpected to me as if I'd discovered the *Ensign* cropping up between the *New Yorker* and the *Atlantic* on the store's magazine rack.

Reading Kirn's collection, I found his treatment of Mormonism unpredictable and thought provoking. Sometimes he seemed reminiscently warm, and other times he seemed to be writing an exposé. To a person who grew up disdaining the predictable, preachy stories available through the *New Era* and Deseret Book, Kirn made me see new possibilities. However, his stance was clear as an outsider looking in, and this left me wanting something more. I craved more realistic, nuanced, intimate explorations of Mormon temptations, cultural foibles, unresolved issues, and struggles for redemption.

From Boston, I made my way to graduate school at Brigham Young University. Leaving a BYU theater after seeing *Accommodations* by Eric Samuelsen, I felt almost high with pleasure and relief. Finally, here was an insider exploring some of our foibles and realities in an original, provocative, authentic way. Shortly thereafter, I took Eugene England's Mormon literature class. His guided cultural tour included Levi Peterson's *The Backslider*, Orson Scott Card's *Lost Boys*, Maurine Whipple's *The Giant Joshua*, and several other works of significant Mormon literature. Since that class, I've remained deeply interested in the nature and possibilities of Mormon literature.

During his class, Eugene England introduced me to the Association for Mormon Letters (AML), an independent literary group. I started attending AML meetings and discussing literature via e-mail on AML-List, and before long I was asked to help transform the AML's printed newsletter into a full-fledged literary magazine, which we named *Irreantum*, a Book of Mormon term meaning "many waters." As editor of this magazine, I saw an opportunity to interview Mormon authors of all stripes and feature them in the magazine.

This collection contains mostly interviews that first appeared in *Irreantum* magazine. However, I also got permission to include a few that originally appeared elsewhere, such as in *Dialogue* or *Meridian* magazines, or that haven't been previously published. Unless another interviewer is named, I conducted nearly all these interviews via e-mail, with some of the questions suggested by other participants on AML-List. In preparing this volume, I gave the authors the chance to update their interviews.

Certainly, not every author I would have liked to interview appears in this book. Some didn't respond to my invitations, and others I simply didn't get a chance to pursue during my five years as *Irreantum* editor (1999–2004). What I like best about this collection is its cultural breadth, from faith-promoting LDS romance novelist Anita Stansfield all the way to BYU-educated playwright and film director Neil LaBute, whose dark, disturbing works have rattled even worldly coastal critics. In between these two extremes, this collection reflects many other cultural positions and outlooks, including those of practitioners of other faiths or no faith. Another aspect I enjoy is this collection's web of community that emerges as interviewees cite each other's work and influence.

I hope readers enjoy learning what and how these Mormon-connected authors think as much as I did, and I hope current and would-be writers of Mormon literature find challenge, inspiration, and community in these pages.

Christopher Kimball Bigelow
chrisbigelow@gmail.com

MARY CLYDE

Mary Clyde
Short Fiction Writer

Interviewed by John Bennion

Mary Clyde has published short fiction in the Georgia Review, Boulevard, American Short Fiction, Quarterly West, *and elsewhere. One of her stories was anthologized in* Best Stories of the South 1999. *Her collection* Survival Rates *won the Flannery O'Connor Award and was published in 2001 by the University of Georgia Press. She lives in Phoenix. The original version of this interview was published in* Irreantum, *winter 2000–01.*

An English professor at Brigham Young University, interviewer John Bennion is the author of a novel titled Falling Toward Heaven *and a story collection titled* Breeding Leah.

How did you begin writing?

I liked telling stories to my brothers and sisters. They were usually patient listeners. In the fourth grade my aptly named teacher, Mrs. Page, encouraged us to fill composition books with poetry. My outpouring was the most prodigious of her many near-retirement years of teaching. It was terrible stuff. But I was on the road to being a writer.

I graduated from BYU and went on to the University of Utah for an M.A. in English literature. I didn't write much until after the birth of my fourth child. Then I began with a short short story. In spite of it also being terrible—or maybe because it was—it felt like I'd come home, like writing was what I was supposed to be doing or, at least, what I wanted to be supposed to be doing. It was like falling in love. I wrote with increasing dedication, and some of my stories began to be accepted in literary journals. Thus encouraged, I enrolled in Vermont College's M.F.A. program in Montpelier.

Who did you study with at Vermont College?

The program was structured so that you worked directly with four mentors. Mine were all excellent: Darrell Spencer, Sydney Lea, Francois Camoin, and Sena Jeter Naslund. I also had workshops with Phyllis Barber and Bret Lott, among others.

Who are the writers you draw from?

I've drawn a great deal from the teachers I mentioned. I've learned from Darrell Spencer, both how he teaches and how he writes. I'm amazed at his use of language and detail. I consciously and unsuccessfully imitate him. I've learned from Melissa Pritchard that every word is important. There isn't an *and* or a *but* that is superfluous. I remember her pointing out in a student's story a line Melissa said must have been left over from the first draft. I thought, *Oh no, you can't even have one line from your first draft?* Well, you probably shouldn't. You reexamine all of it. I admire James Agee's *A Death in the Family.* I love *The Heart of Darkness, Middlemarch, Death Comes for the Archbishop,* and contemporary writers such as Peter Taylor, William Maxwell, Toni Morrison.

Writing is such an isolated act—just you and the paper or computer. One of my struggles is making time to write and still having a life with my family, friends, and church. How have you done it?

It's always a huge struggle. Yet it's life itself—family and relationships—that fuels the writing. Of course, there isn't any way to stop real life while you dash over to your desk and make fictional lives. I frequently work up complicated writing schedules: days on, days off, hours of the day, up early, up late. Living always interferes with writing. I take some small comfort from the fact that this dilemma is shared by every writer I know.

Many of your stories deal with illness of the body and the spirit. Your characters include a girl whose nose was bitten off by a dog, two

young women who have had ileostomies,[1] an infant whose burial urn is abandoned roadside, a man dying of cancer, a young man so petrified of people that he hides in his girlfriend's closet from her family, a girl who watched her youth leader die in a fall from a ski lift. These are sad cases. What brought you to this material?

Some of my stories began with my own experience. My daughter has ulcerative colitis.[2] She had an ileostomy. My former husband had thyroid cancer. I kept wondering about suffering, about the consequences of it, how it mattered, what it meant. I worried about it. I don't worry about happiness. It hasn't kept me up at night.

I noticed that in the title story, "Survival Rates," and in other stories there's a feeling of terror about what's outside the cultivated yards—fear of wilderness and whatever else is beyond human control.

Someone pointed out to me that the javelina are like cancer.

Yes, a frightening image. But you turn the bats in "A Well-Paved Road" into something that signifies wonder.

Wonder and freedom.

This wariness about what is "out there" is linked to another aspect of your stories. The landscapes of the desert seem to bear human habitation reluctantly.

I think that's a typical Western kind of awareness. Water is precious. Cactus is inhospitable. These deprivations make the land spiritually important. Robert Frost, a Westerner only in his first decade, pointed out the loneliness of nature that corresponds with the "desert places" within us.

I find that in your stories the hazards of the world correlate with inner hazards, such as when you have the character say in the last story of Survival Rates, "In jumping, we saved ourselves. In the action, we exercised an option; we made an exclamation. We said, 'We have survived.'" Why are you so interested in the act of survival as a subject of fiction?

I'm interested in how we survive surviving. To that particular character it means that while she had witnessed and experienced pain, she was able to do something that made her feel less hopeless. She also feels the sweetness of survival—of life. Surviving isn't happily-ever-after. Sometimes it provokes despair. At first the narrator of "Survival Rates" doesn't look at his cancer as much of a problem. To him it's his wife looking at the cancer that's the problem. He kind of brushes it off. The poignant moment for me is when he confesses he could die. He realizes he's given up more than he knew he had; he's given up the assurance that he will live. Understanding your mortality—that you've only escaped for a while—is part of surviving.

I've heard Darrell Spencer say that one characteristic of contemporary writers is that they begin at the end of a traditional plot line. The dust jacket of your book cover says that your stories "explore not so much what has happened already, but what happens next." In terms of story, why begin at the end, after the physical action?

I think part of the reason is that in life the physical action is often forced on us. We don't have a lot of say in thyroid cancer or ulcerative colitis or sometimes in accidents or divorce. But what we start to have a say in is what happens because of those events, how we move on or how we don't. I was recently rereading *The Member of the Wedding,* by Carson McCullers. In that book so much suspense is built up about the wedding. The young narrator is obsessed with it. Well, the wedding takes place offstage. When we finally get to learning about it, the narrator is on the bus going home. Of course, what happens at the wedding itself isn't what matters. It's what's around it.

It's the girl's response.

It's her response, and before that it's her anticipation.

Many of your characters are stuck in pitiable situations, but the characters themselves never seem pitiful. The stories are not sentimental, the pity never turns into condescension, perhaps partly because you give them agency and hope.

I have a fondness for my characters—a certain admiration for them, as I do for real people when they struggle and find ways to go on. I don't feel sorry for them, even the little girl whose nose is bitten off. There's the moment she makes a connection with the doctor and I think, *Oh, she's going to be fine.* I've never been able to create a good "bad guy" because I don't understand them. I feel that I understand people like me, who mean well but mess up in varieties of ways. I'm not all that interested in villains. It's a failure of imagination on my part.

I think that some contemporary, linguistically based stories avoid traditional characterization and moral dilemmas in any traditional sense.

I think there's a certain condescension in some contemporary fiction, something superior and negative, as if the characters don't really matter. If the characters don't matter to the writer, why write about them? And why would they interest the reader? That kind of fictional world feels empty and seems to imply that life itself is meaningless. I think when those linguistically based stories first started to appear, we thought they must be brilliant because we didn't understand them—an emperor's-new-clothes syndrome. Also they were surprising, and because they were so different they interested us. Now there's kind of a the-emperor's-naked backlash. We want more depth.

I'm interested in the how of what we've just been talking about. How does a Christian writer move beyond pity?

That's an interesting question. Perhaps by definition, characters who have the possibility of making choices are not pitiable, even if the choice is pitiable. One of the characters you mentioned is so intimidated by his girlfriend's family that he hides in a closet. That's a pretty pathetic response. But somehow, given who he is, to me it is an understandable, even reasonable action. And I rejoice when he emerges. I think he's kind of heroic. We all are in our own way.

Even when the characters are not heroic, you make them appealing because you care about them.

I remember when I wrote "Farming Butterflies." There that kid stood, doing that weird thing with the rivets in his jeans. I was worried about him, anxious that he'd find his way in the crazy situation.

I think your stories are full of compassion, of Christian empathy for your characters. How else does your Christianity play into your writing?

I think it does in a number of ways, often in ways I'm not aware of. Someone pointed out to me that my writing contained an unusually large number of biblical allusions. I hadn't noticed. In the broadest sense, my stories contain the philosophy that there is hope, that we can go on.

In your fiction, these moments of hope, when a character realizes she can go on, are quite focused. In his essay "Against Epiphanies," Charles Baxter warns against the dangers of having an all-encompassing and focusing worldview that is distorting in some ways, some times. But, your stories do bring characters to a clear and specific realization at the end.

I'm a sucker for an epiphany. Sometimes I consciously try to get away from them, but I'm never very satisfied because I do believe a story means that something happens. I think the best thing that can happen is that the character ends up knowing something. Sometimes that's not only the best thing, but it's the only thing—all there is left.

The character in the closet that we've been talking about responds to his girlfriend's beckoning by stepping toward her. That's his epiphany. But it's a quiet epiphany—not something earth-shaking.

Yes, and I guess the epiphanies we and Charles Baxter are really offended by are the ones with turn arrows, road signs, flashing lights—and everything's different forever. But I think the right level of epiphany—if epiphanies have levels—is something more subtle, maybe just some kind of movement, a shift in gears, a quiet breeze. And after all, it is the reader who needs to have experienced something because he's read the story, more so than the character.

I think your epiphanies are very humane and rational and quiet ones.

I hope so, because most of life's epiphanies are like that.

The important ones are. They're very quiet.

I suppose we could both point to work where the writing is self-consciously shaped by a writer's beliefs, and it ends up feeling didactic and obvious, not artistically successful. Yet a Christian aesthetic famously informed Flannery O'Connor's short stories. Her work feels haunted by her religion. She expresses a sharp disappointment in man's failure to act according to Christian principles. In my own work I feel as if my characters and I stumble toward discovery. I'm not trying to sell anything. I don't have many answers. But I do believe that man can grow and that belief in purpose is more important to me than a story where the language is everything.

One of the advantages is that more is at stake than language. There is a moral structure to work against, something rock hard—your Christianity.

Some core of me informs me that this is what I believe. I don't think there's any way to deny it. Whatever I do, it's always there, always pushing me.

You offer your characters the possibility of hope through your basic technique; you focus on what happens to the spirit when the body is failing.

Of course, that is where we are ultimately all vulnerable. What it comes down to for all of us is that our undaunted spirit is fighting the decay of our lives. Isn't this the problem all good fiction forces us against?

[1.] Surgical construction of an artificial excretory opening.

[2.] An inflammatory colon disease.

RICHARD DUTCHER

Richard Dutcher
Filmmaker

Debuting in March 2000, Richard Dutcher's breakthrough Mormon-themed film God's Army *earned over $2.5 million and played in more than two hundred cities, including screens in Canada and New Zealand. While Mormon film existed before Dutcher, he's widely credited for starting the new Mormon cinema movement, with independent Mormon films finding audiences in commercial theaters.*

While highly regarded by critics, Dutcher's second Mormon-themed film, the murder-mystery Brigham City, *performed less well with audiences. In addition to other film-related projects, Dutcher has released a well-reviewed* God's Army *follow-up called* States of Grace *and has long worked toward making a biopic about the Prophet Joseph Smith. The original version of this interview was published in* Irreantum, *autumn 2000.*

Describe your vision for a Mormon cinema.

Mormons are a movie-loving people. Unfortunately, our affection for film is rarely reciprocated. With the exception of church-produced missionary and instructional videos, until recently we were left with no films for Mormon audiences. On occasion, Hollywood misrepresents our history, our people, and our prophets for the sake of mass entertainment. Some Mormons make films for the mass market, and some make "family" films, also tailored to a general audience. To make this work more palatable to the public, they water down our beliefs and genericize our unique perspective. As a result, they have achieved only mediocrity. Certainly they have never strengthened or celebrated our faith.

There is one great rule that our filmmakers ignore: The more unique the story and its characters, the more universal its appeal. Consider *Fiddler on the Roof*. Can you imagine the result if the filmmakers had decided to make Tevye and his family of a generic, unspecified faith? Judaism fills every frame of that great film, yet audiences of all races and creeds have come to love its characters. So Mormonism will fill every frame of our films. By narrowing our focus and by sharing the unique stories, characters, and heritage of Mormonism, we will share our faith with the world.

Our people are hungry for these films, not only in Utah but across the United States and throughout the world in every city where an LDS temple now stands. Movies by Mormons, for Mormons. The uncompromising quality, pure entertainment value, and even the curiosity factor of these films will inevitably build an audience of all creeds.

We have a great purpose. Such an endeavor has not been attempted before. The film medium has been used for so many purposes: occasionally to inspire, often to discourage, and all too often to trivialize or degrade the human experience. We, as a people, have not used this technology to its full potential. We have as yet to fulfill the measure of its creation.

Tell us about your background and influences.

If you've seen *God's Army* then you pretty much know my personal background, although it is thoroughly mixed up among all the characters. I was raised Pentecostal and joined the LDS Church at age eight, shortly after my mother married a Mormon. That was in southern Illinois. My stepfather was an entrepreneurial businessman who couldn't quite achieve any lasting success, so we moved around a lot. I spent my childhood and youth in Illinois, Wisconsin, Kentucky, Utah, Arizona, and Kansas. I had one brother and not many long-term friends, so I discovered books and movies early.

Unfortunately, I can't name any Mormon writers or filmmakers who influenced me. When I first became aware of Mormon fiction in the late 1970s, I was already a student of J.R.R. Tolkien, Mark Twain, and H.G. Wells. I read a popular LDS novel—it should probably remain nameless, but I'll give you a hint: Jack Weyland's *Charly*—and was disappointed. So disappointed, in fact, that I avoided Mormon fiction until very recently.

In a similar way, I became aware of Mormons in film when Kieth Merrill's *Harry's War* was released. But again, I was already a student of so many top-notch Hollywood films that Merrill's stories didn't have much effect on my development. However, the fact that he was a Mormon who also made movies was very important to me. In that sense he was a role model, but I was disappointed that Mormonism, though perhaps subliminally present, was not visibly present.

Even as a teenager I wanted to see Mormonism undiluted on the screen and in novels. Because it wasn't available, I searched for representations of other faiths and found my literary heroes in Chaim Potok and Leo Tolstoy, Bernard Malamud and Fyodor Dostoyevsky. Steinbeck's *The Grapes of Wrath* was an intensely spiritual experience for me. My cinematic heroes are few: Ingmar Bergman for *The Seventh Seal*, Frank Capra for *It's a Wonderful Life* and *Lost Horizon*, Vittorio De Sica for *The Bicycle Thief*. More recently, I was pleased and impressed by Robert Duvall's *The Apostle*, which took me back to my Pentecostal days. I thrive on any serious depiction or study of faith, charity—the pure love of Christ—and religious devotion.

There are so many filmmakers who have influenced me, who have taught me by example the language of film. They have taught me how to say what I want to say. But they haven't given me anything worth saying. I've found that the most technically eloquent often have nothing worthwhile to say. Too often their message is simply that evil is good and good is evil. We all know that story, and too often we buy into it. How many Mormons saw the PG-13-rated *The Cider House Rules* and thought it was a nice movie?

My message, my philosophy, my heart, my voice—all of that comes from the gospel, from the scriptures, from the Spirit, from my own experience. I guess in that sense my greatest artistic influences have been Jesus Christ, Joseph Smith, Isaiah, John, and King Benjamin instead of Woody Allen, Steven Spielberg, and Stanley Kubrick.

Tell us more about how autobiography, imagination, and religious elements work together for you in creating drama.

God's Army is extremely autobiographical. Just about everything that happens in the film is based on my own actual experiences. Granted, those experiences, which happened long before, during, and after my full-time mission, were condensed and organized into a suitable structure for a 108-minute film. In this case, I employed my imagination to organize and present my own experiences and observations.

I see *God's Army* as a study of faith and a character study of individuals at different points along the road of faith. And they're all me at one point in my life or another. I've been Elder Allen struggling for a testimony, I've been Elder Kinegar doubting under the intellectual attacks of anti-Mormons, I've been Elder Banks in Carthage Jail, I've been Benny healed of a permanent disability, and I've been Elder Dalton, faithful and committed and perhaps a bit intolerant.

Writing this screenplay was an amazing experience for me. I used to write more mainstream films, genre films, et cetera. When I finally starting writing about spirituality, faith, and my own relationship with God, the actual act of writing became something transcendent and wonderful. Finally I had learned to use my spiritual life to enrich my writing and to use my writing to actually feed and grow my spirit.

I can't see myself going back to the light comedies and romances and cop or horror stories that I used to write. Why? There are so many other writers who can do as good a job or better than I can with that material. But who can make a film about Mormonism? And of those who can, how many are actually doing it?

It irritates me that Mormon screenwriters haven't been writing Mormon movies. I thought after *God's Army* I would be inundated with LDS-themed screenplays that our writers had written but then shelved because nobody was interested. I was wrong. I've received very few screenplays, because they haven't been written. And it's a damned shame for our screenwriters. It says that we'll write for money but not for passion, art, self-expression, or even for our God.

Fortunately, the same cannot be said about our novelists. I've discovered Levi Peterson, Maureen Whipple, and Virginia Sorensen. They've been few and far between, but at least they're out there. And it's obvious from their work that they were writing from the heart and not for the wallet. If it were up to me, I'd clear the Deseret Book shelves of all the junk fiction and establish these LDS writers as the literary heroes that they are. Maybe our new writers would try to meet these high standards instead of adding to the pile of Mormon pulp.

You've said *God's Army* is for LDS people and you hope the film increases people's testimonies and desires to serve missions. How did you prevent propaganda and preaching from overwhelming your film?

I believe all film can be called propagandistic. All filmmakers have a message, a point of view that they want us to accept and adopt, if only for a couple of hours in the theater. They want to convert us to their way of thinking, of seeing the world. A James Bond movie may seem like a bundle of good fun, but if you wipe off the candy coating and look at the pill the filmmakers are asking you to swallow, you may think twice about taking it into your system.

I don't feel at all shy about confessing an artistic agenda. I'm not out to convert the world, but it is my intention to open myself up through my work and let the rest of humanity see the world through my Mormon eyes. If they like the way the world looks through those eyes, great. Welcome aboard. If they don't, that's fine too. At least we've communicated. They know me better and understand me better, and hopefully they know and understand Mormonism better as well.

One of my other guiding principles in my writing and directing is: You can tell any story if you do it from a faithful point of view. Murder, adultery, struggles with homosexuality, whatever. If you're coming from a place of faith and honesty, you're on solid ground. But if you're finding fault with the Lord or if you're accusing or criticizing the prophets, then you've crossed the line and you're in the wrong.

And here is a good place to talk about what is appropriate and inappropriate in storytelling. I don't appreciate being lumped into the category of family filmmakers. That's not what I'm all about. I don't believe we should define our films by what is *not* in them (bad language, nudity, et cetera). I think we should be far more concerned with what *is* in them. And we should be sure that those ingredients are great characters, great dialogue, deep issues, true doctrine, solid technique, et cetera.

Regarding moral content, I am far less worried about sex, language, and violence than most would assume. Again, you can tell any story if you do it from a faithful point of view. It is a shame that our community holds its storytellers and artists to a standard much more strict than the standard to which the Lord holds his storytellers, the prophets. Think of the strong, often repulsive imagery of Isaiah or John. Think of the violence acknowledged in every book of scripture. Look at Moroni 9:9–10. Can you imagine if any contemporary LDS writer or filmmaker wrote of such things? How will I shoot that scene in the great future Book of Mormon movie? I think our puritan views toward art and storytelling originate more from Protestantism than from the Lord. We need to acknowledge this and move beyond it. Some of the great future Mormon movies will not be family films.

By the way, from my own local church authorities all the way up to basically the top of the church, including the Quorum of the Twelve Apostles, I haven't received anything but positive feedback and encouragement.

God's Army seemed to receive as many good reviews as negative reviews nationally. Positive non-Mormon response is typified by the *Commercial Appeal*: "The film is a dispatch from the other side of the door. Like a foreign-language film from Iran or China, *God's Army* illuminates a culture and lifestyle that will be alien to most moviegoers. It opens a

door to an otherwise hidden world, revealing a group that is no more oddball and no less worthy of understanding than any other."

Regarding the non-Mormon response to *God's Army*, I've been surprised and pleased. It's interesting that when we first opened in Utah, some of the Mormon critics made a big deal about the fact that non-Mormons wouldn't get it all. First of all, they disregarded the fact that I made the film for Mormons. It's strange that they thought *God's Army* was valid or valuable only if it was approved and accepted by the outside world. I didn't really care all that much what the gentile world thought of it.

Second of all, they underestimate Mormonism and its dramatic levels, colors, and possibilities. When we see films set in foreign countries or in unfamiliar religious communities, we are immersed in particulars that we don't understand. There is a lot in Jewish ritual that most of us don't get. Would we prefer to see any Jewish vocabulary and religious observance or even their unique wardrobe eliminated from *Fiddler on the Roof* or even *The Ten Commandments* just so we can fully comprehend what we're seeing? It's clearly ridiculous. Those elements define character, place, and themes. They make the characters real, and once they're real to us we relate to them and their stories can touch us, move us, teach us.

LDS writers who eliminate Mormonism from their work are either ignorant or cowardly. Or greedy, thinking that by stripping their story of Mormonism they will appeal to a broader audience. I believe they are wrong, and I believe the lack of an identifiable LDS presence and influence in American fiction and cinema is the result of artistic and spiritual cowardice.

At the same time, I believe as Mormon artists we are far too concerned with what others within the LDS community think of us. Too many of us are worried that if we make that film or publish that book we won't be called into the bishopric or the stake presidency or the Relief Society. There are a lot of bishops and Relief Society presidents in the church. If you don't get the call, somebody else will, and the work will get done. But if you don't write that great book or make that great movie, who will? I always tell aspiring writers or filmmakers to tell that one story that they have been put on earth to tell. If you knew you had only two years left to live, what is the story you would tell? That's the screenplay or the novel you should be writing. That's how great Mormon writing will emerge. If we overly concern ourselves with the market, we're dead.

With *God's Army*, some viewers were disturbed at the fact that a blessing, a priesthood ordinance, takes place onscreen. What particular challenges come from showing the spiritual in a movie or

play that are different from what authors of nonvisual media (novels and short stories) have to deal with?

I don't believe the whole mini-controversy about a priesthood ordinance taking place in a movie should be taken too seriously. First of all, it wasn't a real ordinance. What you see are actors in a pretend situation. Of the actors who pretend to perform ordinances—Matthew Brown, Desean Terry, Luis Robledo, and myself—only one of us actually holds the priesthood. As for the scene where my character performs a blessing, the ordinance was never carried out in its entirety. The magic of filmmaking allowed me to pretend half the blessing, then stop the camera, and later perform the other half. That was how I felt prompted to carry out the scene. I do understand the anxiety of some viewers, but I believe so much has to do with context and approach. Including the same material in a different film, in a movie such as *Orgazmo*, would be clearly inappropriate. But in *God's Army*, when approached in such a faithful and reverent and respectful manner, it is entirely appropriate.

Some have referred to my dramatization of the priesthood in action as "casting pearls before swine." I find that an unfortunate reference regarding a film that was made for the Mormon people, for my people. Are you calling my people swine? If we're going to bring the scriptures into the discussion—and I think it is entirely appropriate to do so; let's bring them into every discussion—I see these same scenes not as casting pearls but as letting my light so shine. We have to show the world what we have that they don't have, if we want them to take an interest in Mormonism.

One of my guiding principles in making this film was: If it's okay for nonmembers to see it in real life, then it's okay for them to see it on a movie screen. Besides, the guidelines that request we do not film or videotape actual priesthood ordinances clearly don't apply here. Those guidelines are in place to protect the experience of the actual ordinances, to ensure that they are sacredly approached and reverently executed. Can you imagine the detrimental effect of bringing a video camera into a sacrament meeting, of poking the doggone thing into the circle while naming and blessing a baby? The distraction would destroy the reverence and the focus of the ordinance. But in a fictionalized setting, especially when the purpose of the fiction is to promote faith and to celebrate the gifts God has given us, the situation is reversed. To not film the ordinance would handicap the Spirit's effectiveness. It is in the ordinances of the priesthood that the Spirit is made manifest. Again, it is all about context and purpose.

But I guess the best response I can give to any viewers who had a problem with the depiction of ordinances in a film is to let them know that I prayerfully approached these scenes. I prayed about them, considered them, and made decisions that were prompted and approved of the Spirit and thereby approved of the Lord. If they have a problem, they can take it up with the Lord.

Some have expressed the opinion that the last part of *God's Army* is overly sentimental in comparison with the more realistic depiction of missionaries during the first part of the movie. What were some of the reasons you felt this was the artistically correct ending for this movie?

It is interesting that, even in the church, we have such an appetite for darkness. Shouldn't we of all people believe in happy endings? The happiness and affection and the acknowledgment of great blessings in the context of the film is simply an acknowledgment of the happiness, affection, and great blessings I've received in my life. I'm ecstatically married, and I have happy children. I get to make movies for a living. Other than my own stupid sins, what do I have to groan about?

I'm not sure exactly what people find objectionable. Is it that a young man is healed through the power of the priesthood? It happens. Is it that two people marry happily and have a family? That happens too. We've been fed so many lies by the media that we've lost our taste for the truth. And regarding the "sentimental" ending at the beach: Did the critics miss the fact that almost half of Benny's family was not baptized, or that Mangum fell away into fornication, or that Laura's father didn't accept the church and passed away without taking advantage of the gospel? Honestly, I expected more complaints about these shadows than I did about the light. Strange.

I'm almost convinced that most criticisms of the ending have more to do with my execution of the scene rather than the content. I believe if the young Brother and Sister Allen and their baby had been in a sloppy BYU student apartment surrounded by laundry and cheap wall decorations, the scene would have played more successfully. As it stands now, the Allen residence kind of looks like a commercial for Maxwell House coffee. I confess that this is one of the scenes I would have reshot if I'd had more money.

Tell us your thoughts on using symbolism and other literary techniques. Specifically, some viewers have speculated on the reasons for Dalton's throwing his pills away, with one person even suggesting that your reason for including this was so people would have something to wonder and speculate about after the movie was over. Can you elucidate?

Dalton's throwing his pills away has a very solid meaning for me that I don't think is necessary to explain. It is a very real act with profound personal significance for Dalton, but the audience doesn't need to know for sure. He wasn't trading his life, however, as some have suggested. That was not my thinking. In a less public forum, I have been known to reveal the secret—but I may stop.

Usually I am very conscious of and sparing with my use of symbolism. I try my best to communicate simply and effectively what I want to communicate. And I try to be aware of all the messages, whether they are overt or subliminal.

But occasionally a surprise will creep in. One example from *God's Army*: I took great delight in directing the scene where Dalton's casket is carried out of the airport hangar and into the bright white light. As Dalton is carried into the light, the door is closed and the remaining missionaries are left in the dark. A wonderful cinematic metaphor. I loved it. And it works wonderfully.

A surprise came to me in the editing room, however, when we were cutting the scene where Kinegar ditches the mission. It was a night scene, so of course it was dark outside. When Kinegar walks away, he is swallowed by the darkness. When I was directing it, I wasn't purposefully creating the visual metaphor. I was focusing on the performances. It wasn't until I got into the editing room and saw the film footage that I saw what we had accidentally or unconsciously captured. It was a thrilling surprise. A wonderful accident, especially as a contrast to Dalton's exit: Dalton exits into the light, Kinegar exits into the darkness. Perfect.

Talk to us about the future.

I'll continue to write and direct LDS-themed films. Some of them will be marketed as crossover films, as niche products that appeal to the mainstream. Others will be made purely for the Mormon audience, so deep and rich in LDS culture and doctrine and thought that they may repel the gentile world. There's room for all kinds of LDS films, and we have an unprecedented opportunity to experiment. I only hope that the infant marketplace doesn't become glutted with filmed versions of LDS junk fiction. Nothing will kill the Mormon film movement more quickly, and nothing will strangle our influence more surely.

PAUL EDWARDS

Paul Edwards
Novelist

A descendant of Joseph Smith, Paul Edwards built his career at a religious university and then in the central administration of its sponsoring religion: the Community of Christ, headquartered in Independence, Missouri, and formerly known as the Reorganized Church of Jesus Christ of Latter Day Saints. In 2003 Signature Books published his murder mystery titled The Angel Acronym, *and a sequel is forthcoming. Edwards's other publications include religious and philosophical works, writings on the Korean War, books of poetry and essays, and several novels. The original version of this interview appeared in* Irreantum, *autumn 2002.*

How would you introduce *The Angel Acronym* to a chatty stranger sitting next to you on an airplane?

I would describe it as an interesting and spirited murder mystery based on events unique to the Mormon movement and the Community of Christ and suggesting some of the deep advantages and glaring drawbacks of Mormonism and the institutional church. It is a good story with believable characters.

What are your personal motives and goals behind the novel?

I first considered writing a murder mystery dealing with the Community of Christ—and indirectly the Latter-day Saints—right after I retired from several years working within the system. I was considering an intellectual history of the movement but decided that it would be a very short book and no one would read it. If I wanted to consider some of the more interesting social and economic aspects of the movement, then I needed to do something that would entertain the reader and allow the reader to consider some commentary about the movement without seeing it as a threat. The murder mystery seemed an appropriate way to do it. Once I got started, I was having so much fun I did not want to stop.

What audience are you aiming for, and what effects do you hope to have on them? How do you imagine your ideal reader?

In writing the mystery, I anticipated an audience made up of members of the Mormon movement, in all its variations, as well as those who simply like mysteries. My experience has been that mysteries are more fun to read if they relate to something I know about. Thus, I wanted to entertain the reader with a story based on, and in, an environment they knew and among persons they respected. At the same time I was interested in taking a human, and sometimes humorous, look at the organization of churches. Fiction is the exaggeration and extension of what normally is unseen or unconsidered. The mystery allows the author to experiment with deep emotions without being emotional.

How do you expect the novel to be received by mainstream LDS readers? LDS critics? LDS literary academics?

I think the mystery will be well received by the mainstream of the LDS and RLDS communities. The murder mystery is an easy genre to mold around specific events and ideas. I think most readers will identify with the situation and empathize with the characters. So, while the genre is not the sort that excites many literary academics, if they will read it I think they will discover that it contains some excellent and insightful commentary about the common Mormon heritage.

For LDS readers, will you give us an overview of Community of Christ literature and how your novel fits into that tradition?

The Community of Christ has a good but limited literary tradition. There are persons within the movement who have written, some of them widely, but there has been little to be considered literature or poetry. The work available has, primarily, been stories for children and considerations of faith and testimony.

This is, I believe, the first contemporary attempt at a mystery focused on today's church that deals with modern and contemporary issues.

In a very significant way, it is hard for the members of the Community of Christ to consider themselves involved in the "outside" or larger world enough to find its people engaged in life. They are not so much bigger than life as they are "other" to the daily human existence. The movement always seems disquieted to find its people in the mainstream. Until that becomes less true, there will not be a lot of literary efforts.

How much of the story is based on research? How much on imagination? How much on autobiography?

Let me be quick to say that this is just a story. The places mentioned, the various roles played at church headquarters, and the bureaucratic environment are public knowledge. And much of what is written about emerges from my own background. So in that sense it is autobiographical. But, I repeat, it is only a story. No characters and no ideas are reflecting living persons or immediate problems. The conditions have been adjusted to meet the needs of the story. In this case there was not a lot of research necessary other than working out methods by which to commit a murder. But in the most important sense, it is a work of imagination.

Tell us about your writing process for this novel.

I have been engaged in writing most of my adult life. My habit is to get up early, go somewhere and get coffee and a light breakfast, and write at the table for about an hour or an hour and a half. I do that four to five days a week. The rest of the day I go about my other duties: work at the Center for the Study of the Korean War, domestic activities, church activities, research, and study. At this rate I write about fifteen pages a week. Some days I edit, or rewrite, or read and decide to tear it all to pieces. When I am writing, it is necessary for me to avoid places that are too quiet. I have never been very good at writing at a library. It is best to be somewhere where there are people and noise, but where none of it is directed at me. If the telephone rings, I know it is not one of my children.

When I am writing nonfiction, I try to become as familiar as I can with the information and read and reread notes that are the results of my research. Then I try and write the total piece as quickly as I can. After that I go back, and back, and back. In most cases, I will rewrite a piece ten times or more before submitting it to an editor. And, once that is done, I pay attention to what editors suggest. I believe that editors are very significant members of the writing team, and an author should listen to them.

What were the most challenging aspects of writing this novel? What were the most difficult choices you had to make? On the other hand, what elements came easiest?

In this particular case, the most difficult thing about writing the mystery was that I was trying to reach a balance between the story I wanted to tell and the need to consider the feelings and attitudes of those I knew would be its audience. I am not sure how successful I have been. But I have made considerable effort to raise some questions in order to make readers think but not turn them off or cause them to be offended.

A minor trouble was caused by the long-term habit of being able to explain things in a footnote. It is often more difficult to write in the explanation than it is, as in academic works, to simply refer to some authority.

What other books and authors influenced you in writing this novel?

I have been greatly influenced by the novels of Colin Wilson more than anything. Wilson writes in a manner that keeps readers interested while informing them of something or other. I have tried to do that. Of course, as any writer knows, the primary requirement for writing is that you read, and I have been reading mysteries most of my life. I am particularly fond of Raymond Chandler, Hillary Waugh, Ellery Queen (I guess I am showing my age), and the more contemporary author James Lee Burke.

Did you write with a potential feature film in mind? What do you think of that prospect?

It never occurred to me that the film industry would be interested in a murder mystery of this sort. I guess I never considered a film. Of course, that would be a lot of fun, particularly if I were allowed to pick my actors. In my wildest dreams I can see Holly Hunter as the heroine Marie, Tom Selleck as the bishop's agent, and, of course, Sean Connery as Toom Taggart, the hero.

What early experiences and influences shaped you to be a writer? How did you learn the craft? Trace for us how your writing inclination developed and how you first became a published writer.

It sounds like a cliché, but I have always wanted to be a writer. I remember the construction of my first piece of fiction, somewhere around my seventh year. The plot of that work was to later appear in a book I coauthored with my son called *The Brothers Crusoe* [Pelsmith-Monroe, 2001]. Both my mother and father were published authors in their respective fields of English literature and religion. Writing was in the air in our house. At my mother's insistence, I have kept a journal since my sixteenth birthday and write in it five or six times a week. Over the years I have taken advantage of college writing classes and, it seems, hundreds of workshops, one-on-one sessions with established authors, and the crooked path of trial and error.

I do not know how to explain it, but I write much differently when I am doing nonfiction. Formal writing is more stilted, with longer sentences, and—I am told—is hard to read. Fiction comes easier and is, I hope, easier to read. Dialogue seems to come easier since I have been involved in some screenwriting. I love it—I can't think of anything that I would rather do. I write because I must.

What have you learned about marketing yourself as a writer and approaching agents or editors? Where did you send this novel for consideration, and what kinds of responses did you get? How did you end up at Signature, and what has working with them been like?

In the last three decades I have learned a great deal about marketing nonfiction and have developed a proposal style that includes a full description of what I can do to help sell whatever I am offering. In most cases it is necessary to know the audience that the publishers seek to reach and to be sure that what you offer lies within the publisher's part of the market. I have published enough now that I usually work with publishers who know my work and who, if the topic is right, will give me prime consideration.

Fiction is much harder for a variety of reasons. One is the strong competition for the publisher's attention. Another is the large number of sales necessary these days to make publishers happy. They are looking for works that will sell in the tens of thousands, and many good manuscripts can never expect that sort of distribution. I have never used an agent, primarily because I never found an agent who was willing to take a chance on me and, less important but significant, because I was not willing to share the small income available from nonfiction with another person.

In this case I approached Signature because I knew the people there—I have a great deal of respect for what they do and for the people involved in what they are doing—and I thought this particular topic might be of interest to them. I made one other effort to locate a publisher and got an offer, but since Signature was interested I much preferred to work with them.

Working with Signature is always a good experience. The one with whom I have had the most contact is my editor Lavina Anderson. She is a wonderful editor, makes excellent suggestions, and can turn the most difficult sentence into reasonable English. Certainly Tom Kimball has been good to work with on the marketing. In this particular case, since I have so many contacts with the Community of Christ, I can be of considerable value in supporting sales in the Midwest and among members of that organization.

Finally, let me say that I believe it is in the best interests of the Mormon movement to encourage such books as *The Angel Acronym*. Not that mine is of any vast value, but because works like this provide an opportunity to discuss and consider things that might otherwise be hard to produce. I am grateful to Signature Books for helping me accomplish this.

EUGENE ENGLAND
1933 – 2001

Eugene England
Essayist

Interviewed by Louisa Wray Dalton

Considered by many one of Mormonism's most influential twentieth-century cultural forces, Eugene England was perhaps best known for his personal essays, which have been collected in several published volumes. In addition, he founded Dialogue *magazine, taught at Brigham Young University and Utah Valley State College, and played a key role in many other initiatives and institutions. He passed away in 2001. The original version of this interview was published in* Irreantum, *autumn 2003.*

Interviewer Louisa Wray Dalton has a B.S. in biochemistry from Brigham Young University and a certificate in science writing from the University of California, Santa Cruz. She is a freelance science journalist in Virginia.

Do you remember how you first began to generate ideas?

I don't remember having to consciously generate ideas. I usually wrote an essay in response to a need or an assignment or a responsibility or an idea I just couldn't get rid of. I guess if there's anything I would advise essay writers to do, it's to follow up on ideas that grasp them, or themes or images. I think the best subject for an essay is whatever it is that wakes you up in the morning, that you can't stop thinking about. That's happened to me, I think, with my best essays.

One of the first essays I wrote was for the introduction of the first issue of a journal I'd started [*Dialogue: A Journal of Mormon Thought*]. So it was kind of an obvious subject. I tried to defend why we needed, in the Mormon church, a journal that was open to a variety of points of view and why that was consistent with the gospel. For me, it was a personal religious journey and a responsibility to think through why I was doing what I was doing. Very often an essay will come out of a controversial idea—that is, one about which not everyone agrees. You have to defend a point of view. So my thesis, essentially, was that Mormonism needed, and could benefit from, something that seemed somewhat inconsistent with its authoritarian nature—that is, a journal that was not controlled by anyone in authority, but only by the vision of the writers and the editors of how to best explore Mormon thought and culture. I wrote an essay about that.[1]

Not long after, I couldn't get out of my mind some experiences I'd had where I've actually given blessings to my car. It seems like such a strange idea to many people, and yet it was an idea that was part of our culture because we do have interesting stories from the pioneer period of people blessing their oxen, which is very close to a car. Actually, one of the best Mormon novels, Maureen Whipple's *The Giant Joshua*, tells such an incident in fictional form. But it is surely based on traditions in her family. Using that parallel, I told about my experience.[2] Twice, when my car was having real trouble, I actually found myself somewhat automatically putting my hands on its hood, and giving it a blessing, and seeing it recover in what seemed like a miraculous way to me.

So those are, I think, pretty good examples of how essays can arise. Now, I've written other essays about complicated theological subjects. For instance, one time I wrote a book on Brigham Young, and as I researched for it, I found interesting passages where he argued that God is progressing, that God is still learning and developing in his realms—not in relation to us, not learning more about us and our world and how to save us, but simply in some way still growing and learning and developing. Now this was an idea that, as I explored it and expressed it, I found that other people in the church disagreed with. They thought that the statement that God is all-powerful and all-knowing was absolute, and there's no way that he could do anything more.

So I decided to explore that idea by looking up all the material I could from all the different church writers and prophets. What I did was come up with an unusual idea that you could actually, depending on what you meant, describe him as both—as both progressing and as perfect, as perfect in relation to our realm and as progressing in his realm. So I explored that and expressed it as a way of helping Mormons deal with what seemed like contradictory ideas, then seeing that sometimes ideas that feel contradictory may actually illuminate. You can transcend the contradiction. You can actually get a fuller vision of new possibilities. I wrote an essay about that.[3]

Another thing I've loved to do as I've grown older is fly-fish. I've found this special place up above Ogden, the south fork of the Ogden River, up toward the mountain called Monte Cristo, which of course has symbolic meaning: the Mount of Christ. As I thought about fishing, and that fish have always been a symbol of Christ, and about the peace that I experienced there, I thought maybe I could describe what it's like to go fishing. So I wrote an essay called "Monte Cristo" about that experience and the peace it led to in my own heart to do something with skill and integrity.[4] In fact, part of the subject of the essay is a friend of mine. He is one of the best fishermen I know, and how honest he is about his fishing. He never pretends to catch more than he does.

Once you've got your subject—something that wakes you up in the morning—how do you focus that idea? Do you do that simply by writing it?

With my arguments or theological essays, I usually outline—I just do a term paper. In my personal essays, it's more of an organic process where I have an image or something that gets me started, and I work on developing that through association or through telling a story.

I think an essay usually works best if it's organized around a story, an actual experience, or a couple of them that are related. Usually I try to organize the essay around the experience and where it's appropriate develop parts of it for more commentary or a related experience. Probably the best essay I've written was one called "Easter Weekend," which grew out of an experience I had attending a scholarly conference on Shakespeare, a subject I've taught and have strong feelings about.[5] It was kind of a controversial idea that he was a devout although unorthodox Christian and that his plays are really a serious exploration of what can be done about sin, especially the sin of retaliation and revenge, which was something that interested him—how destructive those impulses are. All his plays have some element of retribution and show the destructive effect of it, and I think his best plays show the alternative, which is the only thing that can stop the revenge impulses: unconditional love, which comes ultimately from Christ. So I thought about that and I just began to explore the connections between Shakespeare and the question of sin and hope. I just began to tell about that weekend.

Actually, earlier in that weekend I did something kind of like sin—that is, I went to New York where they have all these people on the streets trying to get your money by playing these con games. One of them, I think, is called three-card monte, where they shuffle cards around and you try to guess, and they have some cons worked out. I watched them a while. I watched some of the others playing the game, and I thought how stupid these people were. Then I said to myself, It looks so easy. The guy said, "Got twenty bucks?" So I described that con in some detail. Then I went back to an experience I had with my father. We were in a car wreck together, and I had been kind of low; I had been doubting my own spiritual qualities. But after the crash, the first thing I remember was giving my father a blessing. So I tried to write about these connections. And of course the essay is ultimately about sin and redemption, but it is told through stories.

If there is anything my essays try to do, it's to take contraries, then prove them by testing them out, by following them through, exploring them, and then seeing new truths emerge.

I see you as someone who very easily and effectively fosters other writers, especially other LDS writers. Do you do that deliberately?

I don't think of myself as a model, but I taught Writing the Personal Essay at BYU and tried to encourage trying that genre. When I teach Mormon literature, I offer as an option for the term paper writing a long personal essay, and I hope that will encourage students to try it.

When I founded *Dialogue: A Journal of Mormon Thought*, I established a section in it called Personal Voices, where we regularly published essays that had this personal quality, and that's continued. For instance, in a recent issue, there are two wonderful personal essays. Paul, noticing numbness in his hand, put himself through an MRI and diagnosed himself with cancer. Very tender and sort of hard to read, but an excellent essay.[6] In that same issue a young woman from Alpine, Utah, has an essay about going to the temple.[7] Just a wonderful and thoughtful exploration of that experience. So the essay tradition is continuing.

Among LDS writers, I think some of the best are Ed Geary, Mary Bradford, Emma Lou Thayne, Louise Plummer, and her husband Tom; all write good essays. I think it is important for writers to read other good writers, not to copy them so much as develop an ability to be sensitive to the same things they are, to pick up on the ways they build up.

What are some of your favorite themes, the ones you tend to come back to?

Spiritual experiences, and mercy.

Why mercy?

I wrote a book called *The Quality of Mercy*.[8] One of the things I am most interested in is how the power of unconditional love can change both ourselves and other people—especially ourselves. One of the points that I want to make in my essay about the spirit of Amos is that giving and serving other people is a wonderful thing to do for them, but ultimately it's the way we save ourselves, because it enables us to accept. If we can give mercy and accept mercy, then we won't judge ourselves. We won't say, "Oh, I don't deserve it," because we've been willing to say, "I'll give even if they don't." I don't think we can accept Christ's love until we get to that point of saying, "Even if I don't deserve it, I accept it." So I think it's a wonderful preparation for the Atonement.

Peace?

Yes, peace is important, of course. It's related to mercy. I really think that's the only way to bring peace in the open. I think force always begets force. I think even arguing violently for peace is a good way to increase violence. And I've been guilty of that sometimes. In my book *Making Peace*, the arguments I make there against violence may not be as important as my essay in there, "Monte Cristo," which describes what peace is like. I'm trying to get to a point where I can describe peace because that may be the best way to help people find it. If I can get through the experience I'm in right now, I'd like to write about it in an essay or book called *Being Here*—what it is like to be, rather than so actively doing or changing.

A lot of your essays deal with gender issues. How have your feelings about gender issues in the church changed?

Well, I think I've gone through a fairly normal liberation, through the effect of my wife and daughters. I grew up in a very patriarchal world and church, where men were in charge and superior and women's opportunities were somewhat limited, and I kind of fell into those patterns myself. Even in our marriage, I think I neglected Charlotte's needs. I think I've learned how wrong I was and how we need to combat this. I really believe what God says in the Book of Mormon, that all are alike unto God, male and female, as well as black and white. We need to think through better what that means, until we really are saying to God, "In what way should they be?" and "Have we failed to make them alike to us?"

I think I've developed better attitudes. Whether I've developed better practices remains to be seen. And maybe what I'm going through right now, where I'm totally dependent on Charlotte and I'm so grateful for her and willing to release myself to her, is certainly part of that. I mean, I've certainly felt, Oh, I wish I'd done this long before, when it wasn't because I had to but because I wanted to. I think she is wiser than I am and stronger than I am, and I could have had—I could have done better writing. I could have avoided some of the mistakes I've made, when I've challenged things I probably shouldn't have. It just caused pain and difficulty there, rather than increased understanding. And if I had listened to Charlotte and not published certain things, it might have been better. So I'm still learning.

One of the things that affect me is your description of things that seem contradictory or are contradictory in the church.

I'm very attracted to paradox and contradictions and really believe that one of the great inspired insights of Joseph Smith is one he expressed by saying: "By proving contraries, truth is made manifest."[9] If there is anything my essays try to do, it's to take contraries—that is, ideas or experiences that seem to deny each other—then prove them by testing them out, by following them through, exploring them, and then seeing new truths emerge. And I think they do. I think there is a truth that comes out of the conflict of justice and mercy that is more complete than either justice or mercy, male or female, or God's progression and his perfection.

So many of my essays have to do with an attempt to prove contraries, to follow through and explore what seems like a contradiction and hope that process itself will reveal truth greater than either part of the contradiction.

How does that happen in the church?

I think we are divided, not formally but informally, between liberals and conservatives. And I think it is the interaction of liberal ideas and conservative ideas that can make a dynamic culture. Out of that come new expressions, new ideas, new thoughts, and tolerance. If we learn to do that with tolerance for each other, that itself is a new truth. I've constantly tried to help Mormons get over using those as labels, name-calling, demonizing each other, and simply recognize them as descriptive. Liberals tend to have a certain kind of approach to life, an interest in freedom and expression and various things, and progress, whereas conservatives have another set of interests they value. It's not wrong; it's different. They are interested in stability, in tradition, and those are great values. And if we didn't have one or the other, we'd be in a lot of trouble.

---

1. "The Possibility of Dialogue: A Personal View," *Dialogue* 1:1 (spring 1966): 8–11.
2. "Blessing the Chevrolet," *Dialogue* 9:3 (Autumn 1974): 57–60.
3. "Perfection and Progression: Two Ways to Talk About God," *BYU Studies* 29:3 (1989): 31–47.
4. *Making Peace: Personal Essays*, Salt Lake City, UT: Signature Books, 1995: 203–22.
5. *Dialogue*, 21:1 (spring 1988): 19–30.
6. Paul R. Cazier, "Stealing the Reaper's Grim: The Challenge of Dying Well," 32:4 (Winter 1999): 115–46.
7. Sheryl Cragun Dame, "Hosannah," 32:4 (Winter 1999): 147–57.
8. Salt Lake City: Bookcraft, 1992.
9. *History of the Church* 6:428.

BRIAN EVENSON

Brian Evenson
Fiction Writer

Interviewed by Todd Robert Petersen

Brian Evenson's short fiction has appeared in several collections and numerous literary journals. In addition, he has published novels and poetry translations and written an opera libretto and two radio plays that were adapted for the stage. Evenson received a National Endowment for the Arts grant, and in 1998 he was awarded an O. Henry Award for his short story "Two Brothers." With a Ph.D. in literature and critical theory from the University of Washington, he has taught at several schools—including Brigham Young University, which he left due to controversy over his writings—and now teaches at Brown University. This interview originally appeared in Irreantum, summer 2001; Evenson states that his thinking has evolved and changed in the meantime.

Interviewer Todd Robert Petersen received a Ph.D. in creative writing and critical theory from Oklahoma State University and teaches at Southern Utah University. He has published work in several literary journals.

I'd like to begin by quoting a previous interview you did with the writer Ben Marcus, in which you assert the following about yourself: "As a writer, I gather a useful tension from the fact that I am a believer, but that belief becomes imperceptible in my prose. I don't know why . . . I don't think that writing, real writing, has much to do with affirming belief—if anything it causes rifts and gaps in belief which make belief more complex and more textured, more real. Good writing unsettles, destroys both the author and the reader." Could you expand on that?

It's grounded in a notion of what writing does. There is a camp that sees writing as mimetic, as describing the real, another that sees writing as trying to convey a message or theme or point, another that sees it as necessarily a product of its time. There is another that sees writing as anarchic, a challenge not only to the notions of order and restraint that impose themselves onto the real but a challenge to the real itself. I have most sympathy with the last camp, though I don't think I fit into any camp completely. Writing, if it is going to be effective, will challenge standard notions of belief. It will tear open gaps and holes where there are weaknesses in the fabric, will call into question received knowledge. But I also think that such writing is finally an affirmation almost in spite of itself. It tears holes, leaves you gutted, but lets you know what won't be torn. It makes things more complex for writer and reader, allows both to move out of the artificial world of Pollyanna.

Can writing work the way other experiences work? There is a habit in the church of loving grief and strife because they are all supposedly for our good and experience. Is the same thing true of literature?

Do you mean the same sort of thing as "Adversity can make you stronger"?

Basically.

Yeah, I suppose so. The one thing to remember about adversity is that it can make you stronger or it can kill you. I think loving strife and grief because they're for our good and experience is a way of saying, "Strife and grief aren't really strife and grief; they're symbols of something else, of experience; let's make them significant, process them into something less threatening." I'm very dubious of symbols, especially symbols that mask the objects that are used to convey them. I think strife and grief are most useful when they're perceived first and foremost as strife and grief, as not signifying something else, and we fully understand their potential to destroy us. If you can process them after that into faith, I think it's a much more durable faith.

Can literature function at all as a kind of training for adversity?

I don't know. It can in a way, but I think that to see it as exclusively that would really ignore almost everything I see as interesting about literature.

What does interest you about literature?

I'm interested in literature that is transgressive, that crosses boundaries and challenges its readers' sense of self, takes its readers apart and doesn't put them all the way back together again. I mistrust literature that has a kind of revelation or salvation at the end. I like fiction that is conscious of form, very careful and accurate in its use of language, well written. I like fiction that addresses serious ontological and epistemological questions but doesn't offer resolutions. Those things seem different than seeing literature as a preparation for adversity. I guess I see the literary experience itself as potentially a kind of adversity, though an adversity shot through with many other pleasures—a challenge in and of itself rather than a preparation for a challenge. Finally, literature can be more productively challenging than anything in life.

How do you think the contemporary literary establishment views writers with any kind of religious affiliation?

It depends on a great many factors. There has been a kind of notion that books about religion are interesting to people and they sell, but the work that gets designated as religious is pretty abysmal. I'm thinking of things like the *Book of Virtues* or Orrin Hatch's "I affirm my faith in Christ for political reasons" book. If I were in charge of sending people to hell, those two would be among the first to go. You might also add Paul Coelho's pseudo-religious pseudo-mystic claptrap, Og Mandino's *Greatest Salesman*, the majority of the Mormon historical novel series, and the unconsidered tales gathered in *Especially for Mormons*.

The flap copy for my novel *Altmann's Tongue* spoke about my Mormonism, which caused some readers to scratch their heads. "Hey, this guy's Mormon, but look at what he's doing here. That doesn't seem Mormon." That's a result, I think, of a simplistic idea of what "Mormon writing" is, an idea very much alive still at Brigham Young University. It's one of those ideas that protect us from the truth of things, shuttling us elsewhere, away from thought. At that point you have the choice of either deciding "This can't possibly be a Mormon book" or you can think "What does this text reveal to me about the interplay of writing and religion that I didn't know before? How does it challenge me to reconsider my own notions about religion?" I think that idea of challenge is still very central to many of the stories I've published.

You know, I think the literary establishment rejects religious writing when they see it as the equivalent of missionary work. Otherwise, there's a certain interest about morality in writing that goes back to Flannery O'Connor, to

Dostoyevsky. In contemporary American fiction, because of O'Connor, there is a belief that religion can be a productive part of a writer's experience—not only as background but in the process of composition. So even though I think there are very few writers who are genuinely engaged with religion, I don't think it's necessarily rejected out of hand.

People have found the same incongruities that you mentioned in Neil LaBute (i.e. "He's Mormon, but there are these horrible things going on in these stories"). It seems like a much more interesting dynamic in the long run than a direct match between the writer and what is written. More often than not, with writers of some religious affinity, people seem to want their lives and work to coincide. This seems like an oversimplification to me, one that benefits readers very little and writers not at all. LaBute is most fascinating to me when I can think, "Okay, this guy is Mormon; what is he trying to tell me?" This kind of approach opens up his work and his Mormonism in new ways. Nevertheless, there are certain successful religious writers like Andre Dubus, who is sometimes right on the money and other times he's saccharine.

Dubus is certainly one who sometimes writes about religious issues quite well, though he too often ends up trading in a religious belief for showboating and sentimentality. I think the more overtly religious stories are not always successful, but a story like "Killings"[1] has genuine religious feeling. I guess what I object to is when religion becomes an excuse to be sentimental.

I should say that people like Dubus and O'Connor, even though they are respected, are exceptions; there aren't a lot of writers like them. I see traditionally a lot of writers who consider themselves atheists who also see themselves as being very interested in ethics. I think that Sartre, for instance, is very interesting in this respect. There are contemporary writers today who have similar interests, but at the same time I think there hasn't been as much genuine interest in ethics or morality, partly because of the superficial emphasis put on ethics back in the fifties and the sixties. The search for Christ figures that went on in fifties and sixties criticism—and which continued at BYU through the time when I was in school in the eighties—was morally motivated, but it was also misdirected, superficial. I think that the drift away from morality and ethics is part of the literary process; there is a kind of turning away that takes place. There's likely to be a turning back at some point, hopefully in more genuine and deep terms.

You know, a lot of people—a lot of Mormons, a lot of writers—are comfortable in ways that impede their ability to be ethical. I think if you reach a point where you're comfortable in a certain way—maybe you don't want to have that kind of a challenge, you don't want to listen to either inner necessity or exterior necessity—that's when you stop talking about ethics and probably also when you stop being ethical.

One of the things that strikes me about that idea of comfort is that, once upon a time, Mormons were a hunted people—you know, with the exterminating order and so forth. Now we're the über-suburbanites, at least in the popular imagination. I wonder if American Mormons aren't too comfortable to consider ethical and social issues with any real intensity.

One of the things that has been very damaging to the creation of a Mormon literature is that in the last twenty years Mormonism has been doing everything it can to move into the mainstream, not only to integrate itself but to ingratiate itself to middle America. When we were hunted, at least we knew who we were. The last few decades have seen a church leadership that seems compelled to make us into a sort of product, to package the religion. Though I know they have good motives, I think this is a huge mistake. In most ways, Mormons are on the way to losing their cultural identity. I think that's one thing that makes the ethical issues less interesting or compelling in Mormon writers then they could be.

You have claimed that "for most Mormon writers, religious belief comes into the literary work superficially—the situations are Mormon, the responses are didactic, the stories are meant to teach easy lessons." What would a subtler and less didactic Mormon literature look like?

First, I don't think good literature is primarily, or even secondarily, didactic. I don't think good literature primarily conveys information; I think it allows the reader to enter into an experience. I wish Mormon writers would stop trying to teach and just write; if you do so but still have something to teach, it'll come out subconsciously, much more naturally, much less woodenly, integrated in the prose. I'm of the opinion that if you really believe something, it will be integrated deeply into your patterns of thinking, and no matter what you do, you won't be able to keep it from expressing itself in one way or another. If you resist expressing it directly, it will express itself subtly, in a way that will reveal qualities of which you were previously unaware. I think that people, through their actions and words, eventually reveal who they are, no matter what they profess on the outside. I guess what I see in most Mormon literature is stories pushing easy lessons that have a kind of Sunday school response, which is a certain set of answers that never change from year to year. You can go into the worst Sunday school classes sometimes, where a question is raised by the instructor; someone raises a response to that, a kind of objection; and someone raises a counter-response. At some point you realize that this is the same thing you heard when you were twelve; people aren't thinking, just regurgitating rote information. We're reading from an internalized script that is keeping us from having to think. That's not something I intend to participate in.

It's those easy responses that I think an effective and subtle Mormon literature would really have to work against. It will require a willingness to just let itself be Mormon. If you write and you're Mormon and you honestly believe, it's going to be relevant to the "Mormon experience" even if it seems far away from that according to superficial consideration. I think Mormon writing has less to do with making statements about Mormonism than it does with having something integrally Mormon about it. It is Mormon in terms of the way language is handled, in terms of the way the words exist on the page.

Even the Sunday school manuals make some attempt to override the reflex responses you just mentioned, so there must be some recognition in Salt Lake that these thoughtless responses are a problem.

Yes, but at the same time we cycle through those manuals every four years, so you're right, there's a certain progress made, but it's progress that's made within the constraints, within the system of repetition. The attempt to override gets worked into the reflex action after a few years. It's the system that's dogmatic. I think that system, which has nothing to do with the gospel—even is counter-gospel in some senses—needs to be called into question.

There could also be that differential between the church and the members and the leadership at play as well.

That might be true, but I think you give people too much credit. You might have introductory classes that are more guided, but I think you reach a point where the best thing to be done would be to get rid of all manuals and say, "All right, you have your scriptures, get together in a group and figure some stuff out." It would be messier, but you'd start to have genuine discussions about things. Of course, if you're the kind of person who wants everything consistent and dogmatic, you live in dire fear of genuine discussion.

Eugene England argues in his preface to *Tending the Garden: Essays on Mormon Literature* that "Mormon theology . . . encourages a remarkable and fruitful openness in relation to current controversies about the nature and power of language—and thus of human thought and literature." Is he right?

Well, I think it's wishful thinking on Eugene's part. I think there is a certain openness available, but I don't necessarily think that it's a remarkable one or even a fruitful one. Plus, I think the openness is only rarely drawn upon. I think what Eugene would like to do, and I agree with him in this, is try to force it to be more open than it actually is. Language is a powerful device; if it is to be effective it must continue to grow and develop.

I guess one other thing I would also say has to do with the prohibition on R-rated movies we have in Mormon culture. There is an acknowledgment there that a certain type of imagery, or a certain type of language when it is coupled with certain images, is powerful, but because it is powerful it is also something to be avoided. I think that sort of power equates with immorality for some Mormons. So you have people who end up going to see mindless movies because they're PG-13 rather than going to see something that is genuinely challenging and interesting and provocative, like Neil LaBute's movies. The PG-13 movie isn't going to do anything for you one way or the other; Neil LaBute's movie, on the other hand, might make you reconsider life. It's those kinds of easy solutions, those blanket rules, that work against thought. It's a problem related to the problem with the Sunday school manuals.

Mormon leaders in the early days of the church had a pretty good knowledge of what was going on in literature. I think that's changed—a lot. I think that the interests of the church leaders have moved away from good books generally. That's not true with all of them, but I also think that those few who still read tilt toward the nineteenth century. There are very few leaders who look actively into twentieth-century works that are interesting.

There is one General Authority who quotes T.S. Eliot from the pulpit in general conference and another who thinks that William E. Hinley's "Invictus" is the greatest poem ever written. In fact, Joseph F. Smith, Orson F. Whitney, and Boyd K. Packer have all quoted from that pretty terrible poem, some on more than one occasion.

Well, okay, T.S. Eliot, who was born in the nineteenth century and died a year before I was born. That's a start. But can't we do any better than that? What about what's gone on in the last forty years?

Lyotard says in his essay "What Is Postmodernism?" that "a postmodern artist or writer is in the position of a philosopher: the text he writes, the work he produces are not in principle governed by preestablished rules, and they cannot be judged according to a determining judgment, by applying familiar categories to the text or to the work. Those rules and categories are what the work of art itself is looking for. The artist and the writer, then, are working without rules in order to formulate the rules of what will have been done."[2] Is there any way, in your opinion, for a faithful Mormon to be truly postmodern or avant-garde?

One can have preestablished rules in one's life, and one can live according to a certain moral code and still have quite a bit of openness in a text. With the Mormon emphasis on choice, making choices, I would think the Mormon writer would feel compelled to write an open text rather than a closed one. You can bring a set of rules to a text and impose them on it, or you can leave enough openness that the formulation of the text may lead you to a new series of possibilities. That's something that Bakhtin discusses in *Problems of Dostoevsky's Poetics*.[3]

He talks about introducing, within the work itself, different ideas without controlling or managing them in advance. In a dialogic text, different ideas, different utterances will knock against one another, will be expressed fully, allowed to live and breathe. In a monologic text, an author imposes a meaning upon a text. I am much more partial to texts that are highly dialogic.

It appears to me that at least one of the concerns for writers who are trying to be faithful and progressive is that an equation is drawn between an artist's work and their life. It seems that many within the church who are trying both to chastise the vagaries of artists and, in some cases, lay a critical hand to their work see the work itself as equal to or coinciding with the life.

I believe in what I do, and I don't want to avoid any kind of responsibility at all for that, but there's not a one-to-one equation between life and art. One lives according to a certain moral code, but if I live by that code and am comfortable with it, why shouldn't I try to understand the whole range of codes that people live by? I see the work of art as engaged in a dialogue with a reader, completed by the reader. It allows a certain interaction to take place with readers that makes them rethink aspects of their beliefs or aspects of their lives, but I think it is a productive rethinking, finally.

In an essay entitled "Art and Morality," D.H. Lawrence said, "What an apple looks like to an urchin, to a thrush, to a browsing cow, to Sir Isaac Newton, to a caterpillar, to a hornet, to a mackerel who finds one bobbing in the sea, I leave you to conjecture. But the All-Seeing must have mackerel's eyes, as well as a man's,"[4] which is his way of showing us the pride in thinking that the human way of seeing things is the way things are. Thus to shade things in a particular way, even against the way that they are, is to do some violence and injustice to God's vision of things.

The notion that Mormons should look at the happy side of things is incredibly damaging. A good percentage of the world as a whole, but especially Mormons, go through their life never really thinking much about what they really believe, or thinking about it only along predetermined channels. I think that a good Mormon literature would have to push readers beyond that. It's not going to be something like: "Here's a guy. He has some doubts—oh, he prays—oh, it's okay, now it's all right. Maybe he still has some doubts but he can handle them. He's going to be all right." These preformulated situations are no good. Good literature has to take the risk of destroying both characters and readers. I think that's what it comes down to. You put a person in a position where they have to make a choice about what they think. That strikes me as a moral act.

If you go a little into Mormon doctrine, a person can argue that a literature like you've been describing is much more like the plan of salvation that Mormons are forever talking about: There was this choice to come; we knew there would be a risk; we proceeded with full knowledge that everyone who was to come to the earth would not make it back. Agency in this form somehow took priority over enslavement even if it couldn't guarantee one-hundred-percent results. It doesn't seem to have gone that way with literature in Mormon culture.

No, it hasn't.

D.H. Lawrence saw morality in fiction as a function of the author's honesty with his material. In his essay "Morality and the Novel," he says that "morality in the novel is the trembling instability of the balance [of the world at large and the author's predispositions]. When the novelist puts his thumb in the scale, to pull down the balance to his own predilection, that is immorality."[5] Have Mormon novelists, Mormon writers, been guilty of tipping the scale in our representations of ourselves and in our representations of those who are not members of the church?

What Lawrence says there is similar to what Bakhtin says. You have to have a certain hands-offedness—if that's a word—to be able to make it work. I do think most Mormon writers have been guilty of tipping the scale. They allow themselves to become propagandists. Some are more subtle about it, but I think all but a small handful do it. There are a few who avoid that. I don't want to name names because I think there are so very few. I think we're guilty, as Mormon writers, of transforming the world into cardboard.

It seems that a lot of writers are also in search of that Holy Grail of "uplift." But I haven't figured out what uplift is.

I don't know what it is either. Sorry. It has something to do with hair, I think. I think uplift is a desirable quality in a haircut.

If uplift is merely what makes us happy, then there's a lot in Shakespeare and Milton that we're not going to read. *King Lear*'s not really uplifting; neither is *Titus Andronicus*.

I think Lear is uplifting. I think it just depends on how you define it. What is uplifting? Is it something that makes you get tingly? If that's it, then nothing I'm interested in is uplifting. *King Lear* is something that makes you think very seriously about all sorts of things and allows you to experience the sublime. I define uplifting as coming to a more complex understanding of the world. What's uplifting about that for me is that it allows our understanding to move slightly nearer to God's understanding. It's a tricky thing, in a lot of ways, to try to work through all these notions, but I really think one of the big problems is that people fall into formulas pretty easily. It's amazing how easily something like change comes in most Mormon novels. It's also amazing how predictable the change is. I see that as objectionable. If we have a cardboard notion of what grace is, we get cardboard grace. Change occurs very seldom, quite frankly. Clearly I'm a nihilist and a pessimist when it comes to that.

Let's see how your inner nihilist responds to this: In 2 Nephi 28:20–21 we read that in the latter days, Satan shall "rage in the hearts of the children of men, and stir them up to anger against that which is good. And others will he pacify, and lull them away into carnal security, that they will say: All is well in Zion; yea, Zion prospereth, all is well—and thus the devil cheateth their souls, and leadeth them away carefully down to hell." Are some Mormon writers guilty of claiming that "all is well in Zion?"

Yeah, I think some of them are. I don't think they all are, but for some, that is certainly the case.

What effect do you think this has on a Mormon audience?

It's harmful, finally, to claim that all is well. I think it's a larger issue than just Mormon writers. I think we have a whole culture that is constantly telling us that "things are rosy; things are okay. We have our leaders here, and nothing's going to go wrong. You don't have to worry about this; you don't have to think. Have a caffeine-free Coke."

Okay, that said, I'd like to pitch a change-up: do you think there's room for satire in the church? Not from our perspective, but maybe from the church's perspective.

I don't know; you'd have to ask the church.

From your own point of view then. Does Brian Evenson think there's room for satire?

Sure I do. I've written satirical work—the "Prophets" story, among other things, about someone trying to dig up Ezra Taft Benson's corpse so as to resurrect him and get him back in charge of the church. Yeah, I'd like to think there's room for satire. The church is an institution, and I think that satire is essential for institutions. It helps them progress.

The problem is, I guess, that Mormon audiences don't cotton well to satire and irony. In fact, this incapacity kind of keeps run-of-the-mill Mormons from enjoying most real literature. What's it going to take, in your estimation, to create audiences for serious Mormon literature?

In any population, the percentage of serious readers is going to be relatively small. It's hard to get around that. If you wanted to get past that, you'd have to have leaders who were willing to take much more active roles in encouraging people to think, in encouraging people to read good books, to go beyond what's easy. I don't think that's ever going to happen, but I'd like to be proven wrong. In terms of targeting people within the church, I guess the thing that needs to be done is to teach people how to read and expose them to new sorts of work. The official publications of the church don't bother to do this—they enforce the norm. You get stories in the official publications that are exactly the kind of thing I've been objecting to. How maddening: you have a forum that can reach a good percentage of the Mormon population, and you use it in fairly banal ways.

There are magazines like *Sunstone* that try to enlighten readers. *Dialogue* is something that tries to do that as well. Both are mixed and often compromise themselves, but both deserve to be repeated. There was *Wasatch Review International*, also mixed. There are several new magazines that seem at least potentially interesting, though it's probably too early to judge them.

What will it take for Mormon literature to assume a place in the culture the way that Irish, Native American, and Jewish literatures have since World War II?

A number of things. First, people have got to stop thinking of Mormon literature as a missionary tool. I don't think literature can be a missionary tool and still be literature.

Second, I think it is also going to take another two or three hundred years, because Mormonism is relatively new as opposed to those other groups you've mentioned. There's been an Irish identity for centuries now, Native American cultures as well. And Jewish literature has been thriving for a long, long time. Compared to all three of those cultures and what they've gone through, Mormon "persecution" is laughably insignificant. We can't measure up to the several millennia of persecution that Jews have gone through.

Third, the church has got to stop moving toward the mainstream. I think that we're coming closer and closer to fading into the general background. As long as that movement persists, we will have a hard time defining a Mormon identity in a way that will be visible, finally, or interesting. Mormons are losing their faces. They're assimilating in a way that will make their literature no longer unique. If we really are a peculiar people, then let's embrace our peculiarity.

---

1. *Sewanee Review,* spring 1980.

2. In Ihab Hassan, Sally Hassan eds. *Innovation/Renovation: New Perspectives on the Humanities.* Madison: University of Wisconsin Press, 1983: 329–41.

3. Minneapolis: University of Minnesota Press, 1984.

4. *Phoenix: The Posthumous Papers of D.H. Lawrence*, New York: Viking, 1936.

5. *Phoenix: The Posthumous Papers of D.H. Lawrence*, New York: Viking, 1936.

JOHN FULTON

John Fulton
Fiction Writer

Reared in Salt Lake City outside the Mormon faith, John Fulton has published stories in fourteen national and international journals. In 2001, he published his first book, Retribution (Picador USA), a collection of stories that was awarded the Southern Review Short Fiction Award for the best first collection published by an American that year. The following year, he published his first novel, More Than Enough (Picador USA), which was selected for the Barnes and Noble Discover Great New Writers series, named the best novel of the West for 2002 by the Salt Lake Tribune, and selected as a finalist for the Association of Midland Authors award for fiction. Fulton lives in Boston, where he is a professor of English at the University of Massachusetts. The original version of this interview appeared in Irreantum, autumn 2003.

How would you describe your novel?

More Than Enough is about a proud family of atheists down on its luck that moves to Salt Lake City in an attempt to turn things around. As so often happens when things are going badly, they only get worse for this family, which struggles to assimilate without much success into Mormon culture. It's the early nineties, a boom time for the whole country, and not only does this family fail to fit into the religious climate, but it also remains poor while everyone seems to be thriving. As a result, the family begins to fall apart, and the central figure of the story, fifteen-year-old Steven Parker, does everything in his power to hold his parents together. In the process, he discovers the limits of family loyalty and the harsh concerns of adult life that pit his mother, Mary Parker, and younger sister, Jenny, against Steven and his irresponsible father, whose failures and dead-end dreams have repeatedly lead the family into near ruin. The novel takes on the central American themes of money, class, religion, and the individual's struggle to define himself against or within these social forces.

What were your motives, goals, and influences in writing this novel?

In many ways, *More Than Enough* was a formal challenge for me. Most of this two-hundred-page novel takes place in one tense afternoon in which everything that has brought the Parkers to this moment of crisis must be clear and fully realized. In one afternoon, I am presented with the challenge of developing characters and delivering them to an outcome that is both inevitable and unpredictable. And by holding myself to the few hours in which the action takes place, I hope to reproduce for the reader Steven and his family's duress as they see themselves unraveling.

I also wanted to write a novel that takes place in Salt Lake City and deals with the Mormons without making either this particular place or its culture appear extreme or cartoonishly bizarre. Whether they are Mormons or not, most people from Utah are perceived by the outside world as Mormon, and therefore weird; they're seen as religious extremists who either are themselves polygamists or who probably lived near and knew polygamists. While living in Europe, I was especially surprised by the prevalence of this perception. A lot of people I met expected me to tell them about all the wives the Mormons kept, the underwear the Mormons wore, and the extreme anxiety the Mormons felt toward caffeine and alcohol. And these people were rather disappointed when I told them I hadn't met a single polygamist. When I would tell people I wasn't Mormon, they hardly seemed to believe a non-Mormon could live in Salt Lake City.

That said, the city is unique for its religious culture, a culture I underscore in the book by making my characters atheists. And while there is conflict between my Mormon and non-Mormon characters, I was determined to show the Mormons in this book in an accurate and realistic light. I wasn't out to underscore a minority of extremists. I was out to show the experiences of real non-Mormons as they clash against real Mormons, a run-in that has to do more with money and class—social forces that exist just about everywhere—than polygamy and what kind of underwear people wear. While these social forces do, I think, appear slightly differently in a setting dominated by Mormonism, the Mormons and Salt Lake remain recognizable and relatively normal in my book.

Finally, I wanted to do justice to all my characters in this book, make them fully human and, to an extent, sympathetic to the reader. The book involves the breakup of a family and impending divorce, so I expect my readers to have a moral response—in short, to judge my characters and their decisions. But I don't want to make it easy for the reader to make a clear judgment. When writing about kids, especially in extreme situations, the tendency can be to present them as straightforward victims and to sentimentalize them. I hope I avoided that. Likewise, I didn't want the parents to be seen as victimizers. They want to do the right thing in a difficult situation and don't always succeed. When a character hurts someone else because there is no way around it or because he or she can't help but do so, you have an interesting situation.

At certain points in the novel, the father, Bill Parker, uses Steven and Jenny as pawns to get their mother back. His use of the kids is both unforgivable and an expression of how desperately he wants his wife back. In the same way, I hope the mother's choices can be seen as both hurtful to her children and, from her perspective, necessary. It's hard to say what a parent should sacrifice for his or her child. Steven's mother wants to believe that leaving her husband is one way in which she can meet her basic needs and so perhaps protect and care for her kids best. But in leaving him, she's traumatizing her kids. I can imagine readers having different reactions to her decisions because her situation is complex.

The minority-within-a-majority theme is something others could relate to from other ethnicities. Could this novel just as easily have been set among a Jewish population or in a predominantly Baptist or Lutheran community? How dependent are your themes upon the action being set among this particular group of people? Is the Mormon community particularly exclusionary?

This is an interesting question and one I thought a lot about as I wrote and revised the novel. And my answer is: yes and no. I don't think the Mormons are a particularly exclusionary religion. In fact, my experience of them has been the opposite. As everyone knows, they're interested in bringing people into their church, and so they reach out. They want to share themselves and their community with others. And, in many ways, I think this novel could have taken place in another setting with any religious majority goading this family of atheists. And yet, had it been about a family in the South attempting to get along with Southern Baptists, it would have been a dramatically different novel.

What I wanted to capture was the sense of place, both socially and geographically, of Salt Lake City. It is, literally and figuratively, a city on a hill. It's not just a religious city but a wealthy and class-conscious city where one's money is expressed by how high up the surrounding hills one's house sits. And so, to a certain extent, money and religion in this city go together, especially as seen through the eyes of an atheist family who live literally and figuratively at the bottom of the hill. And because the Mormons are a family-oriented religion, both Steven and his sister Jenny are able to see in their neighbors, who have large, seemingly close-knit family units, everything they want and don't have.

Finally, the physical space of the West—Utah, Idaho, Montana—is very important and dear to me. I seem to need its landscape, its views, its particular dry air, its vistas and skies in my fiction. I was born and raised in the West, left it at the age of eighteen, have never been able to return, and so I compensate by recreating what I miss most about it in my fiction. For years I lived in Europe, then in the Midwest, and now I'm on the East Coast. And the farther away I get, the more I need to write about the West.

You have the Parkers move from Boise to Salt Lake City. Idaho is roughly twenty-five to thirty percent LDS, and Salt Lake County is barely fifty percent LDS. Why did you feel it was necessary for the Parkers to move to Salt Lake City as a catalyst for change? Would any move have been a sufficient stress on the family to bring about the same result? Would the family have eventually broken up even if they hadn't moved?

The move to Salt Lake City is motivated by the father and his unrealistic sense that any move will somehow bring good fortune. And while the Parker family certainly must have encountered Mormons in Idaho, Mormonism has a cultural cachet in Salt Lake that it doesn't have anywhere else, and this is especially true of the Salt Lake City of the nineteen-eighties and early nineties, when the action of the novel takes place. Salt Lake, after all, is the Rome of Mormonism, the holy city. I thought of placing the story in contemporary Salt Lake, but the city now feels much less Mormon than it did ten, fifteen years ago. On my recent visits to the city, I'm struck by the number of brewpubs and bars that are everywhere now and by a large population of mountain-climbing, nature-loving, slightly left-wing young people who moved to Salt Lake as young adults and who don't tend to be religious. In the Salt Lake of today, the non-Mormons make up a rather visible and vocal group, so much so that, as you say, the non-Mormons really aren't a minority anymore.

That said, I do think the city plays an important role in the breakup of the family. Eventually, the Parker family would have broken up whether in Idaho or in Utah. But the setting underscores some of the more interesting forces behind the breakup—faith, money, and social standing among them.

Some readers feel as though the Salt Lake City setting and the depiction of Mormons in your novel follow in the long tradition (going back to the early nineteenth century) of exploiting existing prejudice against this religious group. How would you respond?

Well, I don't think so. Certainly the beating Steven takes may be seen, at least superficially, as another one of those bigoted depictions of Mormons. In fact, it's more about the way kids simplify issues and underscore differences in order to be cruel. Whether or not the issue of contention is about what kind of God one believes in or what kind of music one listens to, kids will seize upon differences as a pretext for injuring one another. And so will adults. However, the Mormon parents in this novel hardly behave as badly as the kids do. The father of the kid who hurts Steven forces his child to admit he was wrong and to apologize to Steven and his family. He does the right thing. And while Steven may see Curtis Smith, for instance, as the Mormon who breaks up his parents' marriage, I make it clear to the reader that Steven's mother makes the decision to leave his father without any heavy pressure from anyone else. In fact, when Steven first meets Curtis Smith, the future husband of his mother, he's frustrated because this man is so much more pleasant and human than Steven wants him to be. Steven wants to demonize him, but he can't because Curtis is both kind and concerned about what Steven and his sister must be going through. In fact, in some ways, the success of the novel relies on a fair treatment of Mormons. Had I demonized them and made them responsible for what happens to this family, the complexity of the Parkers would have failed to develop. I would have had a bunch of flat characters: the good guys versus the bad guys. That doesn't make for much of a story.

From the acknowledgments, it appears that Ian Fulcher and your brother Ben provided you with the details about Mormons and Salt Lake City. How much time have you actually spent in Salt Lake or among Latter-day Saints?

I lived in Salt Lake from 1977 to 1986, when I left for college, though I always came back to Salt Lake and called it home until I was well into my twenties. If people ask me where I'm from, I tell them Salt Lake and brace myself for that funny are-you-a-Mormon look I often get. I wrote the novel while living in Michigan, and much of the geography of Salt Lake, especially the directions (east, west, south, north) and some of the street names and locations, had become vague for me. So my brother, who still lives in the city, helped me get the details right.

Ian Fulcher is a close friend of mine and a lapsed Mormon who knows a lot more about Mormon theology than I do. Growing up, a lot of my friends were Mormons and Jack-Mormons. My family was rather strict, fundamentalist Southern Baptists. My friends and I found it best just not to talk about religion. So Ian was able to help me out with some fine points and give me some literature that helped with actual doctrine and the sort of language—songs, scripture, et cetera—that Jenny and Steven might hear at Mormon services and from their Mormon friends.

Why did you feel you had to use made-up place names and locations, for the most part?

I made up names and places in order to construct a more fully realized imagined space for the novel. While I might be writing about Salt Lake City, I use it as a setting for a piece of fiction, and so it comes to mean something more than merely a backdrop for action and characters. Imagine the difference in *The Great Gatsby* if Fitzgerald would have referred to East and West Egg as Little and Big Neck, the models for the Eggs that actually exist on Long Island. A lot would have been lost. When Steven, his mother, and sister are driving into the upper Avenues, Steven notices that the streets are named, unlike the lower avenues, and that "rich people like names . . . and no doubt they got to choose what to call their streets." The street names he sees—Milky Way Boulevard, Venus, Neptune, and Mars Drives—are all made up. As far as I know, this neighborhood doesn't exist in the Avenues. But the names get at a truth about the difference between those who have money and those who don't. Those who have it shape their world and their fate far more so than the poor do. Steven doesn't want to believe this, even as he drives through a neighborhood that models itself after the universe and the solar system, that sees itself as the whole world. After all, Steven is poor and needs to believe in the power of his father to rise above his failures and make more of himself and his family. But the presence of this neighborhood and the outlandish language it uses to define itself suggest that he's wrong.

Steven seems to have started out as the antithesis of his father. Steven gets good grades and sees the value of education. But in the end you banish Steven to his father's custody. This leads to several questions about Steven: Do you feel that Steven would have eventually exhibited his self-destructive behavior regardless of his circumstances? That the beating by the neighborhood kids was just a catalyst for the emotions he developed in his dysfunctional family? Or do you feel that Steven might have never acted out if he had not been beaten up?

Steven ends up with his father because, like his father, he's a dreamer who believes more in the world as he wants it to be than in the world as it is. He's so invested in his hopes that he's willing to do just about anything to make the world conform to his vision of it. At the same time, Steven is a smart, very practical kid, and so he can see that his mission and his vision are doomed. It's a painful position to be in, and it makes his self-destructive behavior inevitable, given what is happening to his family.

Steven's behavior is not simply about his circumstances, however. It's also part of the condition of being an adolescent, straddling the fence between two worlds. When he acts out, he's testing his power to determine events and to control others. He wants to know how much his mother loves him. What is she willing to give up for him? Will she stay with his father because she loves Steven? Will she refuse to fulfill her own desires because of her emotional ties to her son? And, yes, his behavior is also an expression of the emotional chaos and desperation he experiences as a result of his family's breakup. On the afternoon Steven's mother decides to take her kids and leave her husband, Steven doesn't know what to do. He is suddenly confronted with his mother's adult motives— lack of money, security, and love—for leaving her husband. And in the face of these baffling but very real and powerful concerns, he can only explode. Finally, one of the lessons he learns in this story is his own powerlessness. His mother is her own person. She has her own needs, her own will, and is willing to hurt him if she has to.

The mother Mary and sister Jenny both adapt by conforming to the local environment; they both show interest in joining Mormonism, seemingly as a coping mechanism. Father Billy and son Steven both resist the status quo of their environment. From your ending, it would seem that you don't reward either Billy or Steven for their nonconformist attitudes. Do you feel that one should conform in order to gain acceptance and peace of mind?

I think Jenny is more of a conformist than her mother. Jenny takes the path of least resistance. She does so because she is more aware than Steven of the social forces at work and their power over her. She also wants to be a part of the social world. She wants to be accepted. She wants to have friends and belong. I'm not sure she's really rewarded for her conformity, however. Unlike Steven, she has to deal with the fact that she is betraying her father. And while she'll live a more comfortable life, she will have to live with this fact.

Mary's position is far more complicated because she is a wife and mother who leaves her husband and, in some way, betrays her children, especially Steven. She might be called a conformist save for the fact that she is acting very much against the accepted social norms for women. I see her as a survivor, as someone who has to make a difficult decision because she believes it will be best both for herself and her children in the long run. Again, as with Jenny, I'm not sure she's really rewarded for the difficult decisions she makes. What I hope the end of the novel shows is the difficulty of her situation. It's a situation in which she gets hurt and hurts people no matter what she does. I hope her situation both provokes a moral judgment from the reader and causes the reader to question his or her tendency to judge the mother in the first place.

You have Steven carry his soiled clothes around for quite a long period of time. This seems to symbolize his inability to get rid of his negative attitudes and also indicate that his experience in the retirement home was an opportunity to get rid of some of these attitudes. What makes Steven hang on? Why wouldn't a teenager so aware of his position of lack not want to have the opportunity to get away from his father, the cause of his lack, and into an environment filled with abundance?

I don't really see those soiled clothes as reflective of Steven's negative attitude, though I do see where your reading makes a lot of sense. Let me first explain, for those who haven't read the book, that Steven, due to stress and exhaustion, has an embarrassing accident, dirties his clothes, and must change and carry around his soiled clothes for the rest of the day in a plastic garbage bag. Those clothes are Steven's, and he won't let go of them because they're part of who he is and who his father is, never mind the fact that they're profoundly dirty. And so, later in the novel, when his mother, with her newfound financial resources, buys him new and better clothes, he won't take them. And as much as Steven wants to own his clothes and his identity as an atheist, an outsider, a dreamer, and a struggler, they're not terribly desirable. They make him suffer, and yet they belong to him and are part of what it means to live as he and his family have for years, threatened by poverty and social insignificance. Giving them up would be nice, but it would also be tantamount to losing his family as he knows it.

The Parkers don't believe in God. But, Steven and Jenny long to believe in something. When Steven is desperate to find a way to keep his family together, he secretly says a prayer to God, which goes unanswered. So, in a way, God has disappointed him too.

Having just moved to Salt Lake City, the Parkers are outsiders. They have no friends, and they don't share the sort of beliefs and values that would make fitting in easier. The fact that they are supposed to believe in nothing beyond themselves, to believe only in themselves, as their father preaches, means they don't have a lot to believe in. Steven and Jenny can see that their family might fall apart any day. Without friends, family, or a God to believe in, they are left with nothing. When Steven wanders through Oak Groves, the convalescence home where his mother works, lost and alone and surrounded by old people who are as alone as he is, he realizes how terrible nothing can be. And when his sister, who makes friends with Mormons and has begun to attend church with them, quizzes him on the Ten Commandments and he realizes that he and his family don't know these laws and have never tried to follow them, he sees that his life has no structure, no direction. It's a frightening realization. And so, when he is most alone, he does say God's name out loud, and he strains to hear some sort of response. He wants to believe that something or someone out there in the universe will look out for him and his family. Of course, what he wants is a simple solution to his problems. I think everyone feels this way any number of times in life. And what he faces here is the fact that there is no simple solution and that he is powerless to keep certain events from happening. In a more cosmic sense, he faces the possibility that there might be nothing out there, that life may be meaningless, especially if it is attended by enough loss and pain.

Throughout my novel, the theme of waste acts as a kind of counterpoint to the theme of God. Everywhere Steven looks, he sees the threat of waste—the homeless people in the restaurant, his father's meaningless spending of money, his parents' dissolving marriage, his father's failure in school, his own injured arm, the aging and ailing people in Oak Groves, the dead Mr. Warner, his own soiled clothes that he carries around. Then, of course, there is the scene in the bathroom where Steven is literally confronted with waste. In the face of this threat, Steven is compelled at points to hope for the existence of something beyond himself and his world.

Are you familiar with other depictions and critical treatment of well-heeled Mormons in literature, such as the work of Levi Peterson? To what extent are you familiar with any contemporary Mormon imaginative writing or writers, such as Darrell Spencer, Walter Kirn, and Brady Udall?

In fact, Darrell Spencer was the first teacher I ever worked with. He was at a writers' conference called Writers at Work, which then took place in Park City, Utah. I must have been eighteen, maybe only seventeen, and I wanted very badly to write. So I convinced my parents to pay for the conference and wrote my first-ever short story, which I'd rather not think about now. I read Darrell Spencer's short fiction early on. I gave more thought to his style—a kind of lush minimalism that really convinces you that, at least in his case, less is more—than I did his subject matter. Does he write about Mormons? I'll have to go back and read him again. Likewise, I've read Walter Kirn and Brady Udall and have appreciated their particular takes on the West, though I wasn't aware that either writer was Mormon. I'm not familiar with Levi Peterson. That said, I think the Mormon experience, and religious experience in general, is rather underrepresented in contemporary literature. I myself am not religious, but the subject of God and how we relate to God remains, in my mind, one of the more important themes for art to take on.

Tell us about your writing process for this book and its journey to publication.

I started out, as do many writers who enter M.F.A. programs, as a short story writer because the short form is ideal for the apprentice writer and ideal for workshops where writers critique each other's work in a few hours. As a professional writer, however, I soon found out that stories are far less marketable than novels. Every agent I approached with my stories liked them and was interested in selling them if I had a novel or part of a novel to sell along with them. While my current agent agreed to sell my story collection, *Retribution*, without a novel—I feared above all else selling an unfinished piece and writing on a contract—she eventually called up to say she had interested buyers if—and I knew what was coming—I also had a novel to sell. So, at last, I caved in and presented the first thirty or so pages of something that I had thought might become a novel, though, at the time, I saw it as a self-contained story. In addition, I wrote an outline to accompany this "first chapter." The outline seemed to have the effect of morphing the concept of the story into a novel. After it sold, I had eighteen months to write it.

Working on a schedule with a deadline, I expected the worst. I thought I'd be calling my agent and begging her to ask my editor for more time. But, for the most part, the writing went surprisingly fast and smoothly. I wrote the first hundred pages or so in about a month. Then I hit a frightening period of about four months in which I couldn't bring the narrative forward. I was blocked, and every effort, it seemed, was hopeless. It turned out that I was trying too hard to follow the outline I'd sold the book with. Originally, my story was going to take place over a period of two years and was going to involve a daring, drug-taking, suicidal femme fatale under whose spell Steven would fall. As soon as I figured out that more than half of my novel would take place over one afternoon and would not include this character—Daisy Lip was her odd name—the project took off for me again. It took about six months to get a rough draft and another six to revise it. For the most part, it was a pleasure to write.

What has been the response to the book?

For the most part, it has been good. The book has gone through several printings in this country, and it has done a lot better than my story collection, mainly, I think, because so few readers out there want to read stories. It was published in the United Kingdom by Random House and may come out in translation in Germany. So some good things are happening. That said, I try not to dwell on it, and I don't go out of my way to read reviews, though I do eventually get around to reading them. My main challenge, and one I don't handle well if I'm fixated on how my books are doing, is getting myself to the writing desk on a daily basis and producing new work.

What are you working on?

I am currently working on a collection of long stories or novellas, forty to a hundred pages in length, which is one of my favorite forms to write, as well as a novel. The novel has no young children or adolescents in it, which is a real change for me. I'm eager to try out new territory, though I'm still dealing with family discord. The novel concerns two adult brothers in a lifelong feud. Among other things, they fight over their aging mother's favor and how best to care for her in her later years. Because one of the brothers is a dentist and something quite terrible goes wrong in his clinic, I have done a great deal of research about teeth and dental procedures. It's been fun to get into the head of someone who does something so different from what I do. Dentistry aside, it is a Cain and Abel story about old grudges and the possibility of forgiveness after years of anger and misunderstanding. The long stories I'm working on all surround people in the grips of terminal illnesses or who have survived the deaths of family members from such illnesses. While the subject matter may sound grim, I don't think it is. The stories focus on the grieving process and the way those who suffer, either directly or indirectly, from terminal illnesses manage to find surprising meaning in a terrible experience.

JACK HARRELL

Jack Harrell
Novelist

A professor of English at Brigham Young University–Idaho, Jack Harrell won the Association for Mormon Letter's Marilyn Brown unpublished novel award in 2000 for Vernal Promises, *which was subsequently published by Signature Books. Harrell joined the LDS Church at age twenty-one, and he has published short stories in* Dialogue, Irreantum, The Storyteller, *and elsewhere and non-fiction in* Popular Music and Society *("The Poetics of Destruction: Death Metal Rock"). The original version of this interview appeared in* Irreantum, *autumn 2003.*

What were your motives and desires in writing *Vernal Promises*? What effect do you want it to have on readers?

For me, the novel is a redemption story. The main character, Jacob Dennison, is a twenty-two-year-old Mormon who believes in God despite the fact that he hasn't attended church in years. He smokes and drinks and works hard every day at a job he hates. Probably every elders quorum president in the West knows a guy like Jacob—a name on the rolls, someone they have a hard time reaching.

I started writing about Jacob because he's the kind of guy I understand. He's a believer, even if his actions don't show it. I grew up in Parkersburg, Illinois, a farm town of 250 people where blue-collar work is the only work and everyone believed in God in some form or another. Most of the men in my family drive truck, most of the women work as secretaries or waitresses. When I lived in Vernal, Utah, it was the same. When Jacob leaves his job in the grocery store and goes to work for his father, selling oil field equipment, he tries to drown himself in drug and alcohol use because he wants to run away from God. Jacob believes in Christ's suffering, but he doesn't believe he deserves it. If he can smoke enough and drink enough, he thinks, God will give up on him, realizing he's not worth the Savior's sacrifice. The problem is, God's love is tougher than that. If there's any particular effect I want it to have on readers, it's the impression that God is just as concerned about Jacob's soul as he is about the souls of "the righteous."

After reading an early draft of the novel, a friend of mine asked me a question: "Why would literary Mormons care about the struggles of a cigarette smoker in a Vernal trailer park?" He really threw me off balance with that one—I hadn't realized some people might be that smug—but I kept working on the book because I believed Jacob's struggle was important.

What prompted you to start writing? How did you learn the craft?

In freshman English, I wrote an essay about my mom's "second life," a life that started when I was five, when my dad left us. I loved the sense of authenticity that came from writing about that change in her life. Her story was real and poignant, it was a story I knew, and no one else in the class could tell it. At BYU, I used my English electives on creative writing courses. The first hundred pages of the first draft of *Vernal Promises* came out of Bruce Jorgensen's fiction class. I wasn't a very good writer, I don't think, but I had a clear vision of what I wanted to say. That first draft grew to two hundred pages before I deleted seventy-five percent of it. I still do that sometimes—write a hundred pages and then delete half of them. I wouldn't call myself a good writer, but I have learned to work hard. In the end, maybe hard work is more important than talent, anyway.

After college, I started reading books published by Writer's Digest—books on plot, character, and the writer's market. Possibly the best book in this genre is Orson Scott Card's *Characters and Viewpoint* (1988). These books have their limits, but they contain a lot of very important nuts-and-bolts information that isn't taught in college English courses. English classes teach criticism. They teach you how to analyze a story once it's made. If you want to learn how to make a story, you have to go somewhere else, because most English professors, schooled in criticism, don't know how a story is created.

Do other cultural influences besides fiction—such as music—play into your creativity?

Music has always been important to me. In my teens I played guitar in a rock band and learned how to work hard at something I cared about. I enjoyed—and in my own way made a study of—bands like Led Zeppelin, Pink Floyd, Rush, Yes, the Beatles, and Genesis (the early stuff with Peter Gabriel). Since then I've gotten into other bands like Pearl Jam, Red Hot Chili Peppers, and Dave Mathews. As an English major, I learned about poetic devices, literary terms, and the evolution of literary movements, which gave me a vocabulary for the things I had intuitively gathered as a teenager from listening to rock music.

After I joined the church, my musical interests expanded to include classical and folk music, but I haven't lost my first love for rock music. Not long ago I was listening to a Pink Floyd song called "Echoes," a twenty-minute piece that moves the opening theme through a kind of trip to the underworld and then to a final, more triumphant reprise of the original theme. I said to myself, "If I can learn to write a story as good as that, I'll be doing okay."

What is your greatest reward as a writer? Do you ever feel inspired in a spiritual way with regards to your writing?

The best reward for me is that private moment when I've written something I'm really pleased with. The real test is: Will I still like it in a week or a month? Often I finish something that I'm very pleased with, but a week later I can see it still needs more work. When that happens, there's only one thing to do: work on it some more.

I often feel spiritually inspired as a writer, but it's not writing itself as much as it is a desire to do something good that draws me toward that feeling of holiness. I believe God wants us to do good things. One person might make a beautiful quilt to show at the county fair, another might restore old cars. I don't know if there's a great deal of difference between the creative drive that makes one person write poetry while another makes fine wood furniture.

Not long ago I was helping my wife paint our youngest daughter's bedroom. I was doing some careful work around the window frame, painting it a different color than the walls, focusing on keeping the line straight. While I worked, I felt that same joy I feel when I try to get a sentence just right. That's the thing that inspires me: putting love into something, trying to do a good job—dressing and keeping the garden, so to speak.

Most fiction is a combination of three elements: what the author has experienced, observed, and imagined. How do those three elements work together for you?

As with most writers, a lot of my fiction comes out of my own experiences or the experiences of people I know. The stuff about drugs and alcohol in *Vernal Promises* is familiar to me because of the experiences I had as a teenager, before I joined the church. But in fiction, what's needed to make a story work is always more important than the question of what really happened. Even if I do start with something that happened to me, it's not long before it's shaped into something new to meet the needs of the story. Then it's no longer my experience; it's the experience of the characters.

Tell us about your writing habits.

I try to write at least an hour a day. I have a hard time writing when my mind is burdened by the cares of the day, so I write in the morning, before my family wakes up, before I teach or read my e-mail or do any other business. I usually write on the computer, and I usually have music on the headphones when I write. Music helps me shut out the real world and focus on the imaginary world of the story.

When I'm plotting, I do a lot of sketching; I put things on slips of paper and arrange and rearrange them on my desk. I keep a writing journal to help me untangle the knots that come up. I research facts—even things like how many miles it is on the highway from one town to the next. For the first chapter of *Vernal Promises*, which begins with Jacob's wife having a miscarriage and going to the hospital, I did a two-hour interview with an emergency room nurse who had been through that sort of thing more than once. I do a lot of outlining, and I revise a lot. Nothing I do seems very good after a first draft. I have to work it over several times before I'm willing to let someone else see it.

What works of Mormon literature have most influenced you?

I admire a lot of Mormon writers—Levi Peterson, Doug Thayer, Lance Larsen, Margaret Blair Young. I took a couple of classes from Eugene England and simply loved him. But the author who has influenced me the most is Flannery O'Connor. I did my master's thesis on her first novel *Wise Blood*, which had a big influence on *Vernal Promises*. I love O'Connor for her unflinching realism about the challenges of being a Christian and a writer. Her letters in *The Habit of Being* contain some great insights for writers, believers, and thinkers. She was all three of those things.

Besides O'Connor, I've loved—and learned lessons from—Wallace Stegner, Raymond Carver, Sherwood Anderson, Barbara Kingsolver, E.L. Doctorow, Nathaniel Hawthorne, Arthur Miller, and even Stephen King. His book *On Writing* is great stuff. Another book that every Mormon writer and artist should read is Chaim Potok's *My Name Is Asher Lev*. And John Cheever—reading one of his short stories is like listening to a chamber orchestra. His moral life was a wreck, but his writing was sublime. That's a conundrum for Mormon writers. We should try to figure that out—the relationship between personal morality and the production of good art.

How does teaching writing and literature affect you as a writer?

The best thing about teaching and writing—especially at BYU–Idaho, where there's no faculty rank and the focus is on teaching first, rather than publishing—is knowing that my writing has no connection to my paycheck. If my writing isn't successful, I still have a job.

The interaction a teacher has with other people is always helpful to the writing life. Among other things, a writer has to be an amateur psychologist. Dealing with a variety of people and watching their lives unfold provide all kinds of valuable insights.

What is your advice for aspiring fiction writers?

Write all you can, knowing that the relationship between raw product and finished product is about the same as the relationship between how many hours an NBA player spends practicing and how many minutes he spends on the court in the playoffs. Find out when you do your best work, what motivates you, what discourages you. Don't try to work and write the way others do. Learn to work with your own temperament and circumstances. Write what you want to write; don't worry about whether or not it will sell. The inauthentic person who tries to imitate others and follow trends will probably just write drivel anyway.

What are your observations about Mormon literature and the Mormon reading audience?

Faulkner says that great literature involves "the human heart in conflict with itself." I believe that's true. But Mormon culture tends to frown upon inner conflict because we associate it with sin. If we're keeping the commandments, we sometimes think we should be completely happy all the time. There's something wrong with that line of thinking. For one thing, it often leads to terrible disillusionment. If a person is living the Book of Mormon injunction to "Mourn with those who mourn," there is going to be some conflict, some pain in that person's heart. Our culture is too concerned with looking happy, looking good, and looking moral. We want to win the respect of the respectable. But this tendency flies in the face of good literature and good religion.

There's a saying that goes: "The gospel comforts the troubled and troubles the comfortable." Good literature is like that, too. I'm not talking about insulting readers or shattering their faith. John Gardner talks about this in his book *On Moral Fiction* (Basic Books, 1978). He says good literature is life-affirming. Good literature offers a paradox: life is very difficult, and it's totally worth it. The first half of that statement makes the second half more meaningful. Sometimes as Mormons we're afraid to talk about the difficult things, but if we don't acknowledge them, we weaken the truth that life is worth the struggle. That's why easy pop literature, in the end, can't offer the kind of gritty life affirmation that gets people through the rough spots.

Is it a worthwhile goal to get Mormon characters and themes before a national audience? Do you think this nation will ever have a Mormon Saul Bellow or Flannery O'Connor, someone winning top awards for literature that deals with Mormon themes, settings, and characters?

Trying to get Mormon themes before a national audience is the wrong way to go about it. The things we struggle with that are important on a human level are not exclusive to being Mormon. Name any Mormon theme—being persecuted, loving our families, having a unique doctrine of God—and these things are not unknown to other groups. We need to focus on what we have in common with others if we're going to speak to them in ways they can understand. Too often our writing is like an inside joke. When a person tells an inside joke, outsiders are alienated.

People are also alienated when we begin with the assumption that we have all the answers, when we put dogma before humanity. People can sense that sort of thing. Maybe we, as Mormons, have grown insensitive to that approach because we've experienced so much of it. Good literature never begins with answers; it begins with questions. When it comes to art, certainty crushes creativity. In order to write things other people will care about, one has to be like a child: purely curious, having more questions than answers.

We also make a mistake when we try to sell people on our lifestyle. I can't imagine anything more boring than a Wasatch Front version of *Lifestyles of the Rich and Righteous*. It's not the Jewishness of Saul Bellow's characters that makes his writing great; it's not the Catholicism of O'Connor that moves us. It's the human struggle we care about. Going back to Faulkner: "The human heart in conflict with itself." Flannery O'Connor constantly received letters from good Catholics asking her to write a novel that showed the blessings of being Catholic. She refused because she didn't want to write bad fiction. Propaganda—information advocating a doctrine or cause—has its place, in the church and elsewhere. But propaganda is never good literature. A novel that tries to prove the church is true will be just as bad as a novel promoting the gay lifestyle or the virtues of working for Microsoft. Good literature is about people, not institutions or doctrines.

While your publisher, Signature Books, produces beautiful volumes, this publisher is not known for selling many copies of fiction titles, occasionally only in the low hundreds. What are your comments on that?

That's an interesting comment on our culture. We know that in America certain things, such as symphony orchestras, libraries, and public television, would not survive without a combination of government funding and public philanthropy. Often the sensational and the shallow thrive, while the deep and meaningful barely survive on grants and donations. Perhaps things in the Mormon community should be different, but they aren't.

Many of Signature's fiction titles sell in the thousands, but it's also true that Signature sells more history than fiction. This may be related to the general notion—a false notion, I believe—that "true" things are more valuable than fiction. In my view, fiction can be more "true" than history. I don't think there's much difference between the Mormon publishing world and the larger American context when it comes to these things. Novels sold in the grocery stores sell better than novels taught in English classes. Maybe most people don't want to be challenged by their fiction because their lives are already challenging enough. I don't know. My book will offer some readers more challenges than comforts. That's why I'm grateful for publishers like Signature Books. I get the impression that a big sell isn't the only thing on their agenda. It's actually pretty refreshing to see that commercial interests don't always pervade everything.

What other writing do you do?

I have some short stories that aren't Mormon in their characters or settings that I'd like to find places for. The novel I'm working on now is about an Idaho state park ranger and a man who was once instrumental in his conversion to the church, a man who turns out to be very dangerous. If the first novel was any indicator, it will probably be three or four years before I'm finished with it, especially since I like to stop from time to time and work on short stories. But that's the good thing about not writing for a living. If it takes me twenty years to finish this one, that's okay—my family still gets fed. That's what I call keeping things in perspective.

SUSAN ELIZABETH HOWE

Susan Elizabeth Howe
Poet

Interviewed by Douglas Talley

Susan Elizabeth Howe's poems have appeared in The New Yorker, Southwest
Review, Prairie Schooner, Shenandoah, *and other journals. Her book of poetry,*
Stone Spirits, *was published by the Charles Redd Center for Western Studies
at Brigham Young University, where she is a professor of English. This interview
originally appeared online in 2003 at* Meridian *magazine (www.ldsmag.com) and
is reprinted with permission.*

*Interviewer Douglas Talley graduated with a bachelor of fine arts in creative
writing from Bowling Green State University in 1976. A lawyer by profession, he
has published two books of poetry, and his poems have appeared in several journals.*

**One of the intriguing elements in a number of the poems in *Stone Spirits*
is your sense of the vast stretch of time and how it can be compressed
into the present. From your poem "Things in the Night Sky": "We are
surrounded by ancient light / We can't see, come millions of years /**

Through space we can't recite." From "The Paleontologist with an Ear Infection": "How can a cry heard one hundred / And thirty-five million years be old?" From "Lessons of Erosion": "To hike to the spires, you climb / Over two hundred million years, / Language and breath your sacrifice."

What is your interest in capturing time in this manner, on such a grand, geologic scale? Are you suggesting the "eternal moment" is simply a compilation of innumerable years, or something else?

My initial reasons for writing about these vast reaches of time is that when I was exploring the three subjects of these poems—the galaxies in the universe, a dinosaur, and the southern Utah landscape—I felt the need to try to grasp those immense distances of time and space. And, indeed, I do feel that they can help us understand the difference between our perspective and God's perspective. If the creation of the earth took four billion years, and humans have been here for only about ten thousand of those years, we can scarcely comprehend the processes of the creation, much less of the eternities. I think we have a tendency to reduce God's power and thought to our own levels, and I think we ought to be a lot more humble than that, aware of the immense difference between God's knowledge and our own.

Lines like these suggest that poetry can almost effortlessly transform the human perspective into a godlike perspective, as for example when William Blake wrote: "To see a World in a Grain of Sand / And a Heaven in a Wild Flower / Hold Infinity in the palm of your hand / And Eternity in an hour."

Do you believe poetry has an inherent power not just to inform our sense of the divine perspective but to actually grant us that perspective on occasion? Do you think it can actually transform us into a more divine nature?

I suppose it is possible, if a poet is both in tune with God and gifted with language, to convey God's perspective in a poem. Whether such a perspective is received or not will also depend on the spiritual condition of the reader. But I think most poetry, including my own, has much more modest aims. The impetus for my poems is almost always an attempt to understand why an experience or image or story has impressed itself so forcefully on my mind—what does it mean to me? And because what makes our lives meaningful is associated with our beliefs, I hope that what I believe—basically, Mormon doctrines—informs my poems in some way. But I would never claim to be able to assume a divine perspective in my poems; I'm much too mortal and limited for that.

Another delightful element in your work is your sense of the comic. It's readily evident even in the titles of some of the poems, such as "The

Paleontologist with an Ear Infection" and "In the Cemetery, Studying Embryos." The idea seems irresistible in your work that the comic perspective is also rather godlike, that there is a gentle omniscient presence looking down upon human affairs and, on occasion, chuckling. Is this intended, or is it reading too much into the poems? What sense of humor, if any, do you attribute to God?

Yes, I believe that God has a sense of humor because humor is associated with happiness and also provides us with a means of coping with grief and distress. So I see humor as good, and I believe that all good qualities originate with God. But again, I don't think that I have the capacity to convey God's sense of humor, just my own. "In the Cemetery, Studying Embryos" is about resurrection, and it tickles me that many readers have seen that. But to think of mortal remains as embryonic in the sense that they are waiting for another birth was just an idea that came to me while I was sitting in a cemetery one day. It certainly arises from my beliefs, but I don't know that I feel comfortable attributing it to God. I don't really feel qualified to speak for God.

You also allow, quite sympathetically, for the tragic, as evident in your bittersweet elegy, "To My Brother in His Casket." How did the writing of that poem help you deal with your loss? Can poetry help us reconcile the tragic?

My friend Peter Makuck, the editor of *Tar River Poetry*, taught me that poetry can be healing to someone who is trying to deal with loss or injury. To write about pain—what has caused it, how it feels—can help the writer release that pain, and readers who have suffered the same or similar experiences are comforted in reading the poems and learning that their own feelings are shared by others. One of the greatest poems to show a passage through grief to eventual resolution and peace is Tennyson's "In Memoriam."

My twenty-year-old brother was killed on his mission in an automobile accident. His death was one of the most difficult losses of my life to reconcile and accept. I hope that my poem is something of a memorial to him. I hope it expresses my love for him and my huge sense of loss at his death.

The opening section of poems in *Stone Spirits* is titled "The world is hard, not of your making," a line taken from the poem "Archangel." A number of the poems describe a physical world that is harsh, where "more ruin waits for weather," as stated in the poem "Lessons of Erosion." How do you reconcile your faith with the harshness of the physical world?

It is not just the physical world that is harsh. Humans suffer horrendous trials; I don't know anyone who hasn't been through terrible pain, physical or emotional or both. I hope that in my poems the harshness of the physical world suggests the harshness of what we sometimes suffer. But if I understand the purpose of life, real high-stakes struggles are necessary or we won't ever grow morally or spiritually. God has honored us with agency so that we can actually become more godlike; Christ has made it possible for us to repent when we mess up, so that we can try again.

One of your finest poems is "Mary Keeps All These Things." Tell us about the inspiration for that poem and how it developed.

One Christmas season it occurred to me that the person most involved in Christ's birth, in addition to him, was his mother, and yet we have no account of the experience from her perspective. So I tried to imagine what the whole long event was like for her and let her speak in her own voice.

What directed you toward poetry in the first place? Were there defining moments in your life when you knew you wanted to be a poet? Whatever possessed you to pursue this "finikin" art, as Wallace Stevens put it?

I wrote poetry in high school and my early college years, but just for myself—I had received no training, not even in high school English classes. In college, I majored in Spanish and minored in French, and then after graduating I immediately realized that I'd majored in the wrong subjects (though they have been useful in teaching me how language works, as well as about some of the relationships between English and other Romance languages). So I didn't begin to train in poetry until my master's and doctoral programs. Then I took several poetry-writing classes even though I thought I would primarily be a fiction writer and a dramatist.

One of the major forces in my development as a poet was a friend in my doctoral program, George Bilgere. He is a very fine poet, and for about a year we had a pact that we would write a new poem and exchange it every week. That constant writing helped me learn the discipline of poetry. What finally turned me to poetry as my primary art form was that I began publishing poems in literary journals before I even had any stories ready to send out. That was a clue to me that I was a better poet than fiction writer.

How would you describe your principal literary influences? What authors do you return to, and why?

Anyone who wants to be a poet should constantly be reading poetry, and so I read a great deal. I try to read the current volume of *The Best American Poetry* each year, and I subscribe to two or three literary journals where I am trying to place poems. This means I am exposed to many contemporary poets, and when I encounter one whose work I admire, I buy that poet's collections and read in depth, trying to look at everything from subject matter to rhetorical strategies to figurative language.

I often copy individual poems into a notebook, because I think such writing helps me observe the individual words and the lines more thoroughly. I memorize a few new poems each year so that I will have them in my head. Some of the poets I have read in depth include Mark Jarman, Chase Twichell, Louise Glück, Billy Collins, Elizabeth Bishop, May Swenson, Mary Oliver, and Maxine Kumin. A couple years ago, I found a remarkable new poet named Morrie Creech. I recommend all these poets very highly; they are a joy to read.

Tell us about your writing habits. Do you work at it every day? Do you have a particular schedule or discipline to stay at the work, even when it's not going well? Do you have any tricks for working through the blocks?

I wish I could write every day, but during the semester I have to devote most of my time to teaching, so I usually write only two or three days a week. I eagerly await summer and semester breaks because then I have more time. It is hard for me to settle in and start writing, so I always read poems for about half an hour at the beginning of a writing session. This moves me over into my more creative self as well as giving me models of several fine poems in my head.

I write first drafts by hand on the back of scratch paper. This lowers the stakes for me. "It's just scratch paper," I say. "It doesn't matter if what I write isn't very good." Early drafts are almost never very good, but they usually have the seeds of what can become a better poem. I always have more ideas for poems than I'm able to get to; I try to work on about five poems in each session, and then I come back to those poems until I haven't found things to revise in about four readings. I wouldn't dream of sending anything out to be published until I had taken it to my poetry group and responded to their suggestions.

How has your work as a teacher of creative writing helped shape your own poetry?

I try to assign exercises that give my students a new imaginative space from which to write a poem, and as often as I can, I also complete those exercises. They have led to some of my best poems, especially in the last few years.

What value do you see in the workshop approach to creative writing promoted by colleges and universities? Are workshops a good idea?

I've found that I can't just turn beginning writers loose in a workshop, because they are not critical readers; they themselves don't recognize the difference between a strong line and a weak line, vague imagery and specific sensory imagery, and so forth. So I don't use workshops in introductory classes. But in intermediate and advanced classes, workshops are invaluable. By the end of the semester, students are able to find other writers whose work they respect, and they often form writing groups with these other class members. Workshops are helpful to me because if a student hears that several other readers don't understand a line or an image, she is much more likely to accept my own criticism of the problem. The main difficulty with workshops is that they can lead to poems that all sound alike; students have to be warned not to try to rewrite another student's poem but to let him know what its strengths and weaknesses are on the writer's own terms.

Do you believe in a Mormon school of poetry, like the Augustans or the Pre-Raphaelites? Do you want to see a body of art that is distinctly Mormon?

In my mind, the question you ask is a question of audience: should there be a body of art created for a Mormon audience, using language and symbols and references that only those within the culture will understand, or should Mormon artists consider the larger culture as the audience for their art? I think that our culture is mature enough to support art for both audiences and that the artist's talent and interests will suggest the audience she should create for. Both can be subsumed under the category of Mormon art. But standards of craftsmanship should be high regardless of audience and regardless of medium. I am encouraged by the excellence I see developing in Mormon art in so many different mediums: drama, film, the novel, visual art, and music, as well as poetry. It seems to me that in many ways our culture is coming of age and that many very talented Mormons are using their gifts to bless our culture and the larger American culture as well.

In summary, tell us how your faith has influenced your poetry and your approach to your work.

The very perceptive questions you have posed in this interview point out how my faith has influenced my poetry. The specific subject matter of my poems is not usually religious, but my perspective on my subject is often the result of my faith. Flannery O'Connor said that her definition of Catholic art was the Catholic mind working on any subject. That is a definition that I apply to Mormon poetry: a Mormon mind working on any subject.

What advice do you have for the aspiring Mormon writer?

I've pretty much already given it: read all the time, read a variety of contemporary poets, give yourself permission to write bad early drafts and then work on them, and get yourself a writing group with other poets whose criticism you respect. One more thing: you have to send your work out to literary journals and keep it out until it is accepted. No one will ever come to you and beg you to let them publish your poems; that's just not how the system works.

DEAN HUGHES

Dean Hughes
Novelist

Dean Hughes has published more than eighty books for children, young adults, and adults. He wrote several Mormon novels early in his career, including Hooper Haller, Jenny Haller, Cornbread and Prayer, Under the Same Stars, *and* As Wide as the River. *After publishing in the national market, he recently returned to the Mormon audience with his best-selling Children of the Promise series of World War II–era historical novels and other novels. In addition, he and his son Tom have coauthored three nonfiction books. With a Ph.D. from the University of Washington, Hughes has taught at Brigham Young University and elsewhere. The original version of this interview appeared in* Irreantum, *summer 2000.*

Trace for us how your writing inclination developed and how you first became a published writer.

Back in my childhood days, I somehow developed a sense that I was going to do something interesting with my life. My teachers told me I was smart and I was a good student, in spite of talking too much. But it was really my mother who made me feel I could do whatever I set my mind to. She read to me and created my first love for books, and even more importantly she welcomed me in from catching grasshoppers and taught me to embroider. Somehow, along with the desire to do something well, she also gave me the feeling that the range of joys in this life is very wide.

I started talking about wanting to be a writer when I was a kid, and by junior high I told people I was going to be a writer when I grew up. I read a lot, started writing stories, had a great creative writing teacher at Ogden High, a man named Wilson Thornley, and just kept believing I could do it. I wrote a novel— a *Catcher in the Rye* kind of thing—the summer after I graduated from high school, and it got rejected. By then I had developed a secret image of myself as sensitive and rather deep—but I was still playing football.

At Weber State I majored in English, took creative writing classes from Gordon Allred, and decided to go on for a master's in creative writing at the University of Washington. I wrote a novel for my thesis but didn't publish that one either. I had already planned to go on for a Ph.D. in literature so I would have a way to make a living. I did that and then found a job at Central Missouri State University. I was teaching a lot of literature classes at first and had little time, but I got interested, because of a children's literature festival there, in writing for younger audiences. I wrote a young adult novel, it got rejected, and then I did a children's historical novel about the early Mormon period in Jackson County. In the meantime I had published some children's nonsense poetry and some stories, but nothing else, and a lot of years had gone by since I had written that first novel.

I was thirty-four when I finally sold that historical novel, *Under the Same Stars*, to Deseret Book, so I had been trying for seventeen years and it was the fourth book I had written. All this was ever so much more complicated than this summary may imply, and the truth is that I quit a dozen times but then couldn't ever stay quit. Interestingly, however, after I sold the sequel to that first novel, I sent a humorous children's book to Atheneum in New York and sold it to the first editor who read it—the famous Jean Karl—and I've been publishing in both the Mormon and general markets ever since.

What are your favorites among your works? If someone asked you where to begin reading your books and how to get the best overview of your career and writing range, where would you point them?

I have written everything from nonsense verse for preschoolers to an adult true crime book. I do sports, but I also do humor, mysteries, historical fiction, and serious young adult novels. I get so many ideas that I can't settle down to one thing.

I'm concerned that some kids overemphasize athletics. Those concerns come out in various ways in my Angel Park books. I try to portray Little League the way it should be: with a coach who teaches kids to play the game well but doesn't pressure them too much about winning. In my soccer and basketball books, I raise questions about the relative importance of sports, the dangers of racism and sexism, and the struggle of growing up in a complicated world. I see nothing paradoxical about writing a fast-action sports book that also raises questions about life. I've had lots of fun with some funny books about Nutty and Lucky, and I think the sports novels are good, solid books for kids—especially some boys who are reluctant readers.

I have always enjoyed writing more serious works. I loved writing *Switch Tracks*, a young adult novel, along with *Family Pose* and *Team Picture*. Another of my favorites, more about my own life than most, is *The Trophy*. I suspect that the Children of the Promise series represents my best work, although that's difficult for me to judge. Also, I'm proud of a young adult novel I recently published with Atheneum called *Soldier Boys*. It's also about World War II, and it includes a prominent Mormon character, but it's for the national market.

Most fiction is a combination of three elements: what the author has experienced, observed, and imagined. How do those three elements work together for you?

I think my work is almost never autobiographical, in one sense, and of course always is. All my characters are me, to some degree. When Alex gives a young woman a blessing in *Rumors of War*, feels the Spirit, and then a few minutes later doubts his own faith, that's right out of my experience as a missionary and right out of my never-quite-as-spiritual-as-I'd-like-to-be life. But I do think I have one gift: I seem to possess a good deal of capacity for empathy. I seem to be able to imagine how I would feel in certain circumstances, and I like to believe I can imagine myself as older, younger, a woman, and of course a soldier, even though I've never been one.

What works of Mormon literature have you personally most enjoyed? What works of general literature?

I really read a lot of different kinds of things. During my years as a literature professor, I specialized in nineteenth-century British lit, with an emphasis on the novel. So I love the great, classic novels. In Mormon lit, Levi Peterson and Doug Thayer are two of my heroes, but I don't think I write very much like them—and, of course, not as well. I love Faulkner and Cormac McCarthy and Ann Tyler and Ivin Doig and a lot of other fiction writers. They're not much like each other, and I'm not much like any of them. I guess they have some influence on me, but I couldn't say exactly what the influence is. I do know that I'm limited in my own talents, so I've learned to do what I can do: tell a good story and try not to get in the way too much. When I try to write great sentences, I usually embarrass myself.

Do you like writing? Tell us more about your writing habits and what motivates you.

I love the process of writing, and I think I have a good MO. I do a lot of prewriting—brainstorming, outlining, describing characters, et cetera—and I write a fast, sloppy first draft. All of that is creative and fun for me, and then, once I have a draft in my computer, I love to revise more than anything. That's the polishing, artistic part of writing, for me.

I do like to sit down at 8:00 in the morning and think of myself as going to work. Usually at 8:00 I don't feel like writing, but by 8:30 or 9:00 I almost always feel sorry for all the people in the world who do anything else. The self-pity usually hits me again in the afternoon, by about 4:00, when I stagger upstairs from my little basement office. I go for a run at noon sometimes, and I can handle interruptions without a lot of problem. I know I'm not a great writer, but I do think I'm a pro. I pride myself on my discipline.

What motivates me? That's always so complicated to answer honestly. I started out, like most young writers, thinking I would get fame and fortune. The fame a writer gets is very limited and gradually means almost nothing, and the money is so unpredictable that it's the scariest part of the life. What I love is to create the stories. I like responses   letters from kids or, now, adult readers and meeting people who want to talk about the books—and I've enjoyed doing school visits over the years, but for me the great joy of being a writer is the writing itself.

You worked for about fifteen years at home as a writer while your wife worked outside. You served as a bishop during much of that time. Tell us more about how your career has played out.

I quit teaching because I was too naive to know better. I don't recommend such stupidity, but I don't know how I could have done it without being naive. My wife, Kathleen, is a very organized person, and she worked as a busy school administrator with big responsibilities. And she likes security. But when I told her I wanted to give up my tenured teaching position to write full time, she leaped off the edge with me, and she trusted that we would land somewhere.

At first I taught technical writing for Shipley Associates, did some writing for hire, and made money from school visits. It took six or seven years to get to the point where I was making a living. Kathy provided the steady check and the insurance benefits, and that's one of the biggest problems for a writer: operating without those paid benefits. But overall it's been a fairly easy ride for me, considering what we bit off. I was able to publish consistently, find new ideas, move into various markets, et cetera.

I was home writing when I was a bishop, and sometimes that meant too many telephone calls, but it also meant I was there when I was needed sometimes. My kids were gone away all day at school, so I had the house to myself most of the year, and when they were home Kathy was home on the same schedule. I loved being home when my daughter needed a ride to dance class or one of my sons had a JV football game or a track meet. I could knock off and be there for all those things.

I hate to admit it, but it's been a good life. Writers love to suffer, I know, and maybe that's why I'm no better than I am. I've had life too good: lots of freedom—even golf on Friday, like a dentist, sometimes—and pretty good financial rewards. Would I recommend it? Well, it takes a certain personality, maybe, and some luck. I would definitely have another career option ready.

How does teaching writing affect you as a writer? Is it even possible to teach creative writing?

I really prefer to write. I like the classroom part of teaching, but I weary of reading student writing—not that it's bad, but there is just so much of it. On the other hand, I find that teaching forces me to take a harder look at my own writing. As I revise, I ask myself how tough I would be on a student for some of my vague descriptions or maudlin sentiments.

I do think that creative writing can be taught. Talent can't be taught, of course, but that's true in any area. I can teach process, and I think that's something creative writing teachers have tended to avoid. To me, the idea that each person has some magical way to write is nonsense. The creative process can be improved and adjusted. Just think how many people opposed using word processors for creative writing when they first came out. Hear anyone saying that now?

By workshopping with students, I can help them see what makes sense in their writing and what doesn't. Every semester I'm stunned by how much my students improve. I really emphasize revision, and that's something students need to work on more than almost anything. What most young writers lack is discipline.

What have you learned about marketing yourself as a writer and managing your writing career?

I think most writers sort of feel their way along in this business, and that's what I've done. My agent thinks I should have developed more of a niche, probably stressing my sports fiction, but I've always done a lot of different kinds of things: middle-grade, young adult, adult, even an early reader book; fiction, nonfiction; LDS, national; humor, sports, serious subjects, mysteries. I do what seems fun, and I write the ideas I get. The one obvious thing I've had to do is figure out what I can sell and what will bring in enough income to feed a family. I've done more series books than I might have done if I hadn't been trying to make a living by writing. Series provide security, and they don't have to be poorly written, but they do tend to use certain formulas, and they're not as satisfying, for the most part, as the more literary novels I've done. Of course, when I speak of series, I'm excluding Children of the Promise, which is a series but is quite different from the more commercial children's series I've done.

I have written a lot of books, and one thing has sort of led to another. I got interested in a Mormon history series because I was living in Missouri and wanted to do children's books. From there I moved to other topics: humor, sports, et cetera. And then other ideas came as I had to take a hard look at how a person could actually make a living writing. Children of the Promise was the outgrowth of wanting to return to historical fiction and realizing that a period as vast as World War II would work only as a big family saga.

Tell us more about your experience with Children of the Promise.

Children of the Promise was something my wife got me thinking about: Why don't you write about the forties? I spent two years reading about World War II before I began writing. The whole experience has been life-altering. I put nearly a decade into the project, and I've never steeped myself in anything so long and thoroughly. I've loved it all; I am somewhat tired now but enormously exhilarated. I've reached a bigger audience than ever before, even with my national books; made more money than I'm used to; and received an overwhelming response. I get letters from adults, who can tell me what they like about the books—really wonderful, moving letters. And my name is actually recognized once or twice a month, instead of once or twice a year.

So it has made a great difference in my life, at one level, and finally not that much difference. But wow! How many things in life are this dramatic, fulfilling, and satisfying? I have loved writing the books. I finished the last chapter with at least as much sorrow as relief.

Will you give us an idea of what your sales have been like? How do the Mormon market and the national market compare?

Sales have really varied over the years. I've had some lean years, but I've almost always done as well as I would have as a full-time professor, and sometimes much better. Most of my books are out of print now, just because books do disappear quickly in the modern market. I've published more than eighty books. In terms of my total sales, I have no idea. I would think the number is in the millions.

I don't think the national and Mormon markets are so different as people might think. Deseret Book is very professional, and as the organization grows it is becoming a little bit too much like the New York publishers: books go out of print faster, you get your editor's phone mail instead of live voice, and all the rest. Certainly, there are some topics a writer can't deal with in the Mormon market, but those things are becoming fewer all the time, and most of the things I can't deal with I wouldn't choose to write about anyway. For a long time I felt that I couldn't write about Mormons in the national market, but I'm seeing some better signs there all the time.

What are future prospects for Mormon literature? Do you think our writers will ever win national awards for fiction that deals with Mormon themes, settings, and characters?

I think the future looks great for Mormon literature. People keep saying to me, "Thank you for telling the truth." I know that my books are pretty safe, but if readers are looking for more realism and less that is promotional and self-satisfying, that's a very good sign. We are getting to be a bigger market, so we can produce books for different tastes and still sell enough to make them worthwhile.

Watch how we'll move into more genres and styles in the next twenty years. In 1979, when I sold my first novel to Deseret Book, there was almost nothing. In fact, in 1975 a Bookcraft editor told me that the company had never been able to sell fiction. Look at us now. But it's a very young art form in our culture, and it takes time. The great mistake is that many fine Mormon writers avoid the market because it isn't good enough. But they are the writers who can bring it here. Maybe I've compromised on some issues over the years, but I would like to think I've helped bring the quality of Mormon fiction to a little higher place.

Do I think we'll have Mormon writers winning national awards for writing about our culture? No question. But we've got to learn to look at ourselves honestly, and not everyone is going to like that. I just don't think that means we have to give up our faith and commitment. There's plenty of room for conversation about who we are without throwing out the basic things we believe and share.

As for me, I'll keep writing for children and adults and for both the national and Mormon markets, but I want to slow down a little. My goal is to write books that are truly fine pieces of art. I don't feel I've done that yet; I always think my next book will be the one I'll finally be satisfied with. I have a feeling I can get better in my old age, and I want to try to do that.

ROBERT KIRBY

Robert Kirby
Humorist

Interviewed by Edgar C. Snow Jr.

While working a police officer, Robert Kirby started writing anonymous humorous newspaper columns. Eventually, he became one of the Salt Lake Tribune's *anchor columnists, widely known for lampooning Mormons while simultaneously practicing the religion. He has published two novels and several compilations of his humor columns, as well as a book about Utah's murdered police officers. The original version of this interview appeared in* Irreantum, *spring 2001.*

An attorney in Atlanta, Edgar C. Snow Jr. wrote a humorous book titled Of Curious Workmanship: Musings on Things Mormon *(Signature Books, 1999). He has published in* Dialogue: A Journal of Mormon Thought, *the* Journal of Book of Mormon Studies, *and elsewhere.*

Can you elaborate on how, when, and where you aspired, or were foreordained, to the calling of Mormon humorist?

I'm not sure. My scholastic and employment record would indicate that I've always been something of a smart aleck, especially where organized behavior is concerned. The Mormon humorist part came later, most visibly when I started lampooning the Utah culture as a columnist for the *Utah County Journal*, sometime around 1992.

One day this light went on in my head, a sudden burst of understanding about the legitimate side to the behavior that once got me suspended or fired. I'm not suggesting any sort of spiritual confirmation but rather that I finally realized I'd been given this left-handed way of looking at things for a reason. Better yet, there was a necessary place for it within the Mormon experience.

There's also the possibility that one too many Sunday school lessons drove me around the bend. If that's true, maybe this is just what keeps me from taking a gun to church. However, judging from the feedback I've received over the years, there are a lot of fellow travelers out there.

I heard you say once that President Hinckley all but set you apart for your position as Resident Fool at the *Salt Lake Tribune*. Could you comment on that and your experience at the *Tribune*?

I wouldn't go so far as to say that I was set apart. It might imply that I have President Hinckley's blessing or endorsement for what I write. I don't. I prefer it that way. As the Lord's anointed, President Hinckley has no business lurking out here on the lunatic fringe with the likes of you and me. But you're probably referring to the time my stake president talked to me about a column I wrote in which I claimed I could beat up President Hinckley. I didn't say I wanted to. I was simply responding to readers constantly asking me if I was afraid of church leaders. In fairness, I also said I could beat up the Pope, Mother Theresa couldn't take a punch, and Billy Graham was sick and therefore no real threat. So why would I be afraid of church leaders?

Anyway, the long and short of it was that my stake president thought that particular column was a bit irreverent. He's probably right. I mean, I freely admit to being more than a little crazy. I ended up talking by phone with the general authority who brought the offending column to the attention of the stake president. It was all in the best of spirits, but they wanted me to know they were concerned about me going too far. As my ecclesiastical leaders, they were perfectly within their rights. They asked me to be more careful. I said I would. On the off chance that President Hinckley was offended, I wrote him a letter of apology. I said I wouldn't write stuff like that anymore, but I still thought I could beat up the Pope. I got a letter back from one of his secretaries two weeks later telling me that the president wasn't offended and wishing me luck.

I would like to point out that my stake president was a good man. He was the stake president because he has talents in that area. That said, he told me that he found some of what I do to be vulgar and light-minded. I'm not offended by that, and I hope he's not offended by the fact that I find some of his behavior incredibly boring. We have different senses of humor. His particular sense of humor probably serves him very well in his capacity as a stake president. I think it's safe to say that I wasn't sent here with the expectation that I would become a stake president. If I had to use his sense of humor to balance the talents and traits I have, I'd probably kill myself.

A lot of Mormons behave as if God grades on the curve. Too often we use other people as the standard by which we measure our worthiness to God. You and I weren't put here to fashion ourselves after President Hinckley. In addition to it being a colossal waste of time, it's contrary to God's plan. God made us as individuals, and our job now is to become the best people we can be, individually. I'm on a rant here. Next question.

President Hinckley is widely recognized as a charming man full of good humor. I often refer to him as "prophet, seer, revelator, and humorist." How do you see his humor affecting Mormon culture?

I don't see his sense of humor changing what Mormons laugh at now, but rather I think it will change how hypersensitive we are to ribbing from other people. His sense of humor is very much a self-deprecating one, and I think he's done a marvelous job of helping us shrug off a lot of that martyr mentality we've packed around since Nauvoo. If you want to be a player in the world religion business, you can't go around sulking because someone thinks you're a bit odd. Humor has this way of making you okay with being odd.

On a Utah level, Mormonism can be stressful. Not only does it require a lot from its members, but there is a great deal of internal pressure—both imagined and real— to maintain appearances. Humor goes a long way toward alleviating the pain of realizing that not only can you never be perfect, but everyone already knows you aren't.

You had a dog once as a missionary companion. Tell me about that experience. Was it a pilot program in your mission?

Toward the end of my mission in Uruguay [1973–75], I adopted a stray dog. We weren't supposed to have pets, but I wasn't a very obedient missionary. I kept the big rules but didn't let the smaller ones get in the way of what I wanted to do. My junior companion at the time was Carl English from New Jersey. The dog in question was a large German shepherd and greyhound mix we called Lurch. The town was San Jose de Carrasco. Tough place. Nobody wanted to hear from us. We had a lot of doors slammed in our faces and quite a bit of name-calling.

I got bored with all this, which is a bad thing for me. I get into trouble when I get bored. One day I put a white shirt, tie, nametag, and pair of gym shorts on Lurch and took him out tracting. The responses were nothing less than amazing. People didn't know how to handle a four-legged Mormon missionary. They weren't ready for humor coming at them from that direction, and it caught a lot of them pleasantly off-guard. It wasn't long before people started watching for us. They quit calling us names. I think they finally realized that we were human. Sharing humor does that.

Elder Lurch didn't catch on as a pilot program. The assistants to the president came out and told us to quit dressing up the dog as a missionary, and we more or less complied. But they also told us to get rid of Lurch, to which I responded, "Or what?" Neither one of them was big enough to make that happen. Lurch stayed with me until I went home, at which point I turned him over to Elder English, who passed him along to the next missionary. As far as I know, he was still there a year later.

I believe you once mentioned that Mark Twain's *Roughing It* is perhaps your favorite book. I see a kinship between Samuel Clemens, that "Wild Humorist of the Pacific Slope," and you, our own "Wild Humorist of the Wasatch Front." I've heard others suggest you are the Mormon Dave Barry. Which do you prefer, and why?

Twain is the absolute supreme commander and high overlord of American satire. I read *Huckleberry Finn* the first time when I was eleven and have worshipped him ever since. Any similarities between Twain and myself are high sacrilege, so quit it. *Roughing It* is one of many favorite books. What I liked about it was the part wherein Twain recounts his visit to Salt Lake City. It was a humorous, even punishing, account of Mormon-dominated early life and a pleasant switch from the corporate spin on Mormon history that I was used to.

As for Dave Barry, I met him the last time he was in Salt Lake. He's every bit as funny in person as he is in print. If I had to choose between being like either of them, it's probably Dave. But I hope I'm cutting my own trail in this business, which perhaps goes without saying. I mean, really, how many religion humorists are there? There certainly aren't enough Mormon humorists. Pity, actually. I think the gospel is the most interesting when it's cast in a humorous light. I'm much more encouraged by stuff that makes me smile.

Which humorists or other authors have influenced you most?

Humorists would be Patrick McManus, P.J. O'Rourke, James Thurber, Lewis Grizzard, and Erma Bombeck. Authors, probably Robert Lewis Taylor, Pat Conroy, Harper Lee, Levi Peterson, Martin Cruz Smith, and James Lee Burke.

But inside the church, I would have to say that the greatest influences on me have been cartoonists Cal Grondahl and Pat Bagley, particularly the early Grondahl cartoon books published by Sunstone. One day I picked up *Freeway to Perfection* and very nearly killed myself laughing. Nothing about Mormonism was the same for me after that. It was so much better, so much fuller. I believe that there are people, some of them future leaders, who have remained faithful because Cal gave Mormons a safety valve. It's unfortunate that his contributions aren't recognized more.

A *Newsweek* article reported that "laughter evolved from the heavy breathing that accompanies something like playful wrestling" and that "ritualized panting—laughter—then might have come to represent the playful activity itself, signaling 'I'm enjoying this.'"[1] Do you have a theory of humor? Why people laugh? Why Mormons laugh?

There are so many positive physical benefits to laughter that it's a wonder laughter isn't included in the Word of Wisdom. It boosts your immune system by activating T lymphocytes and natural killer cells that destroy invading organisms. It increases gamma-interferon, a disease-fighting protein, and best of all it triggers a flood of beta-endorphins. Free drugs, woo-hoo. I think most people laugh simply because it's a pleasure to do so. It's certainly a better alternative than screaming.

I think Mormons laugh—at least within the context of the church experience—because if we didn't, we'd go nuts. This is particularly true in Utah, where pressure to measure up or conform can be severe. If anything, I think this is the secret to whatever success I've had at this. I didn't create the demand. I'm not even all that original in my style. If anything, I'm probably simply brazen enough to write what so many others are thinking. Lots of us have suffered at the hands of gospel Nazis. If it wasn't a strict parent, it was an unimaginative seminary teacher or overly dogmatic bishop.

Laughing at certain things is our way of getting rid of the guilt that we have been taught is the primary vehicle of the gospel, something that is so much a part of being reared in any religion. It's a way of saying that you don't have to be just another cow in the herd in order to be Mormon. Face it—ninety percent of church is moo stuff. Like humor, the true beauty of the gospel lies in its simplicity.

Is there a distinctive Mormon sense of humor? Can or should Mormon humorists create a style of our own?

Since control or correlation is such an indelible part of Mormonism, I think some people would love it if there were a distinctive or approved Mormon sense of humor. That would make it safe for them. But I'm not sure where you would look to find humor that is particularly Mormon. Other than the occasional chuckle elicited during a general conference talk, there's no official church endorsement of humor.

Some years ago, Deseret Book published *Best-Loved Humor of the LDS People*, a book so singularly unfunny that it ought to be at least a misdemeanor to own a copy. What wasn't lame was not singularly Mormon—it borrowed heavily from other faiths, with only slight changes in casting to make it Mormon. If this is our best humor, what we as a people find the funniest, it's no wonder people think we're anal. As for creating our own style of humor, that's something that happens on its own. Humor is whatever makes you laugh, a natural process that fails when you force it or try to corral it.

I heard you once admonish an audience to "hold to the ironic rod." Could you explain that doctrine?

For me, irony is the greatest teaching tool. The psychological world has two poles: the way we want things to be, and the way they really are. Irony is everything in between, particularly any attempts by us to correlate one with the other. The most important lessons life teaches us are the ones we learn by accident, usually at a time when we're clueless as to what's happening.

Mormons are ripe for irony because we're so sure we have all the answers that we can remain oblivious to many of the questions. Unfortunately, life then has to teach us that we're stupid before it can teach us how to be smart. If you look at life with a sense of irony, it doesn't hurt so much when this lesson comes.

I'm over-generalizing, but ironic wit seems to characterize American humor in the eighties and nineties, rather than the wacky gags or physical humor common in the sixties and seventies. I suspect the cause is the rise of comedians such as David Letterman and Jerry Seinfeld, among others. Irony rules. It's hip. It permeates our media, from Sprite commercials making fun of the idea of a commercial while pretending they're not trying to sell Sprite to Alanis Morrisette warbling about irony itself, causing literary types to argue among themselves whether she's using the term *irony* correctly. Will irony eventually become unfunny, to be followed by some other flavor of humor?

I think irony will always be with us because it is so completely human. It's old, at least two thousand years. I think the Savior was using irony when he told everyone to stop worrying about the sliver in their neighbor's eye and pay attention to the plank in their own. The beautiful thing about ironic wit is that it's such a Christ-like form of humor. George Orwell said it best: "The aim of a joke is not to degrade the human being but to remind him that he is already degraded." It's a gentle way of preparing us for the entire point of the gospel: namely, that we can do something about it.

One could argue that, in order to endure, great works of tragedy must contain comic relief, while great works of comedy must contain tragic relief. Do you think that's true?

I think the two are inextricably linked. Laughter and crying are closely related. Both are necessary coping mechanisms. They're also natural contrasts, which is another great rule of life. You can't appreciate something without it having some kind of opposing or countering force. I think it's fair to say that much of my humor about religion stems from having my faith destroyed by black and white thinkers in the church. I had to rebuild my belief in the face of those same people, and humor was the best mechanism for coping with them. Even when made up of good people, large groups are dangerous to individuals. The bigger the group, the lower the collective IQ.

Some Mormon authors believe that inspiration plays a part in their artistic creation. Do you ever feel that you write inspired humor? How do you come up with funny things to write about or funny ways to write about things?

I told you, I'm crazy. But other than that, I'm very much a product of my environment. I sometimes get feedback from Mormons angry about something I've written. Generally, it's e-mail or letters from people complaining that I'm being too irreverent or too punishing. Some contain the accusation that I'm thwarting God's plan by giving people the wrong idea about Mormonism, that I might even drive members into inactivity. I don't think so. Disaffection from the faith was a problem long before I showed up. Only about forty percent of Mormons in the United States attend church regularly. If we had to blame this inactivity on a particular type of Mormon, I very much doubt that we could blame it on humorists. If you asked inactive Mormons what drove them away from the church, they aren't going to say it was because someone made them laugh. I'm guessing that it's the overly starched Mormon who does the majority of the alienating. I know they've inspired me to do what I do. I wouldn't have known what kind of Mormon I was if they hadn't been themselves. And for that I thank them.

As for coming up with funny things to write about, it's easy. I go to church. The basic Mormon ward is such a condensed experience of antipodal human behavior that something's always happening.

Speaking of inspiration, Mormon authors frequently note they're inspired by Orson F. Whitney's observations that we will yet have Miltons and Shakespeares of our own. Will we ever have Twains and Thurbers of our own?

Sure. The church is growing. It's inevitable that we'll have great humorists and lampoonists. Look at the advances in other artistic endeavors. Twenty years ago, there never would have been a Hollywood movie like Richard Dutcher's *God's Army*. Prior to him, films about Mormons came largely from apologists or antagonists, neither of which gave a realistic view of us. You'd have to be blind not to recognize Richard as the first in a long series of movie directors to credibly tackle the Mormon experience on a national level. Is *God's Army* the greatest film about Mormons that will ever be produced? No. But it's definitely a terrific sign of the times. Years from now, I predict that Dutcher will be regarded as the first filmmaker to bring Mormonism out where audiences could see us for what we really are. There's nothing for Mormons to be ashamed of in *God's Army* and loads of stuff to be proud of, namely that we're human beings first and Mormons a much distant second. Frankly, this is something that escapes a lot of Mormons.

As for humorists of world stature, certainly we will have them. Humor is an art form, and art grows with society and culture. So it stands to reason that as the church grows, so will our art. Just as Grondahl inspired me, I hope I've turned on a light for someone else, hopefully someone smarter.

Your first three humor collections—*Sunday of the Living Dead, Wake Me for the Resurrection*, and *Pat and Kirby Go to Hell*—were targeted toward the Utah and Latter-day Saint audience. Then, with *Family Home Screaming*, it appeared you were aiming broader than Mormon culture and the Beehive State, as the book deals with general family themes. Could you elaborate on the audience for your writing?

Family Home Screaming was a definite shift away from a primarily Mormon theme. My daughters were growing up, and I wanted a collection of columns that were inspired largely by the experience of raising them, or how not to do it. I also wanted something for a wider audience. The first three books targeted Mormon life, but life is so much bigger than just that. I think Mormonism will always be part of what I write, but it's not everything there is to write about.

For this reason, one part of the interview with Richard Dutcher in the autumn 2000 issue of *Irreantum* troubled me. Dutcher said Mormon writers who eliminate Mormonism from their work are either ignorant or cowardly. Now that's a bold statement from someone who no doubt would reject any outside attempt at dictating what type of films he should make. As a writer, I'll write whatever I'm moved to write. If my next book has nothing to do with Mormons, that's my business. You go where the story takes you. I wouldn't include Mormonism in my work just because I'm a Mormon.

You've written two novels, and I also recall that you wrote a short story about a missionary that appeared in *Sunstone* (the story, not the missionary). Do you plan on writing more fiction? How about hymns? Did you know we used to spell it *hims* until Carol Lynn Pearson made us change it?

Actually, it's more like *hums*. Most Mormons don't know the words to the songs in the humnal.

I love fiction. You can create the world any way you want it to be. It's a wonderful opportunity to play God and learn that the job isn't easy. My republished novel *Dark Angel* is doing moderately well, with great emphasis on "moderately." This is partly due to the fact that although the book is about Mormons, it is not directed at the LDS audience. As the title suggests, the book contains darker elements. It was originally published in a heavily edited format that I didn't like. That was in 1991. When I reacquired the rights last year, we put out the unabridged version.

The short story in *Sunstone* (July 1999) was "Letters from the Field," a collection of fictional journal entries from an elder laboring in South America. In the course of these entries, you see him change from an arrogant nineteen-year-old with all the answers to someone who just wants to be of service. Yes, I plan on writing more fiction, but I'm not sure that it will be in the LDS market. By the way, *Dark Angel* was my second novel. The first was *Brigham's Bees*, a historical mystery that is now out of print.

When does wholesome humor become the unwholesome "light-mindedness" warned against in the Doctrine and Covenants? What constraints do you feel writing Mormon humor?

First, I think everything has a humorous side to it. Everything. If you haven't laughed out loud in the middle of a personal prayer, then I don't think you are living the full gospel experience. I believe that God has a ripping sense of humor and that he communicates to us through every one of our emotions.

With respect to public humor, the trick is in knowing what you can and should share with other people. When I began the newspaper column, I knew that I would cross the line from time to time. Not because I wanted to, but because no two people can agree on exactly where the line is. D&C 63:64 says, "Remember that that which cometh from above is sacred, and must be spoken with care, and by constraint of the Spirit." But everything in this life comes from above. The entire experience was orchestrated by God. So, which parts are okay to laugh at? The part where you trip and fall down? The part where you trip and fall down in church? The part where you trip and fall down while passing the sacrament?

You get a lot of mail. How many pounds per week? Does it distract from your work, provide a constant supply of new humor material, or both?

I get a lot of feedback. Depending on what I've written, the response ranges from 80 to 150 e-mails and letters per week. It's gone as high as six hundred. Typically, less than five percent of this feedback is negative. Surprisingly enough, most of that comes from non-Mormons. There are more than a few anti-Mormon bigots in Utah, people who think that being in the minority relieves them of any obligation to show basic human kindness or decency. All you have to do to attract the attention of people like this is say that you're a Mormon. They'll tell you all about women and the priesthood, Mountain Meadows, and Classic Coke vs. New Coke. My favorites are the Born Agains. They're the Dobermans of Christianity. Love your fellow man even if it kills him.

As for angry Mormons, hearing from them lets me know that I've hit the mark. Usually it's from someone so utterly humorless that they're arrogant enough to think that making fun of them is the same thing as mocking God. I find this to be almost hysterically funny. Maybe that's what makes their anger so easy to tolerate. Being reviled by some people is a necessary part of what I do. On a personal level, it lets me know who I am. André Gide said it best: "It's better to be hated for what you are, than loved for what you are not." I don't think I've ever written something that someone somewhere didn't find offensive. No matter what happens, someone will always find a way to take it too seriously. What's amazing about this feedback is that people would actually presume to change what I think by insulting me. Weren't they paying attention in Sunday school?

But the vast majority of feedback is positive. Some of it has left me humbled. A woman once told me that my column was the only thing that brought a smile to her father's face in the last few months of his fight with terminal cancer. I still have a hard time thinking about that without getting choked up.

Do you think you will ever hear the words "Welcome to the humor session of general conference"? What's the future of Mormon humor? Any advice to the fledgling Mormon humorists out there?

I hope not. Official endorsement would be the death knell for Mormon humor. As for advice, do what comes naturally. It's in you. Go find it. When you do, don't be afraid to point it out to other people. Some of them won't like it, but that's okay. They're a big reason for doing it in the first place.

Twain suggests there will be no humor in heaven. In your book *Pat and Kirby Go to Hell*, you and your cartoon collaborator, Pat Bagley, go to hell and back, whether in the body or not you probably cannot tell. Will there be Mormon humorists in the celestial kingdom? Terrestrial? Telestial? Outer darkness?

Yes, in all of them. Pat Bagley, who illustrated the four humor books I wrote, has already had his calling and damnation made sure. He's going to outer darkness. I'm a telestial spirit and proud of it. I think what Twain was expressing was his fear that heaven will be very much like church. If it is, why would anyone in their right mind want to go there?

---

[1] "The Science of Laughs," October 9, 2000.

NEIL LABUTE

Neil LaBute
Playwright

*A playwright, screenwriter, and director of films and plays, Neil LaBute burst
onto the independent film scene in 1997 with his Sundance Film Festival sensation*
In the Company of Men, *a film adaptation of his play by the same name. Since
then, LaBute has directed film adaptations of several more of his own plays, and
he has directed three major studio releases based on the writing of others. Born
in Detroit, LaBute grew up in the Spokane area of Washington. After graduating from BYU with a theater degree, he studied at the University of Kansas and
New York University. He joined the LDS faith while at BYU, but he was disfel-
lowshipped for his play* Bash. *The original version of this interview appeared in*
Irreantum, *winter 2003–spring 2004.*

You did your undergraduate work at BYU, and during that time you joined the LDS church.

Yes. I ended up at BYU as if by magic. It was really a kind of fluky thing. In some ways it's hazy enough that I almost don't remember. I had an LDS counselor in school who knew about these nonmember scholarships at BYU, which wasn't a place I ever would have looked into. I had a few LDS friends who were in the performing arts in high school, so I'd had some exposure to the church. I put in for one of those scholarships, and I got it. It made the most sense at the time, so off I went to a place where I really knew virtually no one.

You also did graduate work at BYU?

Yes, I came back six or seven years later and worked on a Ph.D. I did the coursework, did the research for my dissertation, all of that. But then, after the first year, I got a job teaching, because I already had an M.F.A. from New York University. I thought, Why not take the job rather than stay in school and finish, only to be out looking for a job again. So I took the teaching job and never did finish the Ph.D., which is a shame. It's one of those things I wish I'd done.

So you voluntarily went back to BYU, and they accepted you?

I think enough smoke had cleared. I probably left more smoke, unfortunately, the second time I was there for the one year than I did in the previous four years.

Have those two influences of BYU and Mormonism had much effect on how you've been shaped as a writer? Do you think you'd be different now without those two influences?

Undoubtedly I'd be different, both for good and bad. All experience shapes you as a writer. I didn't ever see myself as a Mormon writer, and yet I was, because I was a Mormon who was writing. I've written only one real piece of work that had anything to do, at least in a specific way, with members of the church. Of course, *Bash* was not really widely embraced by the church, to put it nicely.

I'm not really one to do much of what people ask me to do, and there was certainly a sense of the church not wanting me to write anything more about members of the church. Fortunately, I didn't feel any compulsion to do so. I only wrote *Bash* because the idea came to me, and I used the background of the church because it was at my fingertips, rather than doing research on Catholics or Christian Scientists or whatever else. I grew up in a community church with a very general sense of the Bible and faith, a more generalized Christianity than the specificity of a church like the LDS Church. So I used that in the piece to give some specific credence to these characters and their situations. I tried to juxtapose what was essentially the goodness of the church with these characters who were not protected from making mistakes simply by virtue of being members of that church. That's really what the whole piece is about. But it wasn't seen as that so much as—well, I don't think it was ever really pointed at as "This is an indictment of the church" so much as "This is just not very much of a trumpet." Moroni was in no danger of being replaced on the temple.

Did *Bash* have its roots during the BYU years?

Yes. During that second stay at BYU, I started doodling away on something that would ultimately become a portion of that.

Mormon playwright Eric Samuelsen made an interesting comment about your work. He said, "LaBute seems to see little need to dramatically depict characters who seek light and growth and repentance, but he seems to anticipate such growth taking place in the audience."

I think that's a pretty fair statement, actually. It's a fairly accurate sense of my communion with an audience. I'm essentially hopeful that they'll take something from what I'm showing. I've often said that you can achieve goodness by showing bad. It would be hard for me to believe that most people walk away from something like *Bash* or *Friends and Neighbors* or *Company of Men* saying, "I wish I could act like those folks. They have a good way of going about it." I hope they're getting my intent through the force of the work, but that's not necessarily always the case.

You leave a lot of work for the audience to do.

Yes, during and after. That's really the only way I'm interested in doing it, in the same way that I'm interested in that as an audience member. I like it when I'm left with a pile in my lap that I have to sort through on my own. I'm happy to raise questions, but I don't have all the answers. Of course, I can see another way of doing this, but I'm rarely compelled to do it that way.

Have you recognized a lot of rewards from your writing? What do you get out of it personally?

Rather than financially or anything like that, you mean? I feel fulfillment every day. At its worst, it's a kind of drug. You kind of get a jones for it. You really want to get your hands on a keyboard or pad of paper because you feel the need. It's an important form of expression for me, but I don't think of it as therapy. This is not my place to exorcise demons. It is work for me. It's something I enjoy doing. It's pleasure as well as discipline. It serves a lot of functions for me. I can't imagine not doing it.

Do you write every day? You also direct films and plays, so how big a role does the actual writing take in your life?

It certainly has a platform every day. Writing comes in so many shapes and sizes. Some people are funny about rituals and habits, while for others it's a haphazard thing, which is probably truer of someone like me. I don't have a certain specific discipline to it. I don't need to do it in the morning; I don't need to have a cup of coffee; I don't need to be facing east. And I don't sit there and stare at the screen, because invariably I lose those battles. I can't sit there and go, "Okay, be funny now, be creative now, do something worthwhile now." I suppose there are times when I'll type through that, say to myself, "Maybe something will come of this," or I have a deadline and I need to produce because I've been paid. When you first start out, though, nobody gives a shit if you finish today or a week from now. When you're done, you turn it in to whoever you think might be interested in reading it—your cousin, open submission to a play festival, whatever. School is good because writers need deadlines; we're a procrastinating bunch.

Even now, plenty of my writing is just dwaddling around while I'm supposed to be writing for somebody else. I have ideas in my head that I try to get down on paper and see what comes of it. This morning I was up at 5:30 writing, because that's when I woke up, and I wanted to take a look at what I did last night. I'm not writing it for anyone, but I have more outlets now, so I can figure that a piece of work may have a life. I know enough people and I've done enough work that there are ample conduits to production or publication—a sale, if you want to be as base as that. But that doesn't mean it's going to happen.

I think it was Oliver Stone who said, "I write five pages a day even if I throw it out." When I was younger, I thought that must be the thing to do, because Oliver Stone must know. But I came to a point in my life where I thought it might be kind of a hollow exercise if it's just something I'm going to throw out. What I've learned is that it's only as hollow as you make it. If you hold onto those pages, who knows what might be in there: the germ of an idea, a monologue that gets enveloped by something else. And just the craft of it, the labor-intensive act of sitting down and writing—you can get better at it as you hone it. It falls into that tradition of wheelwright and shipwright; there is a kind of skill to it, a kind of craftsmanship that comes from the doing of it. People get better at it, including some students that I've had and continue to have. The more they rewrite something or write new things, the better they're getting.

Do you have a file cabinet full of stuff?

I've got a fair amount of stuff that's sitting there in various states, whether "I'm still working on it" or "I haven't touched it for a while" or "This one's for later, when I don't have anything else going on." That's both film and theater, and even TV now. And short stories, which I've begun writing.

Has anything happened on the TV front?

Only if you count Showtime's production of *Bash*, which I shot from a couple of different live performances. I've had offers to do TV work. I did one project with ABC, and they ultimately felt it wasn't for them because it was a little too much. That was fine, because I got paid really well. It was the kindest, softest, most nest-feathering rejection that I've had, so that was okay. The material wasn't wasted, because it found its way into other things—portions of it, anyway. I continue to have an interest in that skill and that medium, the ability to get out on a weekly or monthly basis to an audience of that size.

The question of audience is what originally brought me to film in the first place. I reached a crossroads where I was teaching and getting produced in various venues across the country, even in places like England on occasion, but I was not the master of my destiny. A company would contact me if they wanted to do something. I'd had an agent since NYU, but because I was just starting out there was only so much they could do for me. Whatever happened happened, and I was not able to capitalize on it in any significant way. At some point you want to have a testament of what you're doing by getting out to a larger audience. I'd seen enough examples of people who were doing that with film work, especially in independent film, that it just made sense that that's what I would do.

I went through an experience with a group of people who were trying to make a film from one of my plays. Although I'd been a film lover for a long time, I'd never been introduced to the world of independent filmmaking and how long it can take to get a movie made. So I sat around with these people who had an option on my work for a year, and it was just unthinkable for me to sit around that long. I was used to finding spaces for plays I'd written or others had written that I wanted to direct and doing a show that cost only hundreds of dollars. The idea of movies is such an extravagant thing. Something that cost even a couple hundred thousand dollars was so beyond my thinking.

Anyway, when they wanted to renew the option, I felt I just couldn't do it. Instead, I went off and tried to make a movie on my own. That ultimately led to *In the Company of Men*, which was not the piece that had been optioned. I found some money, and that was the piece I felt I was most able to do well with the amount I had. I wanted to do a project that people would have to accept on its own terms and not say, "If only he'd had five million dollars, he could have really made a good movie. He had a great story, but it looks like hell." I think it actually works very well the way it was done.

Let's talk about your short stories. They've appeared in *The New Yorker* and elsewhere, and you've published a story collection, *Seconds of Pleasure* [Grove Press, 2004].

I often find that I write my short stories on planes. They've all been relatively short, two or three thousand words. So far, I really don't ever sit down and say, "Okay, now I'm going to write a short story." It's more like I just get into the right groove and one comes out.

Any Mormon elements popping up in your short stories?

No.

Is it really different to write a story, as opposed to a screenplay or a script?

It certainly is. The stories are not necessarily my forte. I've enjoyed it because I enjoy exploring things. It's been fun, and I know I'll keep at it. But it's not a thing that comes as naturally to me as, say, dialogue does. Even the prose that goes into a screenplay is work for me because the mechanics of getting people from place to place and describing places are of less interest to me, in the same way that the camera is not as interesting to me as the things that are in front of the camera. Sitting down and writing a story is always more work than play, more so than a film script will ever be. Not that I haven't felt some degree of personal success in doing it, because that's the only thing worth marking anyway—until you win the Nobel prize, and then you can mark it by that. I can finish a story and go, "Yes, that feels good, I like what I've done." That said, short stories will always be my second language.

Concerning HBO's film production of *Angels in America*, do you have any opinions on Tony Kushner's use of Mormon elements and characters?

I was approached to direct that film, and I chose not to. It was right around the time of my disfellowshipment for *Bash*, and I thought, "Well, that's probably not the best move."

Kushner himself calls *Angels in America* a sort of fantasia. The Mormons are treated in the same fantastical way as everybody else. Kushner understands that his Mormon characters are just human beings; they're just people who are capable of great good and of making mistakes. There's nothing wrong with that sort of portrayal. If the church can't stand up to that kind of scrutiny, then there's something amiss. But I don't think Kushner is pointing a finger and saying, "There's something wrong with that religion." I may be wrong about that, but it's certainly not my feeling, and it's certainly not what I was doing with *Bash*. What I did see him doing right was underscoring that we're all in this together and there's just no way around the idea that this is work, this thing called life. We must be constantly vigilant because it's so easy to stumble, and if you do stumble then you hopefully right yourself, pick yourself up. It's as simple and profound as that.

Have any of the recent Mormon films made it onto your radar?

I've had a couple of conversations with Mitch Davis, who did the missionary film that takes place in the Pacific [*The Other Side of Heaven*]. I thought he did good work there. It seemed to have a wider appeal than most things written by so-called Mormon writers. It was a very earnest, straightforward film. I thought he handled it quite well.

I recently saw *Brigham City*, and it made me hopeful, not just for Mormon filmmakers—I'm not sure that term does anything but marginalize—but for filmmakers as a whole. I thought Dutcher found a terrific way of integrating faith into his narrative without overburdening it. The notions and rituals of the community became a valid and interesting part of the whole without ever feeling forced or manipulative. Religion has been a part of films for nearly as long as the medium has existed, but it's not always very well integrated when it comes to films made by Latter-day Saints. I found Dutcher's use of Mormonism, however, highly effective and nicely restrained—part of the message rather than the message itself.

If the film has a failing, it's the same one that I see in many independent features: the level of talent in front of the camera. Some of the work in the film is very fine, and it was a treat to see people I knew years ago at school up on screen. Dutcher seems to me a careful and gifted filmmaker, but considering him as an actor I found myself less than moved. I think he takes a gamble, holding his own character's emotions in check until the last few scenes of the film, but it doesn't pay off for me. There is obviously a great deal of back-story at play here, but I didn't find his performance providing enough power in the first two-thirds of the film to compensate for his reserve. What is meant to be depth seems merely emotionless. I couldn't help but imagine what an actor like Ed Harris or Bill Paxton might've done with this role. Still, I felt overall that the film was an enjoyable one, and it was great to see something this ambitious and successful come out of an independent production, Mormon or not. I expect good things from Dutcher, if this is any indication of his gifts.

After the *Bash* situation, do you think you'll ever write something else with Mormon elements?

I don't know. I've certainly been asked not to, quite specifically. There was no sense of "You can write some more about Mormons if you like, as long as they're good ones." It was just "We'd like you to steer clear of them." So far, that's been fine, because I haven't had any plans for additional Mormon characters. Doing that would be a real declaration of something—I'm not sure exactly what. So if that happens, it will be a monumental choice that I'm making. I see no particular need to make that choice, because I have no Mormon stories in my head right now.

There are many things I've written where you could say, "Gee, that could have been a Mormon character." In fact, a Salt Lake critic asked about *In the Company of Men*, "Are you making a statement about the church? These guys are in white shirts and ties, and they're very patriarchal." My response was, "I hadn't thought about that, but now that you say it, let me think about that." You don't always know what's filtering its way into your own work.

In bad writing, characters trumpet who they are. There are a lot of people in life who do that too. Others never mention their membership, and I don't think they're any less of a missionary. They do it by their example of who they are, not by overt statements.

Was the church discipline for *Bash* a local action or was it triggered out of Salt Lake?

I think what happened is that some reviews started to come in. Before that, I'd kind of been flying under the wire, in terms of people knowing who I was. I was a relative newcomer to the national scene. When *Bash* came around, it got a lot of publicity.

Calista Flockhart and the cast were trumpeted by *Time* magazine and *USA Today*. Evidently it filtered back to Salt Lake, and they said, "Hey, we need to take a look at this."

A lot of Mormon filmmakers want to achieve a crossover. The example often cited is *My Big Fat Greek Wedding*. Does that line of thinking have any potential?

Of course. Who would have guessed that something like *Fiddler on the Roof* had crossover potential? But why wouldn't it? Everything in it is specific, but when it touches on something universal, that's when people begin to notice and reach out to it. Why should *Fiddler* be any more universal than something written by a Mormon about Mormons? As far as *Greek Wedding*, I didn't think it was particularly good. Could that same kind of phenomenal popularity happen for a Mormon film or play? Of course it could. My heartfelt hope would be that it's actually good rather than makes a lot of money. When we start to equate quality with money, that gets dicey.

JOHN MOYER

John Moyer
Scriptwriter

When John Moyer wrote the screenplay for The Singles Ward *in 2000, he didn't expect it would see the light of day. When HaleStorm Entertainment approached him in 2001 about doing a script for them, he informed them that he already had one ready to go. The success of* The Singles Ward *launched HaleStorm as one of the key players in the Mormon cinema movement, and Moyer went on to earn screenwriting credits on several subsequent HaleStorm films. A native of South Jersey, just outside Philadelphia, Moyer has worked as a standup comedian. The original version of this interview appeared in* Irreantum, *winter 2003–spring 2004.*

What is your underlying drive as a writer? What are the rewards?

For me, writing is simply a form of expression. It's about taking an idea, a feeling, something that's inside of me that generates certain emotions and packaging that in a form that I can share with other people and hopefully create the same emotions or thoughts within them. It's a way to get somebody else to look at the world the way I do, or, if they are somebody who already does, then it's something we can both share together. Either way it creates a bond between me as the writer and them as the audience. Sometimes it has just the opposite effect, and people walk away angry. That's great too. It's all about generating emotion and causing someone to think.

Literary art is a combination of three elements: what the author has experienced, observed, and imagined. How do those three elements work together for you?

For me it's mostly about experience and observance. I take things that I have gone through or witnessed, things that have created extreme levels of thought or emotion, and I recreate them. That was one of the funny things about *Singles Ward*; so many people said, "That is totally unrealistic that he would come home and find his wife drinking and smoking and saying she wasn't going to church anymore!" Well, guess what. That was totally true. I was an elders quorum president at BYU, and I came home one day to find my then-wife drinking a beer and smoking a cigarette, two things she had previously done before joining the church and marrying me. She said she was fed up with church and wasn't going anymore.

After that, we eventually divorced. Going to church was painful because I felt like such a failure. I didn't belong in the family ward, and the singles ward was filled with—well, let's just say so many of the characters I wrote about, that I slowly went inactive. That whole experience and how I felt about the church and God really did a number on me. I wound up writing about it. To this day, I still talk to people who tell me they knew exactly what those characters in the movie were going through.

Another experience was a scene from *The R.M.* At one point I really worked for a rent-to-own company and had to repossess a young child's bed. He was crying to his mom about not wanting to sleep on the floor. That was so hard for me. But I had to suck it up because his parents were negligent on their financial obligation and, like it or not, I was the guy who had to do this job. That was a tough day for me. It was hard. Later on, when I wrote about it, it was a way for me to deal with guilt and a messed-up situation by trying to go back and laugh at it now.

In another scene, Jared has to spend the night in a hotel room with a complete freak. That actually happened to me. Totally true story, though the scene in the movie is a little more toned down than reality. In reality, the guy I was sharing the room with, after reading his *Jesus the Christ* and then falling asleep, starting screaming profanities at the top of his lungs. I got the heck out of the room and spent the night on the couch in the lobby. To me, as jacked up as it was at the time, it was actually a very funny situation that I simply wanted to recreate for the masses.

Mobsters and Mormons had another great example. When we did test screenings, several people were beside themselves at the scene where it's implied that the neighbor, Louise Means, rifled through the Jaymes' mail, snooping to give herself more gossip ammunition. I think the quotes from several women in the test-audience feedback were something like, "An LDS sister would never do that" and "I don't know any LDS women like that." Again, that was based on a true experience. We moved into a neighborhood where we had new neighbors next door. The LDS sister two houses down went through their mailbox one day and told everybody on the block the names of the new people, where they were getting their mail from, et cetera. True story. It was something that upset me and I think speaks of the nature of some of these gossipy Utah Mormons, so I put it in the movie. I think we found that the people who say they don't know any LDS women like that sometimes are the ones of which we're speaking.

What other things do you do besides writing HaleStorm screenplays? Do you earn a full-time living as a writer?

I have been performing standup comedy for the last ten years. Between that and my writing, I pay the bills.

Tell us about your writing process. Does writing come easy or hard?

Writing comes fairly easy. But as with all writers, there are times when I am completely stumped. I just wait it out and know that it will eventually come to me.

For the overall actual process, I do a combination of planning and flying by the seat of my pants. I try to nail down what I call my story anchor points. A lot of screenwriters will say not to get hung up on the page count, but I'm sorry, page count is everything. Why have a hundred and fifty pages that you have to cut down to ninety? I say, do all the cutting as you write. I know by page ten I need to be here, by page forty-five I need to be here, by page seventy here, et cetera. So, I cater to that as I write. I come up with what I want to happen by those pages: the inciting incident, the initial push of the story, the mid-act crisis, et cetera, and then I fill in the blanks of what needs to happen both physically and emotionally from there.

But also, I leave room for stuff that just happens. There are times when something will come down onto the paper and I have no clue where it came from. The character will say something that spins the whole thing into a new direction. I love that. That's when the characters and the story really come alive and become their own beings.

As far as editing, during the first go-around I let my characters say whatever with however many words it takes. Then I go back and trim dialogue. I am often amazed that what took me five lines the first time around can be said in one line.

I do write fairly quickly. When I get into it, I work a solid ten hours a day, six days a week. Of course, I have yet to tackle a script as a father. Having an infant in the house now certainly slows the process down. It's been quite the challenge trying to type and rock an infant seat with my foot, only to have him want to be held. I just have to put everything on hold and hope he falls asleep soon.

I write at home in my office, but I also have a laptop and enjoy going to a couple of places outside the house to work, either the Cougar Eat down at BYU or this bagel place on Center Street in Provo that has a vintage café feel. I enjoy the ambiance.

I can pour out a first draft in about a month or so at my ten-hours-per-day rate. Then I sit on it for a few weeks. But after that first draft is done, after I have poured out so much from inside of me with all that energy, I go through this post-writing depression for a few days. My wife hates it. I become a vegetable. It's like I just spent all this time focused on a purpose, and now I feel like I have no more purpose. It's very strange.

But after that, I go back and tweak. It's at that point that I will let a few key people read it, people I know I can trust to be honest one way or the other. But you have to balance comments from people and learn to sift through things. Recently two very talented, very creative people, who really know what they are talking about, gave me some feedback unbeknownst to each other. One absolutely loved a particular scene, and the other absolutely hated it. What am I to make of that? To each his own; you can't please everybody. Was the scene bad because person X hated it? Was it great because person Y loved it?

You have to listen to people with a wide-open mind. I take everything in and digest it. Oftentimes there are things somebody else saw that I didn't. Or they might have ideas I never thought of. The danger comes when you have somebody who likes the story and wants to see it told their way. Suddenly it's no longer about your story; they start giving you feedback about how they think it should be.

The greatest approach to critique I ever experienced was in Film 101 with Dr. Charles Metten at BYU. He used to yell at the film students, "Don't tell me what you would have done! Or what you would have liked to see! Tell me what you saw!" I apply that to my readers. Don't tell me what you would have liked to read or what you would have written. First, tell me what you actually read; then, if there is a void, let's talk about how to fill it.

But you also need to know when to just trust your own instincts. I mean, obviously if you have thirty people reading a script and they all say the same thing, you know there's some truth to whatever they are pointing out. Other times, you just need to shut that all out and go with your gut. Have some confidence in yourself as a writer, and don't sway with the breeze. At the same time, surround yourself with key readers you know you can trust.

Which is your favorite from among your movies? Which is your least favorite? What's your all-time favorite scene, and which scene do you most regret?

I would have to say my favorite to date is *Mobsters and Mormons.* That's my baby. I wrote it, produced it, directed it, and costarred it in. For good or for bad, it's all me creatively. Yeah, there are things that I look at and wish I had done differently, but as a whole it's all me. And that I am proud of.

Of the other films, the ones that I only wrote, I don't think I have one favorite. To me they are apples and oranges. Each one has elements I love, just simply like, and completely despise.

One of my favorite scenes would be in *The R.M.* with the juxtaposition of how elders quorum and Relief Society teach, the sisters taking so much time and preparation while the brethren just seem to throw things together, if at all. My father-in-law and mother-in-law both taught lessons at the same time. Somebody came up to my father-in-law once after church and asked if the elders had the same lesson as the sisters. He said, "Yes, why?" The fellow responded that the sisters had some big chart, with music and treats, but not the elders.

The scene I regret most is the courtroom scene from *The R.M.*, which I did not write. I had a courtroom scene in my original first draft, but, alas, through rewrites outside of my control and that I did not agree with, it became what you see in the final product.

But from something I did write—I don't regret the scene, but I would have written it differently now. That's the scene where Jonathan and the temptress played by Michelle Ainge go to her apartment toward the end of *The Singles Ward.* I think it could have been lightened up a bit. There were some moments that could have conveyed the message while still being fun. But then again, I don't know. What's done is done, and it's in the BYU archives for time and all eternity.

What is your greatest fear as a writer?

Not getting paid anymore. That sounds terribly superficial, but it's true. I do what I do for art's sake, but I also do it for the money. In some respects I am a literary whore. But that's okay. In all seriousness, I think the only thing that would lead to not getting paid is dried-up creativity. And I hope that I can be constantly producing fresh, funny material.

What is your response to people who get offended by your work and don't understand what you're trying to do? Does that happen often?

I could care less. I know there has been a lot of talk about us not being able to handle criticism. But I can handle it. What I don't understand are people's anger, their outrage, and their offense at these movies. It isn't a lot in the grand scheme of things; there really are only a few compared to the overwhelmingly positive response. But I remember one woman who made a comment about how, at a singles function, someone suggested there be a showing of *The Singles Ward*, and she quickly shot down that suggestion because the film was so inappropriate. Or the person who suggested on Deseret Book's website that the soundtracks to the movies were slowly leading their children down to hell. Huh? Whatever.

On the other hand, those comments really amuse me. I enjoy hearing and reading them because they really are good for a laugh and make great fodder on my website. I got an e-mail from a guy who told me that what I did sickens him. I suggested a blessing.

I recently spoke to John Lyde, director of *Take a Chance,* in which he was kind enough to give me a small acting role, by the way. John said he'd read some comments by some LDS folks who were outraged and offended that the two lead characters, played by Kirby Heyborne and Corbin Allred, wore tank tops in the movie. I mean, seriously people, get over it and get a life.

How much have your HaleStorm screenplays been changed from your original vision and manuscripts?

Well, in *Singles Ward*, none of the cameos were written by me at the time I wrote the script. They were all added after the fact. I did write Richard Dutcher's scene, though. It worked so well with the girl getting offended at watching *God's Army*. It was my commentary on uptight Mormons. Gordon Jump wasn't really a celeb cameo; that was a character I wrote in the script, and Gordon played him. And I think he played it well. That was his last movie, I believe.

But as for the rest, they were added as various Mormon celebs came on board. Some worked, like Steve Young's, which I thought was a great gag, but some didn't. I was distracted by "Hey, let's take thirty seconds out of the story to parade these people across the screen."

The R.M. changed even more so. I would say the final product was about seventy-five percent close to my original. I am not saying that what changed was bad or that I didn't agree with it all. Some things didn't work for me, and I didn't agree with them. Others I really liked, and I was the first person to say, "I didn't think of that, and that really worked." The scene where Jared talks on the phone to Kelly and asks her out wasn't in my original version, and it works great and gets a huge laugh. The story behind that was that one of the movie's investors really had that happen to him, where he called his friends back to tell them that the girl he'd just asked out said yes, and it turned out he accidentally redialed the girl.

The critics haven't exactly been kind about the HaleStorm films, have they? Are the critics right or wrong?

I think many of the criticisms are valid, but many are not. Wow, could that have been any more middle of the road, ambiguous? I sound like a politician. But seriously, are the films technically flawed? Heck, yeah. But we're like the plastic surgeon from *Batman* who worked on Nicholson and accidentally turned him into the Joker. His response was, Look at the tools I have to work with! We have low budgets and tight schedules, and at first we had no clue what we were doing. That's no excuse, but it's true, and technically the films have gotten better looking.

They have criticized the jokes and the stories, but are they wrong? Not to them or to the people who agree with them. But there are a whole lot of people who don't agree with them. The bottom line to me is that when it comes to film, or music, or art, there is no right or wrong. It's simply opinion.

But again, what does amuse me is the intensity that some people have for hating these movies. I mean, there are many LDS artists who have this idea of what LDS films should be in order to qualify as good or acceptable, et cetera. And if they don't meet their own personal criteria, then these films are garbage, bottom line, and don't deserve any respect. That I don't agree with. Again, it's a matter of opinion.

One of my all-time favorite comments about my movies was the guy who said, "What does it say about the Mormon audience that *Singles Ward* has become a must-see among Mormons? Are we, who believe we are admonished to seek after the best of everything, not getting the message? Are we, like the unenlightened world which we regularly condemn in our sermons, so shallow that we embrace the obvious over the aesthetic?" I just love that comment. It makes me laugh every time.

Some critics have suggested that under the fun and games, your scripts—especially *The R.M.*—contain some savage satire of Mormon culture. Some have suggested, for example, that you're exploring an almost sociopathic lack of genuine love and affection in Mormon families; that's at least one way to interpret a family forgetting to tell their missionary they've moved. Is this your intention?

First off, I have gotten some good chuckles out of people who have pontificated about my movies. I remember reading something someone posted on AML-List. I believe she was a grad student somewhere and did some type of thesis or paper on *Singles Ward*. She went on and on, elaborating on what certain things meant, what the filmmakers were trying to say, and what we had intended or were trying to do, yadda, yadda. I just thought, *You couldn't be more wrong, and you really have no idea what you are talking about.*

The family in *The R.M.* forgetting to tell their son that they had moved was about how busy our lives get with the church, so busy that we sometimes put more effort into everybody else's salvation before we worry about our own families. I wasn't trying to say there is a lack of genuine love or affection; I was saying that sometimes we just get caught up elsewhere.

There is a line from *The Home Teachers* where Nelson admits he missed his son being born because he was out on splits with the missionaries. I knew a guy to whom that actually happened. He got so caught up in service, thinking he was doing good, but he was neglecting something more important in his grand scheme of things at the time.

To me, if there is any savage satire, it's in *The Singles Ward*. We have these groups of people who want to get married because they are told it's the thing to do. So they do it, sometimes at great expense. And when it doesn't happen fast enough, they get depressed and they feel like failures. And the ones who get married but wind up getting divorced really feel like failures and are looked upon with suspicion by everybody else.

I felt a lot of anger at what I went through. Not just at the church or the members, but at myself too for the stupid mistakes I made in my own decisions to get married. I have seen single adults go through many of the same things as I did and sometimes worse. I have seen outrageously clueless attitudes about marriage. Those were all the things I wanted to hit on with *Singles Ward*.

Your work clearly plugs into the work of other Mormon satirists, such as James Arrington, Eric Snider, Robert Kirby, and, going back some years, Sam Taylor. Are you influenced by other LDS humorists?

I read their work. I think Eric Snider is a brilliant writer. He gave me feedback on the *Mobsters and Mormons* script, so I guess you could say I am influenced by him in that way.

One might argue that there are two strains in LDS humor, the John Bytheway/Alan Cherry school, in which the idea is to combine humor with an inspirational message, and the James Arrington/Robert Kirby school, in which the idea is to just make fun of the culture and allow the audience to arrive at whatever conclusions they want. Do you agree, and, if so, which school do you see yourself favoring?

I think there is a happy medium, a combination of both. I can't take credit for some of the more emotional scenes in the movies, such as Jonathan crying on the mountaintop in *Singles Ward*. That was written by the director. But the overall message of *Singles Ward* was something very personal to me—that is, do the right thing for the right reasons. I got married to get married and took no thought for what I was really doing because I just thought I had to get married or I would be a loser in the eyes of my fellow church members. So I did, and look where it got me the first time around. I felt strongly about conveying that message in the script through humor, satire, et cetera, and I think it worked, and I have spoken to people for whom it rang home both from a comic perspective and a spiritual one. And as a writer, I was overjoyed that I was able to communicate effectively and touch people that way.

You got into a tiff with the director Richard Dutcher, didn't you? Some diary excerpts on your website mentioned it. Have you reconciled these differences?

I wouldn't say a tiff. Well, maybe. But I never had any hard feelings toward Richard. I was confused about some of his public comments, so I used them for fodder on my site at www.johnmoyer.com. I get a ton of traffic there. Don't ask me why, but people go there and actually read the things I write, and they complain when it's not updated. So I had to get some filler. But in the end, Richard and I chatted, and all is well. I consider Richard a friend and have considerable respect for him.

Where would you like to see Mormon film go in the future? What is the most glaring absence, in your opinion, of a Mormon film that hasn't been made yet?

I have no clue where Mormon film should go, to be perfectly honest. But what I would like to see is filmmakers within the church rise up and make it among the Hollywood elite. I think using Mormon film as a springboard to that is appropriate.

Glaring absence of a Mormon film yet to be made? Hmm, I don't know—aside from the perfectly obvious Book of Mormon movie done *Lord of the Rings* style with a hundred-million-dollar budget. But that ain't happening.

What is absent among the filmmakers is solid sense of camaraderie. There's an old saying among standup comics: Standup comics love to watch other comics bomb. I think there's a lot of that floating around the LDS movie community. Everybody wants to make a film to outdo everybody else, and when somebody else's film comes out and does well, there is bitterness, and when it doesn't do well there is glee. There's a sense of arrogance that somebody else doesn't know what they're doing and can't do it as well as I or we can. Why can't we just support everybody else and help each other up the ladder instead of trying to walk over everybody to get to the top? A house divided against itself cannot stand. LDS film can be a solid force for good. And Satan would love nothing more than to see anyone get destroyed in the process, if he can use it as a tool to bring an individual or individuals down.

In addition, I would like to see audiences be a bit more supportive. When *Singles Ward* came out, it was the number-two film at Carmike's Wynnsong theaters in Provo. The number-one film was a hard R-rated movie with extreme sexual themes. I mean, what does it say when the theater that services probably the most Mormon area in Utah has that going on?

What new directions do you see your writing taking in the future? Do you anticipate trying out any different styles or genres?

I am breaking away from the LDS film niche. At first I was trying to raise money for a non-LDS film, but I found investors eager to do something LDS-oriented. I had a script that I wrote about a mob family from Jersey, where I grew up, being placed into the witness relocation program among an all-Mormon community in Utah. That was, of course, *Mobsters and Mormons*. I figured that would be the best of both worlds: something that non-LDS people could enjoy but that would also appeal to the original LDS fan base. It's written from the outsider's perspective, and there are no inside jokes, so it's akin to Harrison Ford in *Witness*. It's really paid off. We made the movie for $350,000. We took a different approach and played it in theaters for only three months, not the usual ten months that *Singles Ward* and *R.M.* played for. We did about $420,000 in theaters for its limited release, which I was pleased with. Then we went to DVD right before Christmas. The DVD has skyrocketed. It's been the fastest-selling HaleStorm DVD to date. I am proud of that.

Whatever I plan to do now, I can tell you this: I won't be having any Mormon characters in it. It's time to move on.

RACHEL ANN NUNES

Rachel Ann Nunes
Novelist

While Rachel Ann Nunes is primarily known as the author of numerous LDS women's novels, she also writes science fiction and fantasy for young readers and picture books. Since her first novel was published in 1996, she has become one of the best-selling authors in the LDS market, known particularly for her Ariana series and her picture book Daughter of a King. *Nunes started out publishing with Covenant Communications and later released original works or reprints with Cedar Fort, Spring Creek Books, and Deseret Book. In addition, she offers advice and support for aspiring writers through a group called LDStorymakers (ldstorymakers.com). The mother of six children, Nunes lives in Pleasant Grove, Utah. The original version of this interview appeared in* Irreantum, *winter 1999–2000.*

Please tell us about your personal background and how it relates to your writing.

I was born on May 7, 1966, in Provo, Utah, the second child of eight. My mother taught me to read when I was four, and my father, a French professor at Brigham Young University, passed on to me his love of foreign places and people. I believe it was their literary influence that set me on the path to writing. I grew up mostly in Provo and Highland, Utah, and also spent time in Kansas while my father was pursuing his degree.

When I was eleven, I went with my family to France with BYU's study abroad program, during which time I roamed Paris and the surrounding area with my brother, who is two years my senior. I know to some that may sound strange, two young kids riding the subway and buses, exploring as they pleased, but it was a different world in 1977. There were no drive-by shootings or terrorist bombs—at least publicized ones—and kidnappings were rarely in the news. At the time my mother had six children, age thirteen and under, in a tiny apartment. She couldn't leave with all the young ones, and it was impossible to keep the older children inside. So my brother and I roamed, sometimes taking our nine-year-old sister along with us. It was a very informative time for me. Some of these experiences in France I would later write about in my novels.

From May 1987 to November 1988, I served an LDS mission to Portugal, where I met my future husband, TJ. Later, he immigrated to the States and we were married. After having three children, I realized that I wasn't content with my role in life. I had everything I'd been taught as a young girl to want—a good husband, children, a house, two cars—but something vital was missing. I had been told in my patriarchal blessing that I had the gift of writing and that my words would go out among the nations and change lives for the better, but I was so far from that goal that it seemed impossible. I kept telling myself that I would write when my children were grown, but that was an eternity away. I realized that I had to do something about it right then. That's when I began to study every book I could find about writing. Though I had been writing sporadically over the years, I wasn't making progress. My husband bought me a real computer (instead of the K-Pro I'd been using since I was seventeen), and I started out writing two days a week. Soon I was writing every day, often with a child on my lap. I continued reading and studying about writing, and I returned to college at BYU and Utah Valley State College. About this time, I began writing feature articles for the local newspaper, and I also wrote several nonfiction stories that were accepted by the *Ensign* (published in July and August of 1996) and a fiction piece that was accepted by the *Friend*. Finally, in 1995 I wrote and sent in the manuscript that would become my first published novel. That was two years after I became serious about my writing.

Not only do my children provide good writing material, but they keep me from becoming too obsessed with my work. I still write every day, Monday through Friday. I write because I must write. If I don't write, I'm not happy. If

I compare the gospel to breathing, for me writing is like eating. To live I must write. I've known since I was twelve that I was going to be a writer. It was all just a matter of time.

How would you describe your books, your purposes for writing them, and the responses you've received from readers? Is the *romance* label correct for your books?

I was surprised when people called my first novel a romance because I considered the romance secondary to the growth of the main character as she comes to understand how the Atonement works in her life. But I am comfortable with the label as long as it is considered in the classic sense or the mainstream sense and not compared with the garbage that characterizes the romance genre today. I am not aware of following any formula. I see scenes that need to be written and connected with other scenes, and that's what I do.

My first purpose for writing a novel has been and will always be to tell a good, compelling story. But with the publication of my first novel, that purpose was modified. I was unprepared for the overwhelming response I received from readers. Women and even men wrote to tell me their lives had been changed for the better by reading my novel. Instead of this reassuring me, I began to feel a heavy responsibility that temporarily took away the fun of writing. Suddenly I was supposed to write a story that not only entertained but also held a deep spiritual meaning that could make a difference in someone's life. No longer could I simply write for the fun of putting words on the page and seeing the images in my imagination come to life. Instead, I had to consider how my words would be taken by people who were possibly living in a similar situation. It was almost as if my characters had to be perfect examples, even while making the terrible choices that created a plot worth reading—a seemingly impossible paradox.

Ultimately, the responses from readers changed the way I looked at writing. I recognized that I had a great opportunity to do more than just tell a good story. I could influence a large number of people, for good or for ill—and deep down I wanted such an opportunity. I discovered that when I let my heart run with the concept of making a difference, allowing myself at the same time to follow my intuition and feelings, that the joy of writing returned with more force than I'd felt before. And somehow I also found the character balance I needed.

Now when I plan a novel, I purposely tackle an important issue that I feel many Mormons—especially women—might be dealing with. I've written about topics such as drug addiction, AIDS, the death of a child, infidelity, divorce, organ transplant, financial difficulties, miscarriage, abuse, and abortion, to name a few. And I am amazed at how many readers write to say that their lives resemble the fictional lives of my characters and describe how the novels have helped them deal with their own problems or have simply given them a sense that they were not facing their problems alone. People suffer for so many different reasons, and knowing that others share and understand what they are going through makes a big difference in the way they look at their lives. I guess I can say that now my purpose in writing LDS fiction is to make a difference in people's lives while at the same time writing a compelling story that will keep just about anyone turning the pages.

As for who is reading my novels, if my fan mail is any indication, quite a few men are reading my work, though not nearly as many as there are women. Like the women, the men say that they enjoy my novels and usually give me an example as to how a story affected their lives or their emotions. Men often express surprise that they enjoyed a so-called romance novel.

Most fiction is a combination of three elements: what the author has experienced, observed, and imagined. How do those three elements work together for you? How much of what you write is autobiographical?

My fiction is certainly a mix of these three elements, though I find that as time goes on, my own experiences are showing up less and less and the things I hear about or observe are making up the difference. Imagination plays a huge role as well, and it is the vehicle I use to transfer my experiences and what I observe to a usable form. It is the connector, expander, and explainer. I believe that without an active imagination, it is impossible to be a good writer.

One example of using my own experience is in my first novel, *Ariana: The Making of a Queen*, when I wrote about an underground train that breaks down. Ariana's brother hangs on the overhead metal bars in the train to make her forget her fear. A similar experience happened to me when I was in France, except that it was my brother and I who played on the bars to comfort our little nine-year-old sister. Ariana and her brother also roamed Paris together, as my brother and I did. In that same novel I used some of my real-life missionary experiences, from street meetings to actual discussions.

However, the overall plot of the novel was inspired by a woman I met in the mission field. She had experienced tragedies in her life that impressed me, and I wanted to write about a woman who could go through something similar and be stronger for it. But the way the events happen in my novel, as well as the ending, came purely from my imagination. In the final manuscript there is no resemblance to a real occurrence except two or three basic facts. Nevertheless, Ariana has become a real person to me, and writing about her is like writing about an old friend.

I've often used my children and their reactions in my novels, especially my second book, *Ariana: A Gift Most Precious*. For example, one of my daughters went through a tough adjustment when I had a new baby, and her attitude was perfect for the newly orphaned Marie-Therese. In my novel *To Love and to Promise*, I used my own experience with miscarriage along with the experiences of three other women to form a composite story with which many women can identify. That novel was one of my hardest to write, and I remember crying many days while I was writing. I wrote that novel while three of my friends were having severe marriage difficulties, so they became the inspiration for part of the novel. The rest of the scenes and most of the dialogue came strictly from my imagination.

That's about how it goes with all of my novels, except in my adventure-romance series. Those are almost pure imagination, and they have been really enjoyable for me to write. Even so, I am careful to research details so that the stories are still plausible on some level. It may be unlikely such a story would happen, but it could given the right circumstances. Through those novels I can live out fantastic adventures while never experiencing any danger.

Do all your books have happy endings? How do you handle flaws in your characters? How do you balance portraying things realistically versus idealistically? What about potentially explicit things like sex and violence?

I like happy or at least hopeful endings. I don't think such endings cause readers to have unrealistic expectations in their own lives. Readers understand that a novel is a slice out of the entire life of a character. In the sequel, if there is a sequel, more things will go wrong, but in this novel the character will come to some sort of reconciliation with the problem at hand. That's real life. Either we triumph over our problems and go on to face more, or we don't and we quit growing. As Latter-day Saints, we believe in the happy ending. What could be more happy than eternal life? Isn't that the goal of every Latter-day Saint? Sure there will be problems, even death or worse, but in the end we crave and plan for ultimate redemption. Even with a story such as my novel *Ariana: A Gift Most Precious,* in which a couple dies and one of their daughters will soon follow them in death, there is hope because of their belief in eternity. I like my serious work to reflect that ultimate hope.

All my characters have flaws, from a lack of self-worth to serious sin such as abortion. I like to see a character grow in the course of the novel, especially the sinner, but I don't believe all non-Mormons in our novels should convert. I have characters in some of my novels who have grown significantly yet have not accepted the gospel. People keep asking me when I'm going to baptize them, and my answer has to be maybe never. In my works, I explore a wide variety of flaws because I think it's these that make novels and our lives more interesting.

I try to be realistic, with the exception being my adventure-romance series, in which the unrealistic makes for a better adventure. Yet I do like my characters to be striving for the ideal. I think also that my writing has developed over the years. I was more idealistic with my first novel, more realistic—almost pessimistic—with my second, and more of a combination with my subsequent work. To give an example of the realistic, I had a choice in one of my novels to have a baby be born with HIV or not. Her mother, a repentant convert, had AIDS, and there was a good possibility that this child could be born free of the virus like her older sister, but my sense of realism wouldn't allow that to happen. I knew that in the real world the innocent suffer and people who have repented still have to pay the consequences of their sins.

In writing about potentially explicit things, I tend not to go into great detail. If a person slept around to get money for drugs, I say that it happened, but I don't feel it's necessary to go into the seedy hotel with her and show the occurrence step by step. Unless it's vital to my story, I don't include the details. Readers are smart, and they will imagine better than I could write it. In my novel *Ariana: A Gift Most Precious,* Ariana remembers the night her twins were conceived. I write simply that it was the night she and her husband made love in the rain. That's enough to evoke an image for a reader. I don't need to write about him tearing off her clothes or her lips quivering with passion. That's not the story I'm trying to tell. The purpose of that inclusion was to show that the rain held special memories for Ariana now, as opposed to the tragic ones it had once held for her. With violence I do the same thing. In my adventure-romances, there are several scenes where people are shot and killed. I say they are dead and even show it happening, but I don't feel the need to write about the blood spattering on the wall and the brains leaking onto the floor. For me it's unnecessary and not the story I want to tell. I give enough of the image to make it seem real but do not dwell on the horror. I have to admit that occasionally I do get a great idea for a horror story that could possibly rival one of Steven King's, but I'll never write it because I don't care for the images and I don't want them in my mind.

Tell us more about your writing habits.

There are no conditions I consider necessary for a good writing session. I write through everything, including moving to a new house or holding babies on my lap. Every morning after my children leave for school, I sit down at the computer until I finish my goal: two thousand words a day when I'm writing, ten to twenty pages a day when I'm rewriting, and fifty pages a day when I'm editing. I have to stop many times, but I leave the computer on until I'm done. I don't care about dirty dishes, laundry, or even getting dressed until my goal is met. There will be plenty of time for household chores later, but I must write before my brain grows soggy.

I never use an outline. I occasionally write notes at the bottom of my computer file to make sure I remember to include certain points. This helps get it all straight in the first draft. I do a lot of editing while I write but don't expect it to be perfect the first time through. As my plot develops, I go back and rewrite during the first draft. Once a novel is done, I will do a thorough rewrite and then several edits before I send it to my editor.

The easiest novel for me to write was my first one, *Ariana: The Making of a Queen*. Everything fell into place almost immediately, and there was little research involved. However, I have come to consider research vital to my work. Research is one of the most rewarding parts of writing. I love learning about everything and am especially gratified when someone picks up my novel expecting that I have the details wrong and finds that I've done the footwork. An example of this is in my second novel, *Ariana: A Gift Most Precious*. I did extensive research on AIDS, which I had previously known almost nothing about. Later, a woman who worked on an AIDS hotline and another whose brother's death was a result of AIDS told me how much they appreciated the reality I portrayed. I've always done most of my research on the Internet, either on official websites or e-mailing people in the know, but I also call and talk personally to some experts. More rarely, I'll check out books from the library or buy books. I've found guidebooks particularly helpful with my books set in France and Boston. With my motherhood responsibilities, I've never had the time to research something in detail at special university libraries, but so far that hasn't been a problem. I'm thoroughly convinced that if it isn't on the Internet, I don't need to write about it. I check the facts in all my novels, down to the name of the restaurant on the ferry that my characters use to cross the English Channel in my novel *Love on the Run*. I'm sure I've made some mistakes, but it won't be from lack of effort.

It is sometimes difficult for me to stop writing even once I've met my daily goal, but my children are good at reminding me that it's time for them. I try to write only while they are in school, and usually I maintain that schedule even during heavy deadlines. Many people ask me how I do it all without outside help. The secret is that my husband is very supportive, and we share the housework equally. The children have a list of chores they are required to do every day. This keeps the house clean and me sane.

Do you ever receive criticism from LDS members who feel like you are neglecting your family in your pursuit of a writing career? If so, how do you respond?

Actually, I have never had anyone voice this opinion to me except one man who attended a writing meeting where I was the main speaker. I had mentioned that I no longer ironed my husband's shirts because he has two hands of his own and does a much better job of ironing than I ever did. This man asked me if I thought my husband would like to have some ironed shirts once in a while instead of a wife so concentrated on her work. I replied emphatically no. My husband loves me and knows how I detest ironing. Since he doesn't mind ironing—and he never burns himself, either—why should I stop writing to do it? I can find a lot of better ways to show my husband how much I love and appreciate him.

I must also add that I am very careful to tell people that my children and family always come first with me—and they do. One of the reasons I love writing so much is that I can be at home with my family. I want to be where I can stop what

I'm doing to be with my children when they need me. When I say family comes first, I don't mean the housework, or the laundry, or the yard. Those things won't make any difference to my family in a hundred years. But stopping my writing to build a Lego tower or listen to my child will make a big difference.

As an author, you do a fair amount of reaching out to the public. Tell us about your book signings, website, and speaking engagements.

Writing is a very solitary profession, even at my busy house, and so I greatly appreciate hearing positive feedback about my work. This means I generally enjoy book signings, even though it's challenging for me to get time away from my family to attend them. At book signings, people often ask questions about how I came up with the idea for a novel or if I'm going to do a sequel. It's fun hearing their experiences with my work and telling someone who actually cares what I'm planning to write in the future. I especially love doing book signings with other authors. It's rewarding to spend time with people who are—well, just as crazy and focused as I am. Unfortunately, if you get more than two authors together, book signings usually aren't extremely productive selling-wise.

Sometimes book signings can be difficult. Most fans are polite and don't stay too long, so that I can talk with others, but occasionally I'll have someone, who perhaps hasn't even read one of my novels, stand there talking to me the entire time I'm signing. This scares others away, and sometimes I've even worried about getting home safely. But this is a rare occurrence and is easily solved by walking over to chat briefly with store personnel.

Having a web page is wonderful. It helps me keep in touch with readers by letting them know about future works and answering a lot of questions they may have. People can tell me what they think on my survey without requiring a personal response. This cuts down on the amount of time I spend on fan mail, which I love but which takes away from the time I have to write. Readers can also join my e-mail list so they can hear about new releases as they come out. My web page and my e-mail address appear in each book now. I always write back to fans—eventually. Turnaround on my e-mail responses is usually less than a month, as opposed to up to six months with a normal letter. My web page is at www.rachelannnunes.com.

I have been asked to speak at many writer symposiums, library functions, and schools. I enjoy sharing my love of writing and my methods with these groups. But what I enjoy most is speaking at Enrichment meetings. I share with the women the road I followed to become an author, especially the challenges, the feelings of inadequacy, and the guilt over the possibility of neglecting my family. Many of these women ask me how I accomplish all that I do, especially when they learn that my house is relatively clean and my children are well adjusted. I tell them how I set my priorities to accomplish my goals. I encourage them to search for and develop their own talents. I stress that the most important thing to me is my family but that they are not the only important things in my life. We have been given talents that our Father wants us, even commands us, to develop. Often the fulfillment of these talents does not come easily and requires a great deal of effort on our part, effort that is so worth it in the end.

I also encourage women to take a good look at their lives and see what they are doing as opposed to focusing on what they aren't accomplishing. Many women are so overwhelmed with the huge list of expectations given to Latter-day Saints that they feel discouraged. After the meetings are over, I take the opportunity to talk individually with the sisters who approach me. Many share their personal trials as well as experiences they've had while reading my novels.

I am increasingly asked to speak at Young Women gatherings using my picture book *Daughter of a King*. I love doing this presentation for the girls because I strongly feel that if they can internalize their divinity as daughters of a Heavenly King, everything else in their life will make more sense and become much easier.

What kinds of things do you read? What are your observations about the Mormon literary scene? Any comments about top-selling LDS romance author Anita Stansfield?

I read a great deal of science fiction and fantasy, but I also read just about anything else I can get my hands on. I go to the library and come home with stacks of books. Often I will not read a book all the way through if it doesn't interest me. I honestly can't say that any one genre has affected my work more than any other, though I do try to learn something from each novel I read, even if it's how not to write. I don't have any favorite Mormon fiction yet—and I've read a lot—but I'll keep reading.

I feel the Mormon market is largely untapped, and I'd like to see more people reading LDS literature. I think those who buy LDS books often do so as gifts for others instead of for their own enjoyment. I think the average Mormon reader wants a good, realistic story but still clings to the desire of a hopeful ending. I would like to see novels published in the Mormon market with a more general hero or heroine, instead of someone explicitly and completely LDS who uses only the gospel to solve their problems.

The gospel is the answer to many things, but our Father also gave us intelligence to work out some problems on our own. This is an oversimplified example, but I guess what this boils down to is that I don't want characters to pray over what they should serve for dinner. Additionally, in many LDS novels I've read, I feel I'm being preached to, while the religion in others seems more natural, even necessary. It's this naturalness I would like to see more. I would also like to see some good LDS science fiction published, as I love to read and write science fiction myself.

I wrote several of my novels before ever reading any of Anita Stansfield's books, so I can't say she inspired my writing at all. However, over the years we've become friends, and her dedication and her persistence inspire me greatly. When people began asking me to speak at Enrichment meetings, she helped me focus on what I wanted to convey and how to best do that. Our work is similar in that we are targeting the same market and both deal with contemporary issues, but her novels definitely contain more steamy scenes that are more typical of the romance label. She has a great deal of witty dialogue that I appreciate but spends almost no time on description, which I enjoy. I don't know that one way is necessarily better than the other, just different.

My Ariana novels are unique from any other LDS writer's work that I'm aware of in that they are contemporary novels set in a foreign country. The heroes are native French, not just there on holiday.

Will you share with us sales figures for your books? Is it possible to earn a living writing for the LDS market?

I generally sell between fifteen and twenty-five thousand copies of my novels, but I'm hoping over time that will increase. My picture book *Daughter of a King* sold over thirty thousand copies in the first year and over twenty-five thousand more in the three years since. I expect to continue to sell more every year as long as I keep publishing, with each new book sparking the sales of the previous ones. I could support my family on my earnings, but not at the level to which we are accustomed. I couldn't pay for my children's private school, for example, and I would have to move into a smaller house. There are few LDS-market authors I know who support their families solely with their writing.

However, I believe we have really just begun to tap into the LDS market. There are still many people out there who don't read LDS novels. I am constantly surprised that those who often criticize what is being written are the same people who haven't read a good deal of what is available. Yes, there is a lot of poor writing out there, but at the same time there is a lot of worthwhile literature being published.

I derive a profound joy from writing, and I believe that I will continue to write for the rest of my life. There are dark moments when I want to give it all up, yet these never stem from the actual writing but from conflicts that come with writing, such as a trying conversation with my editor, irritation with marketing or publicity, or conflicts with family time. I have been writing between two and three books a year, and I will continue at that pace for as long as I feel like doing so. It's difficult to see where the future will take me, but I know writing will always be a part of it.

CAROL LYNN PEARSON

Carol Lynn Pearson
Poet and Playwright

A professional writer, speaker, and performer for many years, Carol Lynn Pearson has made a significant impact both nationally and within the Mormon culture, in several different genres. Within Mormonism, she is best known for her poetry, her inspirational books, her children's musical My Turn on Earth, *and her screenplay for the educational film* Cipher in the Snow. *Nationally, she is known for her autobiography* Goodbye, I Love You, *which tells the story of her marriage to a homosexual man, their divorce and ongoing friendship, and her caring for him as he died of AIDS. Her one-woman play,* Mother Wove the Morning, *has been performed over three hundred times internationally. The mother of four grown children, Pearson lives in Walnut Creek, California. This interview is previously unpublished.*

Tell us about when and how you came to be a writer. What early experiences and influences shaped you?

My first memory of writing is when I was in fourth grade in Gusher, Utah. I won four dollars in a school-district essay contest on "Why We Should Eat a Better Breakfast." But it was in high school that I began to take writing seriously. I wrote poems as an outlet for my considerable adolescent angst. I still have in my filing cabinet a file marked "Poems, Very Bad" and one marked "Poems, Not Quite So Bad." Gradually, I guess, I wrote some that I thought were okay. Also, in high school—the late, great Brigham Young High school in Provo, Utah—I was editor of the school paper.

An extremely important thing I did in high school was begin keeping a diary. Very soon I was hooked. Evidently it offered a safe place for my thinking. I now have a whole shelf full of hand-written bound books and nearly six thousand pages of diary written on typewriter and now computer. That has been inexpressibly valuable in my life, both as a human being and as a writer. It has forced me to examine my life as I have lived it, and I have often found that as much of my experience as I can put into words, that much I have power over. Many of my writing projects have been directly helped by my diary. For example, in writing *Goodbye, I Love You* I was able to go back through the years and establish certain dates and facts and feelings to which I would not otherwise have had access.

By the time I was in college, writing was an important part of my life. I won a literary magazine's poetry contest and wrote assemblies. As a theater major, I performed in many plays, twice winning the best actress award, which gave me deep personal experiences with some of the great plays.

You write in several genres: plays, poems, memoirs, and more. Tell us a little about your feelings, approaches, and outlook regarding each one. Most of your work has been autobiographical rather than fictional, correct?

Playwriting is a favorite form of mine. I believe that theater is a magical art. The printed page can last forever, but there is nothing quite like the immediacy of experiencing something in the dark cathedral of the theater. Drama, I think, is a religious experience. And I believe Arthur Miller's statement that "the mission of the theater, after all, is to change, to raise the consciousness of people to their human possibilities."

When I wrote *Mother Wove the Morning*, my one-woman play about sixteen women throughout history in search of the female face of God, I thought about making it a book, perhaps a novel. But I am not a novelist. And when it occurred to me that this might be a play, I knew it was the correct choice. I became a priestess-performer in the temple of the theater, invoking the lost part of deity, and the power of that phenomenon made up for my own weaknesses and created a remarkable event.

Musicals carry the possibility of touching the heart in an unusual way. I think my musicals *The Order Is Love* (about the Saints living the United Order in Orderville), *My Turn on Earth,* and *The Dance* (about three Mormon couples at a stake dance) provide charming and moving explorations of LDS life and beliefs.

I have recently completed writing *Facing East*, a serious drama about an LDS family whose gay son has just committed suicide. Much of my writing has been dictated by my life experiences. I have a calling toward certain subjects, and I follow it.

Poetry is where I began. I'm not a great poet. But, very importantly, I am a useful poet. My poems have been used by thousands of people to help them make sense of life and give them encouragement. I love writing short things; one of my good gifts is brevity. And somehow poetry became my first best expression. It was a cultural fluke or synchronicity or whatever that my poetry collection *Beginnings* took off the way it did and really put me on the map. I haven't written poetry for many years, except very occasionally. My interests are otherwise. And the time of my poems being big sellers is past.

Yes, some of my work has been autobiographical. Many of the poems have been. Certainly *Goodbye, I Love You* and *One on the Seesaw: The Ups and Downs of a Single-Parent Family* sprang entirely from my life. And more recently *Consider the Butterfly*, telling forty-four of my personal experiences with the phenomenon of synchronicity, is very autobiographical.

But there has been a large body of work that has been fictional, such as the short Christmas novellas *A Stranger for Christmas, The Modern Magi, A Christmas Thief, The Christmas Moment,* and *The Christmas Play.* And the series of little philosophical/inspirational books that began with *The Lesson.*

I have also written a bit in the humor category, such as the series of little notebooks that began with *The Busy Bishop's Notebook*, little jottings from the to-do list of the harried bishop. The most successful was one that has just been reprinted, *The Model Mormon Mother's Notebook.* I am committed to bring more laughter to Mormondom and have just completed a Mormon joke book. Eclectic as I am, there is also a T-shirt of mine on the market:

> Wheat for Man—D&C 89:17
> Chocolate for Woman—M&M 24:7

Something critical to know about my work is that early on I fell into the blessing/limitation of being able to/having to earn my living as a writer. I have been extremely fortunate in that much of what I have wanted to write has also been successful commercially. But as a single mother, I never had the option of doing experimental writing just for the fun of it. If I didn't write, or if it didn't sell, we didn't eat.

Do you have a sense of breaking new ground in Mormon culture?

I broke ground in the field of poetry. Huge numbers of LDS people who had never read poetry found my work attractive and accessible. Clinton Larson, a poetry professor at BYU, said that I set back Mormon art fifty years. But I think I did encourage a lot of other people to both write and read poetry.

I've broken ground in subject matter, both in writing about homosexuality and in some of my feminist writing. *Daughters of Light* was one of the first things that looked at spiritual gifts in early Mormon women. And *Mother Wove the Morning* was a very bold piece.

Which of your works is your personal favorite? Which was hardest to write? Which do you think will best survive the test of time?

Very hard question to answer. Personal favorite: I could not have gone to my deathbed without writing *Mother Wove the Morning.* I came here to do that. Hardest to write: *Goodbye, I Love You.* Survive the test of time? Probably some of the poems.

Which of your works seems to have struck the deepest chords with audiences and readers? Do you have an ideal reader/viewer in mind? In what ways do you think you've developed as a writer during the course of your career?

Goodbye, I Love You struck a very deep chord, clearly because our LDS culture had done such a horrendously bad job of dealing with the subject of homosexuality and such a huge number of families and individuals were in enormous pain. *Mother Wove the Morning* was very successful because of the hunger of huge numbers of women and men left Motherless by our church and our culture.

No, I don't have an ideal reader in mind, just one who wants to think a little out of the box. Yes, I've developed significantly in the course of my career. Last year I wrote a play, *Pieces of God*, that is the best thing I've ever done artistically. I would never have had the depth, taken the risks, or pushed my personal boundaries this much even a few years ago. And it was a deliberate decision to do something I would be artistically proud of, whether it was ever produced or not.

Who or what are your main artistic influences? What works of Mormon literature have you personally most enjoyed?

My main artistic influences have been the poems of Emily Dickinson and the plays of such as Tennessee Williams and Arthur Miller. As far as Mormon literature, I've most enjoyed *The Giant Joshua* by Maurine Whipple, the short stories of Don Marshall and Doug Thayer, and the poems of Emma Lou Thayne.

What are your greatest fear and pleasure as a writer? What do you see as your dominant themes?

My greatest fear may be not living long enough to get as good as I believe I can get. My greatest pleasure is making myself laugh or cry at the keyboard and then hearing from others that my work did the same for them.

My dominant themes are building bridges between people, inviting the outcasts back into society, and having trust in a world that often seems untrustworthy.

Tell us more about your writing habits and approaches.

My writing habits—when a day permits—are to get done in the first part of the day all the stuff of life that needs attention, then clear my plate and my mind and devote myself to my creative work. Often life itself interrupts and more important things come up. For example, this week I have my granddaughter Sydney here for the week going to art camp, so I am driving and spending delicious one-on-one time with her. Huge interruption of my writing schedule, but more important than anything else.

A ritual that I have is to light a candle that burns by my computer when I am writing, sort of a symbol of receiving and giving light and warmth. I can't afford to have many conditions to my writing. Peace in the house and peace in the mind are all that I need.

I do a lot of research, go through multiple drafts, and usually outline, except for very short things. And I *always* insist on reader feedback. I e-mail things to a select group and ask for their best responses. Often I have groups over to my home to read a work. I couldn't do without seeing what works and what doesn't in the eyes of people I trust.

My Mormon background shows up in most of my works. But in my more mature years, I find myself being much more global in my interests. Hence, a lot of my more recent writing has less specifically Mormon elements.

I don't get very realistic in terms of sex and violence. The new play I mentioned, *Facing East*, has very realistic emotional violence but no physical violence. And sexual things are important in it, but not in a way that will be explicit.

Do you think this nation will ever have a Mormon Saul Bellow or Flannery O'Connor?

There probably will be such people. One thing that will have to occur is for the writer to view herself or himself as a citizen of the world who happens to be a Mormon, rather than as a Mormon who needs to speak to the world. Some of that is happening, I think.

What's your view of the creative writer's role in building up Zion? Do you feel that you write divinely inspired work?

I think the value of literature in building the community and keeping the community honest is huge. We can't do without self-reflection, and a writer's obligation is to do that for self and for community, I feel.

Sure, my work is inspired. My own creative imagination is deeply connected to my spirit, which is deeply connected to the Spirit. And whatever leads to good is of God. Much of my work has led to good.

ANNE PERRY

Anne Perry
Novelist

*Born Juliet Hulme in London in 1938, Anne Perry suffered ill respiratory health as a child and was sent to live in more favorable climates in the Bahamas and New Zealand. (*Lord of the Rings *director Peter Jackson's 1994 movie* Heavenly Creatures *is based on events from Perry's childhood.) In 1967 Perry moved to California, where she joined the Mormon faith, and some years later she returned to the United Kingdom. She broke into publishing mysteries in her late thirties and has since published more than thirty mystery novels, many of them bestsellers. In 1999 she published* Tathea *with Deseret Book, an epic fantasy and allegory of the plan of salvation, which was followed by the sequel* Come Armageddon. *Perry lives in a converted, twelve-room stone barn on two acres in the Scottish village of Portmahomack. The original version of this interview appeared in* Irreantum, *summer 2001.*

What early experiences and influences shaped you to be a writer?

I have always wanted to be a writer as far back as I can remember. My mother read to me often and also made up her own stories to tell me, full of imagination and humor. As far as I can recall, my own earliest writing was very episodic and more for my own entertainment than anyone else's—possibly best forgotten. I don't think formal education had a great deal of effect on me, except perhaps the learning of Latin, because it is an excellent discipline in the use of language and logical thought. Informal education is another thing altogether. To read and learn for the love of it is like opening a window onto the world, not only as it is now but also as it has been at any time you care to think of.

How did you get involved in the mystery genre, and who are your main influences?

I wrote historical dramas for years without success, but the first mystery I wrote, *The Cater Street Hangman*, was accepted in 1976 and published early in 1979. A mystery enforces a better plot structure. Naturally I made the second book as much like it as possible, and the third, et cetera—until the eleventh, when I changed publishers and at last got books contracted in advance and began to feel some stability and confidence in my career. By then I was known for mysteries, and that was what the publishers offered to buy.

What keeps me in mystery? Mysteries are what I am contracted to write! It really is as simple as that. I love fantasy and historical drama, especially with a political or religious theme. However, only one in twenty published authors makes a living from writing, which means that the other nineteen have to do something else as well in order to survive. It is a buyer's market, not a seller's. For me, the lack of freedom to change is the only problem. Most of us like a little variety and like to try new things.

I think the main influences—on my mind, at least, if not my style—are fantasy or philosophical writers, such as G.K. Chesterton, Charles Williams, and other poets of the early twentieth century. I believe Dante to be one of the greatest writers and thinkers in Western history. I admire profundity of thought and feeling and marvelous skill with the music and the meaning of language.

Trace for us some highlights of your professional writing career. What has been the role of literary agents in your success? What is your best advice for aspiring fiction writers?

I made my first sale by at last writing a story with a properly crafted plotline and by acquiring a literary agent. The only real test in my career came with changing my U.S. hardback publisher around 1990, but since then I've seen a steady rise in sales, a little more with each book over the years. There were no enormous leaps. Foreign sales are different. The Germans have published seven editions of *Face of a Stranger*! I don't really know why, but I am delighted. My total number of books in print in 2000 was approximately ten million.

I have had only the one U.K. agent, MBA Literary Agents, but three different people there over the years. Since April 1984, Meg Davis has been my agent at MBA Literary, and her role is pivotal. She discusses the outline of a book before it is begun, is always available for comment along the way, and then, when it is finished, discusses the book again and offers comments for whatever rewrite is necessary after my own two or three drafts. Of course, she also does the selling and legal work and gives advice on any other matters arising.

I also have a foreign rights agent in the same agency, Susan Smith, to deal with languages other than English, which at present are German, French, Spanish, Portuguese, Italian, Greek, Japanese, and Russian. I have a United States agent in New York, who is extremely important. His name is Donald Maass, and he deals with U.S. and Canadian rights and is also a very good friend and adviser on stories. He sees the outlines in advance and offers suggestions and help.

My best advice for fiction writers: write what you care about. If you don't know, you can always find out; but if you don't care, why should anyone else? Be prepared to rewrite as many times as necessary. If you can find a friend who is a good, constructive critic, read aloud to him or her. It catches a remarkable number of simple errors. Encouragement is marvelous, and we all need it. But someone who will tell you what is wrong is helping you far more. We don't go to the doctor when we are fine!

And get a good agent! That is, one who will help you write in a better way what it is you want to write and then be able to sell it for you, if that is possible. Find one who will be honest with you as to that likelihood but will not try to make you write what you do not believe.

Tell us about your writing habits and processes. What other duties and pleasures do you balance your life with?

I write from eight in the morning until eight or nine in the evening every day but Sunday. Writing is a job, not a hobby. Of course, I break for meals and a walk now and then, and this time includes every other thing apart from the actual work of writing a chapter. There is mail to be answered, the office management to direct—I have a very competent person to do the work—telephone calls, et cetera. Other than that, there is research, planning, and individual small problems to deal with. But I spend all day working, like most other people.

It takes me about four months to do most books, longer for *Come Armageddon*. This is necessary because delivery dates don't wait—being late is unprofessional and will make for failure. Some publishers can cancel the contract if delivery is late, and it is also unfair to the publisher. They have plans and schedules to meet too and cannot do their jobs if manuscripts are late. I publish two books a year, plus I do short stories, a little editing, articles now and then, interviews, and tour America usually once a year. I also go to France, Spain, and Germany now and then to promote books. I do the occasional signing, conference, and so on in the United Kingdom—I am actually writing this in a hotel in Edinburgh; I'm here for a signing. That fairly well takes up the year.

To write, all I need is a good pad, a good pen, and somewhere to sit. My study is the best, but an airport lounge will do! Or a hotel room, or anywhere I can sit still. One learns to ignore other conditions or people around. I don't use a computer, but my secretary does, and I do second and third drafts from the printed pages—but again by hand. I just prefer to.

A book usually takes me three drafts—except *Come Armageddon*, which was six or seven. Since all my mysteries are historical, a great deal of research is needed. It doesn't happen all at one time. There must be a certain amount done before I begin, in order to make sure the story is historically accurate and feasible. After that there are specific incidents and facts to check. By now, after thirty-five books on Victorian London, I should know the general facts and atmosphere.

I outline every scene, where and when it takes place, who is present, and what is to be accomplished as far as the plot and relationships are concerned. It usually runs to approximately a legal-sized, single-spaced page per chapter, and there are between twelve and fifteen chapters to a book. *Come Armageddon* was an exception, where there were forty-one pages of outline.

Other duties or pleasures? Church callings, friends—that's about it. Reading, music, the garden, and so on get fitted in during the odd break. Reading is necessary, music can be played while I work, the garden I walk around, but someone else works it. There are two acres—it is a full-time job.

Most fiction is a combination of three elements: what the author has experienced, observed, and imagined. How do those three elements work together for you?

I think this is true, but in my case it is not a conscious blend. I draw on imagination, but it must be prompted by experience and observation. I start at a known point and work from there. If it seems honest to what I know and feel and is right for the story, I use it. If you're not writing what you felt, experienced, and know in some form or another, you're not writing honestly. It may be greatly transmuted, but you're writing who you are.

Which of your titles are you most proud of? Which of your novels has been the hardest to write?

If someone I had just met were to ask which of my books to begin with, I would suggest *Face of a Stranger* because it is one of the best and the beginning of a series. The beginning of my other series was written eleven years earlier and was my first published book. I am least proud of my earliest works, because I hope I have improved since then. If not, I have wasted a lot of years. I am most fond of *Come Armageddon* because it is the most complex and the one in which I have said entirely what I believe about the nature and purpose of human life and man's relationship with God. It was also the most difficult to write, for that reason.

How would you describe your two mystery series? How do you come up with your characters?

The two mystery series differ from each other in setting by about twenty-five years; therefore, social conditions are different. The earlier setting was actually the later to be written and is a little darker, dealing with more complex principal characters. It concerns mainly legal, medical, and military subjects. The other series, in which there are more books, is set at the end of the nineteenth century, when there was more freedom for women and more glamour and excitement, and it deals with social and political issues.

The creation of characters is a subconscious thing, built on faces and impressions and on hard work in creating their backgrounds and motivations. I identify most with Pitt and at times Hester—I think! Great-aunt Vespasia is in many ways my favorite.

Tell us a little about how you discovered the LDS Church and what role it plays in your life today. What Mormon literature have you read?

How did I discover the church? I was looking—the whole story would be an entire article in itself. Why did I join? I knew it was the truth. When? April 22, 1967. As far as the role it plays in my life today, if you believe a religion to be true, it has to be the driving force of everything and at the core of who you are. I am sure you don't want a sermon on that!

I have read a number of church-related books but almost entirely factual. I particularly favor Hugh Nibley. I think I have all his works. As far as Mormon literature is concerned, I presume that means fiction, poetry, et cetera. I am afraid that is pretty well a blank. Remember, I live in the far north of the Scottish Highlands. We do not even have a temple in this country; the nearest is in England. And of course no church bookshops.

What are your observations and hopes regarding the Mormon culture as a literary marketplace and audience?

I have thought quite a lot about my hopes for LDS culture and the LDS literary marketplace. As a people, we sometimes miss the point that really good fiction will deal with a great and universal truth about human nature. If a story is entirely pleasant and comfortable, raises no disturbing issues, does not make you think or feel anything you have not experienced before, and all ends as you would like, then it is hardly worth bothering with. It is comfort food for the mind, but it feeds nothing. And still in the food analogy, it is so sweet that it is likely to do you some harm. Too much sugar not only rots the teeth, I think it rots the mind also. Neither the Bible nor particularly the Book of Mormon is free from the gruesome, and the Book of Mormon has the least happy ending I have ever read!

To be really good, a work must be original and not derivative, and that calls for a lot of courage, because there is always the risk in breaking new ground that you will make mistakes and be criticized and misunderstood. The comfort zone contains no growth—and I think no good literature, because there is nothing profoundly creative in it. Of course, it may be very competent and comfortable in that it tells you what you want to hear and what is already familiar. It requires no effort of mind or emotion to read, and there are times when we all need that and times when we don't.

Tell us about how *Tathea* and its sequel evolved. What was it like to move into the fantasy genre?

I began *Tathea*, at least in concept, even before I found the church, but it developed gradually, and I only pulled out the first draft, from my bottom drawer, and wrote the forerunner to that story a few years ago, which turned into *Tathea*. The story itself was profoundly changed and became *Come Armageddon*.

It was exciting and frightening to publish in another genre, but, as you see, it was not a departure but a return. I enjoy fantasy when it extends the mind and is deeply moral, as a lot of it is. It is one of the oldest forms of storytelling—and teaching. Look at the myths and legends of any civilization.

What kinds of responses to *Tathea* have you received from LDS readers? Has the novel reached non-LDS audiences?

I have received some wonderful responses to *Tathea* from LDS readers, including one person who wrote to me: "It is not a book, it is *the* book." It has not reached as many people as I would have liked. However, it has reached a general audience, and their response has been good also, although it is not an easy book because it makes fairly plain that the path is upward and steep and there are no guarantees of reaching the top.

Regarding your mysteries, one reader posed the following question: "Does she have it in for the upper classes? I've read only a few of her books, but the villains are always aristocrats who consider themselves higher life forms than the rest of us." Another reader argued that your most insistent themes "are about faith in the value of honest human relationships and in the possibility of a society in which all citizens

have equal rights." Are these comments on target, and how would you respond to them?

Regarding the question about the upper classes, that reader has certainly read only a few of my books! All classes have their heroes and their villains, but in shades of gray, not black and white. But it is a fact of writing about all classes that it gives the reader no satisfaction to find that the person to blame for a crime is someone they have not known throughout the story or someone whose circumstances largely explain what happened. It is also a convention of mystery that you cannot blame the butler!

I don't know about a society in which all people have equal rights—before the law, certainly, and equal opportunities as far as that is possible. We are not all equally clever, beautiful, talented, or loveable. Nor are we all equally brave, diligent, honest, compassionate, or generous. It is a very large subject. I think I'll settle for equal before the law and equal opportunities to have the education you can and will use.

Have any of your books been made into movies, and are any in the pipeline? Have you been or will you ever be involved in other literary sidelines, such as reviewing books and teaching writing?

The Cater Street Hangman was made into a two-hour television pilot, and I hope more will be made in time. Period film is always expensive, for obvious reasons, but we have an excellent script for *Face of a Stranger* and are hoping for the necessary finance, et cetera.

I have been for many years involved in writing short stories, occasional articles, and a little reviewing. I have never been invited to teach writing but would certainly consider it seriously if I were.

What can Mormons learn from the mystery novel? Have LDS themes and beliefs entered into your mainstream writing? Do non-LDS publishing professionals and readers seem to have any special reaction to your being LDS?

What can Latter-day Saints learn from mystery books? That depends on the nature and quality of the book. If it is a well-written, fairly serious one, then we can learn a great deal about human nature, how tragedies happen and how we deal with them, possibly even what can be done to prevent them in certain instances, and perhaps a deeper understanding and compassion for other people in a variety of situations where we ourselves may never be. If nothing else, we could learn to judge less swiftly, to hate the sin but not the sinner, and to recognize that many sorts of pain can be learned from.

Yes, LDS thoughts must permeate everything I write, because that is who I am, but most of it is of a fairly subtle nature. I care most about issues like the fundamental value of agency, responsibility, not exercising unrighteous dominion, compassion for those who are different from oneself, and the belief that we can govern our own lives more often than we think. These themes are deeply LDS, but not overtly so.

I have never had a comment on my religion from a publisher, but more readers than I can count remark on my values, even if some of them do not know where they originate. My mystery books have even been used in high-school ethics classes. To me that is the ultimate compliment.

LEVI PETERSON

Levi Peterson
Fiction Writer

Levi Peterson is the author of A Rascal by Nature, A Christian by Yearning: A Mormon Autobiography, *published in 2006 by the University of Utah Press. His earlier books include two collections of short stories,* The Canyons of Grace *and* Night Soil; *two novels,* The Backslider *and* Aspen Marooney; *and a biography,* Juanita Brooks: Mormon Woman Historian. *He compiled an anthology of Mormon short stories titled* Greening Wheat, *and he has written many essays and articles about western American literature and Mormon culture. He serves as editor of* Dialogue: A Journal of Mormon Thought. *The original version of this interview appeared in* Irreantum, *September 1999.*

Many consider *The Backslider* as the preeminent contemporary LDS novel. What were your impulses and intentions in writing the novel? Did you have a sense of breaking new ground?

I had always planned on writing a novel. I don't know why it didn't occur to me that I might write more than one. I began writing *The Backslider* a long time before I came up with that title. I had in mind a novel in which the protagonist's reaction to his brother's self-emasculation would form the center of interest. I was thinking about this topic by at least 1976. This interested me because I believed I could discern an impulse toward self-emasculation in myself as a boy. I read a chapter at Lavina Fielding Anderson's house in 1978. There were a lot of postponements and delays, though I never stopped thinking about *The Backslider* for any length of time. I wrote the stories in *The Canyons of Grace* and gathered the stories in *Greening Wheat* and saw both those works published before I made *The Backslider* my primary endeavor about 1983.

The most important transmutation in creating the action occurred when I stopped being interested in why Jeremy had emasculated himself and started being interested in what would become of Frank. I had three or four chapters completed before I was seized quite suddenly one summer day in 1983 and started writing the present first chapter in which Frank is a half-comic rebel ranch hand. It was only then that I began to think of Frank as the backslider, the ardent rascal who hopes the Big Son of a Bitch in the Sky isn't paying attention to his latest sin. A California physician scolded me by letter for having Frank think of God in the foregoing blasphemous way. I replied that a realistic characterization required that statement from Frank and that it did not necessarily reflect my own views. But the truth is that Frank's hatred for God isn't a literary invention. I hate the same God Frank hates. The only out for both of us is the Cowboy Jesus.

As long as Jeremy was my chief interest, there wasn't much possibility of a happy ending. Though I toned down the earlier overt symbolism of the pit that Jeremy digs near the end of the novel, its validity remains. For Jeremy, this world is hell and all one can do is wait for a ladder on which to climb out of it. Frank, on the other hand, was salvageable in this world as well as the next. But his circumstances were such that the salvaging would have to come about miraculously. A year or more before finishing the novel, I was thinking that Frank would have to undergo an epiphany of some sort. But what it might be completely baffled me. It seemed something only a little short of inspiration when, nearing the end of the entire writing process, I thought of Marianne's accounts of her daydream of the Cowboy Jesus and saw that he was exactly the one to appear to Frank.

I had no ideas about breaking new ground. I was simply writing as I felt I must. At that reading at Lavina's house in 1978, my audience sat in what seemed a stunned silence. I had some inkling at that moment that they had not seen tough realism applied to a Mormon setting.

Tell us more about reader response to *The Backslider*. What kinds of things do you hear? What are total sales, and is it still selling?

The Backslider, published in 1986, is still in print. The first edition came out in a glossy blue cover with cattle and a cowboy on it. I liked that one very much. When that sold out, Signature Books reduced the plates photographically and printed the presently available mass-market paperback version that shows a youth sitting in an open pickup door. The first artwork for the new cover had a bra dangling from the pickup window. I liked that, but given Mormon taste I suppose it is for the best that the bra is gone from the cover of the published work. Signature Books is currently preparing to republish the novel in a new, bigger format.

Aspen Marooney, published in 1995, is also still in print. *The Backslider* outsells it two to one. The University of Utah Press published my biography, *Juanita Brooks: Mormon Woman Historian,* in hard cover in 1988. Later it reprinted it with glossy paper covers. Of all my books, this biography had the most spectacular beginning. The first printing sold out in two months. The topic had something to do with it. But I had also been awarded the $10,000 Evans biography prize, which came with considerable high-class promotion. I remember a reception at the hotel on the University of Utah campus with totally fancy hors d'oeuvres. I thought, "Dang! This is how the rich and the powerful live." There was a big crowd there that night. That doesn't hurt an author's self-esteem any.

Returning to *The Backslider:* I had unsolicited responses to it from almost the start. A cousin, a lawyer, told me on the steps of a Salt Lake courthouse that the book had reactivated two friends of his. A woman wrote that the book made her less despairing of her backsliding son. Another woman said it reconciled her to her father's suicide. An informal group of women in Salt Lake named themselves the Backsliders. As far as I know, they are still in existence. I have visited with them twice.

Almost all my respondents have been Mormon. However, the book has been taught in college classes in at least three states outside of Utah. A gentile friend taught it in an honors course at Ball State in Muncie, Indiana. He sent me the responses of the students, none of them Mormon. They were highly positive. Patricia Limerick, of *New Western History* fame, used the book in a history course at Colorado State. She chose it for what she considered its accuracy of detail about rural Mormons.

I think many people like *The Backslider* because the characters and setting strike them as authentic. Many like it because of its hopeful religious message. Many seem to like it for its tough realism—that is, its R-rated treatment of Mormon life. Perhaps many like it for its quality of pace. By the time I was writing the final drafts, I had realized the importance of pace. There are innumerable brief episodes in the novel. Topic and scene change rapidly. My fiction since *The Backslider* has the same quality, the stories in *Night Soil* and *Aspen Marooney.* For a story that lacks pace, read my piece titled "The Gift," which I included in *Greening Wheat.* It bothers me now to read that story. I itch to speed things up in it.

Could you comment a bit on that story's background? How would you revise it if you were to play Henry James and rework your early stories?

I condensed "The Gift" considerably before publishing it in *Greening Wheat*. Almost invariably I have liked a condensed version of something I have written better than the previous longer version. However, later I began to wish I had condensed it even more. Pacing, as I use the term here, refers to the succession of incidents in a plot. I like a plot with many happenings. I try to make character devolve in relation to these events. Pivotal events will show something new about the character. I try to invent events that will have an intrinsic interest for the reader. The best kind of incident interests the reader regardless of its contribution to character or climax. Obviously proportion figures into incident. I would rather abbreviate an incident than belabor it. I don't want the reader to become bored with it before I finish it.

I have just reread "The Gift." Its incidents are interlaced with description and explanation. I had revisited Liege, Belgium, less than a year before writing the story, and I was eager to include the sights and sounds of that remarkable city. I think also that I conceived of my audience as intellectual readers who would be interested in the philosophical implications of an existentialist come into contact with a Mormon missionary. Perhaps I have shifted my concept of audience since then. I assume my reader wants, as I say above, intrinsically interesting events. So I don't think I could condense the story simply by eliminating the sights and sounds of Liege and somehow toning down the philosophical considerations. I would have to recast the story drastically, coming up with an entirely new set of incidents. Probably it wouldn't be a better story. It would certainly be a different one.

With *The Backslider*'s success, does your other work feel slighted? Have you wanted or expected to equal *The Backslider*'s success with another work? Is there a downside to *The Backslider*'s success?

I think my recognized successes are the stories in *The Canyons of Grace* and *The Backslider*. I think both *Night Soil* and *Aspen Marooney* have created much less interest. I do not reread the stories in *The Canyons of Grace* without considerable impulse to revise them. However, there is scarcely anything in *The Backslider* that I have an impulse to change. Still, *The Canyons of Grace* seemed to come on the scene of Mormon letters at a very propitious time. I recall the non-Mormon referees and editors at the University of Illinois Press congratulating each other in documents—copies of which ended up in my hands—on this find they had made in my stories. Thomas Lyon, non-Mormon compiler of the centennial anthology of Utah literature, *Great & Peculiar Beauty* (1995), included the title story from my collection despite objections by his colleagues that it was too long; it is, in fact, the longest piece in the anthology.

I will say of *Aspen Marooney* that I did not calculate its probable effect on readers. I wrote it in the middle of working on wilderness essays, a project that I later abandoned. I went home to Snowflake, Arizona, for my fortieth high school reunion and came back to Ogden and wrote a short story set in a similar reunion in Richfield, Utah. That story evolved incrementally into a novel, which explains why it has four points of view. If I had set out to write it as a novel in the first place, I am sure I would have had a single point of view. Point of view, of course, is a flexible device. An author can achieve multiple points of view while sticking to, say, a single third-person central point of view by having characters narrate anecdotes and assert opinions. I don't know why it should matter that I have four points of view in *Aspen Marooney,* but I think it troubles some readers.

I don't think there is a downside to the success of *The Backslider.* As for wanting to equal or surpass its success, yes, of course, I would like to with every new piece I write. I do not expect to do so, however. I think its conflict is so central to my personality that, even if I were younger, I would not again achieve the vitality I had while writing it. I was lucky too in taking up the central theme of all Christianity, Christ's redemption. Though it is impossible to predict the future of *The Backslider,* I take some comfort in the idea that this theme will keep the work alive. Right now, twenty years later, it goes on, very modestly selling by simple word of mouth.

What are your thoughts on Signature Books as a publisher, and what has been your experience or observation related to other LDS publishers?

Signature has been crucial to my writing career. It is probable that *Greening Wheat, The Backslider, Night Soil,* and *Aspen Marooney* would never have seen print without them. I do not know the owner, George Smith, well, though I have had a few conversations with him at conferences. I have always respected Scott Kenney, who was in charge when *Greening Wheat* was published, and Gary Bergera and Ron Priddis, who accepted *The Backslider, Night Soil,* and *Aspen Marooney.* Gary and Ron urged me to tone down the obscene language and graphic description in all three of those works. There came a time during the process of publication when Ron phoned me and said he and Gary wanted to go to lunch with me. I knew cleaning up some scenes would be the topic of conversation. After I had done the cleaning up, I liked the result. I don't know why an excess of the R-rated seems essential to maintaining my creative energy while I am writing early drafts.

Signature promoted *Night Soil* in a big way. They flew me to Phoenix and arranged a TV interview down there. We went as far north as Idaho Falls. They overestimated my marketability and found fit to remainder large numbers of *Night Soil.* I bought quite a few copies myself. (I saw on the Web a used-book dealer in California who wants $145 for a signed copy of *Night Soil.*) Gary and Ron got Deseret Book to sell *The Backslider* under the counter. If you asked for it at the main store at downtown ZCMI, you could get it. The branch stores would order it for you. I don't know whether they still do that. My books that are in print can be ordered online through both Barnes & Noble and Amazon. Barnes & Noble has a nice bio about me. I think it is Amazon that numerically ranks each of its offered works against all their other sales. The ranking of my books is not flattering. That ranking process is, I must say, an interesting way to sell books.

I have not submitted anything to one of the mainline Mormon publishing firms. I assume none of them would accept something I had written. I am glad when reviews of my works appearing in local newspapers give a realistic appraisal of their content. I don't want people buying my books and then feeling angry about their R-rated quality.

How would you sum up the current state of Mormon literature? What do you think the future holds?

The current mainline Mormon literature is fecund, alive, creative. The publishing industry aimed at faithful Mormons is enormous. Mormon genre fiction is coming into its own. Orson Scott Card and Gerald Lund have established themselves as best-seller classics. I am impressed by the literary hopes and ambitions expressed by others. I can only assume there are many, many other gifted Latter-day Saint writers out there aspiring to create outstanding Mormon literature. I think this trend will only increase as long as American civilization is ascendant. All this does not apply to literature of an extreme liberal quality. Liberal Mormon writers have almost nowhere to go now to find a publisher, and their works have never sold well among the Mormon public.

***The Backslider* was shopped around to some national publishers before ending up at Signature. What was that process like, for *The Backslider* or any other of your work?**

When I first began writing stories seriously, around 1976, I bought the current *Writer's Market* and used its brief descriptions to help me decide where to submit my stories. It was there I found notice of the University of Illinois Press's short fiction series and sent a single story with a letter of inquiry. That of course eventually led to the publication of *The Canyons of Grace.* I was luckier than I had any idea. There were brief reviews of my collection in newspapers and magazines in Chicago, New York, and Los Angeles. I am sure that is why W.W. Norton invited me to submit my next work to them. In late 1983 I sent the first chapter of *The Backslider.* They liked it, so I sent the completed chapters, about half the novel. They said it wouldn't sell in their market. Houghton Mifflin, Doubleday, and two New York agents to whom I sent the manuscript all likewise said the novel wouldn't sell in their markets and refused to take it on.

In general the Eastern publishers and agents who looked at my manuscript liked it as long as Frank was a true backslider. But when he got serious about his Mormonism—too serious, of course, since his monk-like practice of his religion is one of the novel's major issues—the Eastern press lost interest. I recall that the brief Kirkus review said that the fictional interest of the stories in *The Canyons of Grace* barely "mumbled through the thunder of the message." I decided that the reviewer hadn't really read the stories. I think it is true that people who write book reviews on a schedule become scan readers, or at best they read hurriedly. So maybe the editors and agent who read my draft of *The Backslider* simply weren't willing to grant the premises of the conflict. That would have required them to accept the legitimacy of Mormonism as a worldview.

I submitted the manuscript to Signature Books in early 1986. By then, Gary Bergera and Ron Priddis were in charge of Signature Books. The firm had done a reprint of *The Canyons of Grace* and in 1983 had published *Greening Wheat.* They paid the University of

Illinois Press a modest sum for the reprint rights to *The Canyons of Grace*. My share of that was five hundred dollars. So I got no further royalties on the reprinted version of *The Canyons of Grace*. I wasn't resentful, just curious as to how publishing works.

I began the research for my biography of Juanita Brooks in 1985. I would never have invested the enormous time that project took without the prior interest of the editors at the University of Utah Press. Both Trudy McMurrin and Norma Mikkelsen had proposed that I do the biography, Norma being the one in charge when, in 1985, I settled down to the work. My little essay about Juanita as a tragedian, which I read at the 1976 meeting of the Mormon History Association, had much to do with their confidence that I was the one to write the biography.[1]

I submitted the manuscripts for *Night Soil* and *Aspen Marooney* to Signature Books immediately upon completing them. I knew I had some prior advantage with Signature, and I doubted whether any other publisher anywhere would take those works. It is an unhappy fact for the new writer that a prior acquaintance between authors and their publishers often exists. Some writers can go to a writing workshop, strike up a friendship with an editor at midnight in a bar, and soon place a manuscript. That isn't one of my talents, but I know a friendly relationship between writers and publishers operates as a major principle in the publishing world.

What will it take to get publishers to respect Mormonism as a worldview? Is this disrespect simply bigotry, or something else? For example, could writers change things by building up a body of work too good to ignore? Or do we need a body of militant Mormon critics to insist on the humanity of our worldview, to advocate for us the way, say, feminists have advocated for women's writing and experience?

There are many variables in the public's taste in books. It is possible that it is not my Mormon subject matter but my incompetent writing that has kept me from a success like Judith Freeman's. If Mormon subject matter has something to do with it, I would explain it in this way. Freeman's Mormon protagonist in *The Chinchilla Farm* is on her way out of Mormonism. As I said, the New York publishers who looked at *The Backslider* liked it as long as Frank was a confirmed backslider. They stopped liking it when he got serious about his religion. Why can't readers accord the same dignity to Mormonism that they do to Judaism? It is not bigotry but covert fear. Mormonism is one of the most aggressive religions in the world, and it is getting bigger and bigger. You cannot give a fair reading to literature that you think in its deepest intent aims to subvert your spiritual bearings. The irony for me is that I have never thought of my writing as subverting the faith of someone who is not Mormon. I have never thought of it as faith-promoting. It surprised me to learn that many Mormon readers consider it so.

The educated public is now generally willing to grant the premises of Catholicism, Judaism, and so on in fiction even if those faiths are far from their own. But in their thinking Mormonism has remained an uncanny cult. I recall that Daniel Curly, editor of *Ascent* and one of the referees to whom the University of Illinois Press gave my manuscript collection of short stories, dismissed "Road to Damascus" as being "very crude in spite of being one of the two published stories—it was published in something subtitled *A Magazine of Mormon Thought.* And it reads that way." Obviously he had never seen a copy of *Dialogue.* Potential readers can't suspend the assumption that a story that seems sympathetic to Mormonism will prove polemic. I see signs of change in this assumption. But there have been signs for decades. Who knows when it will actually happen?

In the June 1999 *Sunstone*, Dean May has a memoriam to Leonard Arrington. He says, "Historians and other observers still do not see Mormons as part of the West." Did you notice that in your work with Juanita Brooks? Did the disrespect for Mormonism affect how her work was received? Has it affected how people react to the biography?

There is some truth in Dean May's assertion. But of course it is not absolutely true. Any course in general Western history includes the history of the Mormons. It is possible that historians and social critics don't quite know how to fit modern Mormonism into the modern West. I am not sure Mormon observers know how to do that. Explaining what it is to be a Mormon in the modern West is one of the tasks I have assigned myself in my autobiography.

My brother Charles, for many years a professor of history at Utah State University and editor of the *Western History Journal,* has told me that Mormons who belong to the Western History Association have not integrated well with the large majority of non-Mormon members. Among other things, scholarly organizations are social clubs. It is a rare Mormon who can hobnob easily at midnight in a bar with a group of half-drunk, cigarette-smoking colleagues. Charles says that is exactly what is required for other historians to accept that the Mormons are part of the West.

Juanita Brooks had little opportunity to fraternize with non-Mormon historians because she was an amateur rather than a professional historian. She collaborated with Robert Glass Cleland, a prominent non-Mormon historian, in the editing and publication of John D. Lee's diaries. Both *The Mountain Meadows Massacre* and *John D. Lee—Zealot, Pioneer Builder, Scapegoat* were published by non-Mormon presses outside Utah, and both were abundantly praised in scholarly journals and big-city newspapers. We must remember that many Mormons consider Juanita's writings as anti-Mormon. It is perhaps that quality that has made non-Mormon editors and critics accept her work.

Bias shows in almost all historiography. The bias of Mormon historians supports their faith. That may have something to do with non-Mormon historians of the West wishing to ignore their existence.

You've been involved in the Association for Mormon Letters, Sunstone, and other alternative community efforts. What are your thoughts, observations, and hopes related to the LDS literary and intellectual communities?

I joined the Mormon History Association at its inception and read my essay on Juanita Brooks as a tragedian at one of its early conferences. It seemed natural to join the Association for Mormon Letters when, just a year or two later, it was founded. I attended the first Sunstone symposium feeling doubtful that its announced theological theme would generate much interest. I came away excited by the prospect of a forum where Mormon issues could be openly and honestly debated. I have supported the MHA, AML, and Sunstone because, first, I saw that my own writings would fare better in a climate of opinion amenable to them and, second, because I believed they were liberalizing influences on Mormonism. By liberalizing, I mean I believed they pointed in the direction of desirable change.

I became a board member of AML before 1980 and served as president twice. In my later years on the board, I have always supported a roster of nominees for the next year's board balanced between the liberal and the conservative. I have seen conservative AML boards gravitate toward the liberal. I believe writing, reading, and studying literature liberalizes—that is, it induces change. I think, for example, that no matter how often higher officials at BYU change the composition of the English Department there, sooner or later a new set of professors will become restless and begin saying and writing things that make their supervisors uncomfortable. The only way to avoid this is to abolish the English Department entirely and any other department that studies literature in depth.

I see in the AML-List e-mail group numerous remarkable personalities who like to talk with each other about Mormon literature. Most of them seem to be faithful, active Mormons. They have a refreshing confidence that a person can be both a fervent Mormon and a writer or reader of high-quality literature. I hope they do not, one or many, come to the disillusionment I have seen several other groups of fervent Mormons with literary interests come to. I do not include myself among the disillusioned of any generation. I have never been surprised by the movement of the massive mainline conservative church against any new generation of liberal Mormons. I have always expected it.

What works of Mormon literature have you personally most enjoyed?

I have read and respected many novels and collections of short stories and essays by and about Mormons, among them Vardis Fisher's *Children of God,* Maureen Whipple's *Giant Joshua,* Virginia Sorensen's *A Little Lower Than the Angels,* Richard Scowcroft's *Children of the Covenant,* Gordon Allred's *Valley of Tomorrow,* Donald Marshall's *The Rummage Sale,* Linda Sillitoe's *Sideways to the Sun,* and Eugene England's *Dialogues with Myself.* I have always been interested in Clinton Larson's poetry because he was my professor in courses at BYU. I greatly respect the careful realism with which Benson Parkinson treats Mormon missionaries in *The MTC: Set Apart.*

The book that had the most impact on me was Douglas Thayer's *Summer Fire.* I read it during the summer of 1983, at the moment I had decided to infuse the chapters of *The Backslider* with comedy. I was impressed by Thayer's relentless simplicity of style, appropriate to the teen mentality of his major character. Hitherto, except for the new comic first chapter, I had written the chapters of *The Backslider* with the dignified elaboration of style of my stories in *The Canyons of Grace.* I rewrote the existing chapters of *The Backslider,* making them partly comic and recasting them in a very simple style suitable to Frank's mentality. In a later revision, I struck a compromise between this very simple style and what I thought was a subtle complexity of style that allowed a knowing and ironic narrator to share thoughts alongside Frank.

How did you come to writing in general and to Mormon writing? Who were your teachers?

I decided to major in English at the beginning of my sophomore year in 1952 at BYU. I was nearly nineteen. Instantly I had the ambition to become a writer of fiction. I took creative writing courses at BYU, one from Clinton Larson, two from Thomas Cheney. Although my early stories weren't successful, already they depicted Mormons in sin and turmoil. That topic came to me by nature. I think I am a realist by nature, also, and therefore had to stick to people and scenes I was familiar with.

As for teachers who influenced me, almost the entire English faculty at BYU in the 1950s had an influence on me if for no other reason than that they were the primary influence on my literary values. Besides Larson and Cheney I think of P.A. Christensen, Bruce Clark, Orea Tanner, Karl Young, Marden Clark, Woodruff Thompson, all keen minds, all good influences. Later at the University of Utah, while doing doctoral work I was especially influenced by my dissertation chairman, Don Walker, who has in fact remained my lifelong friend. To a considerable degree, most of these teachers diverted me from the writing of fiction to the writing of literary criticism. That is what university English departments teach best. But as I say, they gave me a thorough workout in the general principles of writing, and they honed my literary values. I do not regret being diverted from writing fiction while I was very young. I really hadn't figured out what I wanted to say. That is something I have against creative writing schools and undergraduate creative writing majors: they try to teach young people to write fiction before they have read good fiction.

People often assume you are a lapsed Mormon or estranged from the church. If it's not too personal a question, how would you describe your relationship with the church?

I value my membership greatly, and I attend sacrament meeting with some regularity. I served as a home teacher for more than three decades in my Ogden ward, where I was also sometimes asked to teach the lesson in the high priests group. I was asked to attend the high priests group at about age fifty for social reasons, though my priesthood is that of elder. I am often invited to stand in the circle when babies are blessed and children are confirmed in my extended family. Some time ago my son-in-law asked that I be the one to baptize and confirm him a member of the church. Some years ago when Lavina Fielding Anderson and others were excommunicated, my stake president asked to visit me in my campus office. I considered this a great concession on his part. He asked for my feelings about the church, and when I had told him, he urged me to attend to the commandments more faithfully, shook my hand, and left.

What projects are you currently working on?

I do little personal or creative writing at the moment, being preoccupied by editing, teaching an online class for Weber State University, and helping care for my two grandsons. Luckily, I finished my autobiography before I undertook the editorship of *Dialogue*. Having kept diaries and copies of my letters for many years, I had plenty of sources to draw on while writing the autobiography. I felt a double obligation to report factually on what had happened to me and at the same time recount incidents and emotions that would interest readers. I feel writing an autobiography is as much a creative act as writing a novel. As for the future, I intend to return to writing fiction when I am through editing *Dialogue*. Because I am old, I plan on writing about elderly Mormons in sin and turmoil. I notice that while my capacity for sin has diminished with age, my interest in it hasn't.

Tell us a little about your personal background.

I was born December 13, 1933, to Joseph and Lydia Peterson. My father had four sons and two daughters by his first wife, who died. My mother had two daughters by her first husband, whom she divorced. Together they had five sons, of whom I am the last. To this day I remain affectionately involved in a numerous extended family. I grew up in Snowflake, a Mormon town in northern Arizona. Though I have spent most of my adult life in cities, I have no affinity for urban existence. The rhythms of life in Snowflake were very satisfying, making me forever wish, as I drive through any little Mormon town, that I had grown up there.

From 1954 to 1957, I served as a missionary in Switzerland and Belgium, then part of a single French mission. In 1958 I married Althea Sand, one of the few non-Mormons attending BYU. I acquired B.A. and M.A. degrees from BYU and a Ph.D. in English from the University of Utah. I taught English at Weber State from 1965 to 2000. Though I served as department chairman twice, I always considered myself a teacher. My wife and I bought an old two-story house in Ogden in 1966 and spent years renovating it. We sold it with much regret in 2000 and bought a condo in the Seattle area near our daughter Karrin and her husband and sons.

[1.] "Juanita Brooks: The Mormon Historian as Tragedian," *Journal of Mormon History* 3 (1976): 47–54; reprinted in *Tending the Garden*, edited by Eugene England and Lavina Fielding Anderson (Salt Lake City: Signature Books, 1996), 135–145.

JANA RIESS

Jana Riess
Author and Editor

Since 1999, Jana Riess has served as Publishers Weekly's Religion Book Review Editor. *Among other works, she is the author of* The Book of Mormon: Selections Annotated & Explained *and coauthor of* Mormonism For Dummies. *Raised by an agnostic mother and an atheist father, Riess earned a master's degree from Princeton Theological Seminary and a doctorate in American religious history at Columbia University. An LDS Church member since 1993, she lives with her husband and daughter in Cincinnati, Ohio. The original version of this interview appeared in* Irreantum, *spring 2003.*

Trace for us your pathway to *Publishers Weekly* and how you feel about your work there.

I adore my job. In graduate school, I had always intended to pursue a teaching career with writing on the side, as most professors do. But in my final year, one of my advisers did not receive tenure, a devastating blow for her and a shock to all the rest of us who thought she had done everything right. We came to believe that Columbia's decision to deny her tenure was essentially a political one. I was so angered by the capriciousness of it all that I began having serious doubts about whether I wanted to continue in the academic path I'd chosen.

A few months later, I got a call from a friend who reviewed for *PW*, saying that the Religion Book Review Editor position was open and that it didn't require moving to New York. (For me, NY is a great place to visit. Period.) I was terribly excited and put in my application immediately. I had been reviewing religion books for *Kirkus* all during graduate school, so I had a little experience.

I've loved all of my experience at *PW*, particularly being able to pick up the phone and interview any author I find interesting. That is, hands down, the best part. Well, that and the free books. And working from home.

From where you're sitting, do you see many Mormon-related books?

In 2002—the Salt Lake Olympics year—we saw a crop of new books on Mormonism, but most of them were of the "Find the dangerous truth beneath the friendly Mormon exterior!" variety. For example, I remember one specifically aimed to help evangelical women witness to their Mormon women friends. That's not exactly progress.

However, I do sense a new openness to Mormonism in publishing and in our larger culture. Knopf recently put out Richard Bushman's excellent biography of Joseph Smith. Doubleday partnered with Deseret to release the first-ever trade edition of the Book of Mormon. St. Martin's has done a few Mormon-related books, including one by Coke Newell that I didn't particularly like but which must have done pretty well, since they brought it out in paper. There have been a couple of other tentative forays by the national houses, but New York publishers aren't yet taking Mormons seriously as authors or readers. Academic presses, however, are beginning to be aggressive about acquiring books that deal with Mormon themes. "Mormon studies" is becoming quite a hot subdiscipline in religious scholarship. And since university presses tend to be a few years ahead of the curve of commercial publishing, this is a healthy sign.

What it will take to release the floodgates, of course, is a hit. Once a publisher has commercial success with a Mormon book, all the other ones will scratch their heads, wonder why they didn't see the market before, and jump on the bandwagon. The market is there; they just don't realize it yet.

What are your personal favorites among Mormon literature? What are your observations about the development of Mormon literature?

I'm a great lover of fiction, but I haven't been terribly impressed with LDS commercial fiction. It is at the stage now that CBA [Christian Booksellers

Association] fiction had reached about ten years ago: characters are predictable, the novels are message-driven rather than character-driven, and most stories end with a predictable and obligatory conversion sequence. This is not to say that CBA fiction is all grown up; it is still very uneven, and much of the industry is stuck in the old models, because they continue to sell well. But some CBA fiction has matured significantly, and authors like Jamie Langston Turner, Athol Dickson and Vinita Hampton Wright make me hopeful for the future of the genre.

It's fascinating to me that LDS fiction started gaining success roughly in the same way that CBA novels did: with historical and scriptural fiction. Certainly the success of Gerald Lund taught LDS publishers that Mormon audiences were very interested in faith-promoting, fictionalized interpretations of history. I'm not a Lund fan, but this was an important step. The next step was to improve the quality of those historical novels, which is where Dean Hughes comes in. You asked about my personal favorites, and he's certainly on the top of my list. I could quibble with little elements of his writing style, but not with the characters or the overall storytelling. I am continually impressed by him, particularly by the love he has for all his characters—Liahonas and Iron Rods, traditionalists and feminists, true believers and skeptics. The guy is so balanced, and he has great respect for the reader's intelligence and faith journey.

"LDS commercial fiction" and "Mormon literature" are not necessarily the same thing. So, the next step will be to develop more of the latter, to tell stories that are darker and deeper. If the LDS model continues to follow the CBA trajectory, these will not sell particularly well. That's a sad market reality. But courageous writers who are willing to tell authentic stories—Terry Tempest Williams, Levi Peterson, and Brian Evenson come to mind—will still be read and discussed when copies of faith-promoting pabulum sell for ninety-nine cents on eBay.

But on the commercial side, the next step is something we already see happening in LDS fiction: the niche factor. We don't just have romance and suspense; we now have "romantic suspense," which is its own thriving genre. And we do have some successful genre authors on the national scene. Orson Scott Card is an important writer in sci-fi and fantasy, a market that has proven to be very receptive to LDS writers. Anne Perry is an acclaimed mystery novelist, and for good reason: her Inspector Monk series is one of the most psychologically intriguing and well-written series you'll find anywhere. And Stephenie Meyer is becoming a recognizable force in the YA market. So, there are LDS authors who have made a name for themselves in the various niches. That trend will certainly grow.

What's your impression of today's Mormon reading audience? What, in your opinion, should be the role of literature in Mormon life?

One thing that tends to surprise non-Mormons who make assumptions about our subculture is what a well-educated crowd we are. As a religious group,

Mormons rank high in affluence in this country. Studies have shown that for Mormons, higher education is usually tied with higher, not lower, retention rates—in other words, educated members tend to stay in the church. All of this translates into a large audience of potential readers and book buyers.

Moreover, ours is a faith that is grounded in story. I was talking with a friend about this, and he reminded me that the Joseph Smith translation of the Bible is not simply a correction of theological or doctrinal errors that Smith saw. Instead, he is inserting characters, dialogue, and settings. He is weaving stories.

Despite these factors, our faith has developed into something that is very cautious around issues of ambiguity and conflict. We don't want to rock the boat, and we think there must be something wrong with other people if *they* want to rock the boat. But great literature, like great art, emerges from authors challenging expectations and shaking people out of their comfort zones, while simultaneously reaffirming core values.

I'm not saying that every LDS novel needs to be a Great Work of Art. In fact, I'm astonished when literary types pooh-pooh the importance of the commercial market, because history shows that commercial success trickles down to enlarge the entire market for a certain type of literature, whether it's intentionally literary or "just" commercial. I really take issue with the cultural elitism that says that great books cannot also be widely appealing. In the Mormon scene, we need to help erase the divide between the writing that is self-consciously literary and the writing that is done to sell books.

One more thing: LDS publishers estimate that as many as eighty-five percent of book buyers in LDS stores are women, which is even higher than the CBA estimate of sixty-five percent. So, for any literary genre to be commercially successful in the LDS market, it has to appeal to women.

What are some recent trends in the religious publishing market?

Distribution has been a huge problem in the CBA and the larger, secular American Booksellers Association, and this is something that affects publishers and, by extension, readers. We continue to see the barnesandnobleization of the book market, a trend that is fabulous for some authors but very hard on independent retailers and small chains. Most CBA publishers have jettisoned their retail stores or spun them off into a separate brand. I wouldn't be surprised to see this happen with Deseret and Seagull, since most retail stores are bleeding and can really eat into a publisher's profit margins. However, I don't know how those chains in particular are doing. Deseret, in fact, has actually been expanding its retail division, and has had success with innovative bookselling ideas, like putting a Lion House Pantry in some of its stores.

In recent years, many publishers have trimmed their lists, choosing to focus their energies on fewer books rather than publishing slews of them in the hope that one will be a bestseller. This does make it harder for new authors to get published, since the houses have fewer slots open and they're less willing to spend the money that it takes to build a writer's career. But the religion category continues to perform rather amazingly well, so that squeeze is a little less obvious for religion authors.

What are some noticeable gaps in the Mormon library? What are some key books in other cultures and religions that you would like to see modeled in Mormonism?

Over the next few decades, I'm sure that we will continue to see growth in the church, though it will primarily happen abroad. This shift is already occurring, since conversion rates in North America have dipped somewhat. The silver lining of this particular cloud is that when religious groups experience periods where they are not inundated by new converts, they can start growing up sociologically and can meet the deeper needs of the people who are already part of those groups. We will see a maturation of Mormonism in North America, and this will affect the kinds of books that are published and read.

As the membership matures, we will see the emergence of more independent Mormon voices. I am not talking of ones that are critical of the church; I am talking of voices that connect the Mormon experience—which has been all too insular—to the wider world. We will see more interfaith books, more books about ethics on the job, more Mormon books about aging and travel and spiritual gardening. It's odd that for a church that speaks so stridently about not being just a Sunday religion, LDS books tend to be overwhelmingly about theological topics and less about how Mormons can engage the wider world. I personally would like to write a book about Mormonism at the movies—not about how Mormons are portrayed on film, but what we as Latter-day Saints can learn from popular culture.

As for key books in other religious cultures, I think we need more Philip Yanceys and Max Lucados in Mormondom. We need writers who are thoroughly steeped in scripture but know how to relate it to everyday life. One of my biggest style complaints about LDS writing is that our nonfiction authors will make two declarative statements of their own and then back them up with six long quotations from general authorities. That style makes for badly crafted writing.

We also need writers who adhere to both sides of Reinhold Niebuhr's famous injunction—writers, like preachers, need to comfort the afflicted and afflict the comfortable. We have any number of writers who do the former but too few who attempt the latter.

Any author contemplating a Mormon-related book faces particular struggles regarding audience. Should the book be aimed at non-

Mormon mainstream readers? Should it be aimed at Mormon readers? Is there a way to simultaneously address both audiences?

I'd advise any writer to just write. If you consciously tailor your craft to fit the needs of an imagined market, your writing will suffer. Having said that, though, I'd add that it is possible to speak to both audiences simultaneously, because superb writing will always transcend boundaries. One problem is that most Mormons who grew up in the church—which includes almost all LDS authors—have a tendency to assume a language and a worldview that will simply not be understood, let alone shared, by a non-Mormon audience.

If a national publisher wanted to break into the Mormon market, what would be your advice for how to do so?

I think national houses need to realize the importance of imprimatur in Mormon culture. Yes, some things will fly under the radar and enjoy grassroots support, but church members respond much more enthusiastically to a message that they know is approved. Major national houses that want to do Mormon books should consider copublishing with LDS houses to dip their toes in the water. Random House, for example, did extremely well with its first Mormon copublishing venture, which was President Hinckley's *Standing for Something*. (How can you lose?) That set the stage for other NY-SLC deals, which is an ideal collaboration. A Mormon publisher can get the book on the LDS bestseller lists and create important buzz on the Wasatch Front, but it doesn't have the clout or distribution to create a national hit like a New York house does. In the copublishing scenario, everybody wins.

Of course, LDS publishers are going to get on board only for books they know are orthodox. What about edgier projects that have the potential to offend their core audiences? This is tricky, but we will see it happen. HarperSanFrancisco did the Ostlings' book *Mormon America* in 1999, and that book had legs in both the LDS and national markets without any kind of official imprimatur. So it can be done.

It seems like Mormonism's well-known proselytizing imperative would make it harder for publishers and readers outside the faith to trust us. Do you think that's true? If so, how can that be overcome?

Yes, this is a serious issue, but not just for Mormons. It's a problem in the CBA as well, particularly in fiction. I mean, a nonfiction book can proclaim a very narrow and/or highly politicized point of view and is entirely within its rights to do so. But fiction should serve the story first and the message second; fiction must be true to itself. Craft must come first.

I am horrified when people—not just Mormons—ask me for advice about how to publish their issue-of-the-week novel about the dangers of cloning, or the perils of teen sex, or whatever. "Fiction seems like the best medium to get this message out," one would-be author told a publisher friend of mine. Well, my friend said, did you also get up this morning, feel upset about this issue, and decide to write a concerto about it? The author conceded that he didn't know how to write a concerto. My friend pointed out that he ought to treat novel writing with the same respect. It takes years of crafting to hone a voice, and the literary muse is not well served by people who want to hijack the novel as a vehicle of social protest. Please note that I get just as ticked off when liberals do this as when conservatives do it. That's how we got *The Da Vinci Code*.

It really boils down to a question of propaganda. There is such a thing as good propaganda, stuff that is well written and entertaining. But it's not literature. If an author writes a novel in order to hammer home a social point, then character and plot have taken a back seat to propaganda. Yes, propaganda can serve a useful purpose and even last beyond its immediate social context—think *Uncle Tom's Cabin*. But it doesn't acknowledge the very essence of creativity or storytelling.

I've come a long and very soapboxy way from your question about Mormonism. Yes, anyone who wants to be published in the national market needs to overcome the idea that literature should be a vehicle for religious proselytizing. We can do authentic books that are thoroughly grounded in the Mormon tradition without that attitude.

Do you think this nation will ever have a Mormon Saul Bellow or Flannery O'Connor, someone winning national awards for literature that deals with Mormon themes, settings, and characters?

Oh, yes. I just hope I am alive to see it! I do think it will take some time. When President Kimball spoke twenty-five years ago or so about the development of the Mormon arts, I think it helped many in the Mormon community see the tremendous possibilities. But these things take time. Flannery O'Connor had nearly two thousand years of Roman Catholic tradition and experience to back her up, not to mention a rich history of her religion's investment in the arts. When Saul Bellow and Chaim Potok told stories, they were standing in a Jewish literary tradition that extended back three thousand years. As Mormons, we may be grafted into that literary tradition, but our religion is less than two centuries old. Our stories are still emerging.

Also, our stories may be less interesting now in our era of assimilation and comfort than they were at the religion's founding. Great stories usually emerge out of painful experiences. But, ironically enough, it is our current assimilated, comfortable status that will guarantee a publisher and an audience for those stories. What a catch-22.

How do Mormon-market publishers compare with national publishers and other religious-market publishers?

What's really surprising to me is how similar LDS publishers are to evangelical houses—surprising because these two groups don't typically communicate well with each other. They really deal with many of the same issues, the same core constituencies. Someday they ought to have a summit!

One difference is that the LDS market is blessed with lower returns of unsold books from stores, even single-digit returns, a phenomenon that increases profitability and decreases the risks associated with publishing. I'm sure that the LDS returns rate would be the envy of the rest of the publishing world, if they knew about it.

Like all publishers, Mormon houses have to pay close attention to the bottom line. Profit margins in publishing can be very slim, and the LDS market has traditionally given pretty generous royalties to authors. This is changing to be more in line with the royalty scale of other houses.

The LDS Booksellers Association (LDSBA) is a trade organization of about 250 LDS-market retailers and wholesalers, and their annual convention provides an interesting window on the Mormon culture. What are your impressions of that group and their role in the development of Mormon literature? How do they compare with the much larger Christian Booksellers Association and other religious-oriented trade groups?

The CBA is a four-billion-dollar-a-year industry, so of course the LDSBA is only a fraction of that size. One publishing executive told me several years ago that it was about a $100-million annual industry, and I'm sure it has grown since then. I think many people in New York publishing would be surprised to see how quickly the LDS market is growing. Covenant Communications has doubled in size in the last few years. Deseret has had some substantial bestsellers recently with six-figure sales. Smaller houses such as Cedar Fort and Signature continue to do well. Signature, in particular, is a house to watch because they are willing to take a chance with material that other houses might deem too controversial. They have done some very good fiction in the past.

When I attended LDSBA for the first time, it was quite helpful. (Of course, it's always difficult to see the kitschy elements of your own culture on display, which is why I could walk right past the "Evangicube" at CBA without batting an eyelash but was marginally disturbed by the temple checks I saw at LDSBA.) But besides that, it's very useful to see it all firsthand. It's a fine opportunity to learn and to meet people in the industry.

Some time ago, the Utah media got into an uproar over Deseret Book banning Richard Paul Evans's novel *The Last Promise* because of the book's alleged immorality. What is your take on that situation, and what future ramifications do you think it will have?

Well, as a self-described "liberal" Mormon—funny how the folks at work think I'm so conventional and the people at church think I'm a flaming left-ist!—I have to come right out and say that I think censorship in almost any form is bad. But as someone who hangs out in religious publishing, I know that this increased inventory conservatism is the trend across the board. Mormons have the unfortunate tendency to isolate themselves and their subculture from the rest of the world and imagine that their struggles are unique. But what happened at Deseret Book had already happened with other books at Family, Lifeway, and other Christian bookstore chains. When Deseret says the company made this decision because of feedback from customers, I absolutely believe that, because that is the way it has happened in the evangelical market. In fact, in the CBA the content rules are far stricter. A friend of mine and I were laughing recently about a Christian chain returning thousands of copies of a novel because it had the word *hell* in it. If Christians can't say *hell*, my friend asked, then who can?

This is a much bigger issue than simple censorship; it is at root an identity issue. With Deseret, part of the problem is that the secular chain bookstores—and even Wal-Mart and Costco—now carry many of the products that folks used to buy at Deseret stores. They also offer them a little cheaper, so why buy them at Deseret? By taking a stand on what it perceives as questionable mate-rial, Deseret can carve a niche for itself in a market that is becoming increasingly blurry for consumers and thereby raise the level of consumer trust. They're creating a brand. It's actually a really sound marketing decision, even though it's troubling from a literary perspective.

I just hope they'll still carry all the Harry Potter books.

As everyone knows, recently Mormon cinema has blossomed. What lessons and implications does that new movement have for Mormon books?

Before I answer that, let me just say how thrilled I am to see the rather sudden evolution of LDS filmmaking. When I saw *God's Army,* I was very im-pressed, but *Brigham City* just blew me away. What a powerful statement about estrangement and forgiveness. And of course I'm also enjoying the more frothy and campy send-ups of Mormon culture. I'm really looking forward to all the forthcoming films.

I think that the growth of Mormon cinema is directly relevant to our conversation about books, because it's not just Mormons who are driving this interest in LDS films. Other people are curious about our culture. I first found the video for *God's Army*, for example, by chance in the video store of Winchester, Kentucky, where we were living at that time. We had hardly any Latter-day Saints in our town. The film's presence there represented more than just the fact that Excel Entertainment has remarkable distribution. Other people want to understand their Mormon neighbors, particularly as Mormonism moves out of Utah and becomes more integrated with national life.

How did you come to join the LDS Church, and how has that affected your literary outlook? What's your current stance toward Mormonism?

By "current stance," I'm guessing you mean whether I am active. Well, I've been the Gospel Doctrine teacher in my ward before, which probably tells you that (a) I am very active in church and (b) God has a fairly perverse and well-developed sense of humor. More recently I've been in the Young Women presidency and was the Primary chorister. But I have also had periods when I needed to take a break from church, including one yearlong sabbatical from the summer of 2000 to the summer of 2001, a time that was very spiritually fruitful for me. I hope to take a sabbatical from church activity every seventh year or so.

How I came to join the church . . . that is something of a long odyssey. I suppose that, in a sense relevant to your other questions, mine was a textual conversion story: I fell in love with the Book of Mormon. It just pierced my heart. The other stuff came later—and is still in process—and some of it has been difficult. I don't culturally resemble most other Mormons I know, a chasm that used to bother me but with which I am now more comfortable.

I told my bishop after my sabbatical, "The church drives me crazy sometimes. But it is also the only institution that keeps me sane. And if you can't understand that intuitively, I'm afraid I can't explain it to you." That about sums it up. I am a food-hoarding, temple-going, tithe-paying, coffee-missing, very prayerful Mormon. I do, however, abhor Jell-O, which I expect will someday result in my excommunication.

You wrote your dissertation about nineteenth-century female Protestant missionaries who tried to save Utah women from polygamy. One reader asks: "There are few books currently available written by women scholars who understand the mindset of our nineteenth-century sisters. Your articles, including your Protestant missionary article, are just the kind of scholarship many LDS would like to see

more of. Do you have any intention to publish a full-length book about nineteenth-century Mormon women?"

Yes, perhaps someday, and thanks for that kind feedback. I have to say that when the *Lexington Herald-Leader* article about me was picked up by a syndicate and appeared in newspapers around the nation, I was pretty astounded by the e-mails I got from people who wanted to read my dissertation. (Who wants to read *anyone*'s dissertation?) But there are many people out there whose grandmothers and great-grandmothers were Protestant women missionaries to Utah, and they were interested in it as family history; there were also e-mails from people who wanted to know more about Mormon interactions with other religions in the nineteenth century. So, I was delighted to learn that there are people out there who would buy the book besides my mom.

I am trying, through my Mormon studies and also my research on Mary Baker Eddy, to keep a foot in the door of scholarship while also working in publishing. I've had a few informal conversations with friends who edit at academic houses, and they're interested. But I know that I'd want to do major revisions and additional research to turn my dissertation into a book, and that would require more time than I now have. Also, I'd need to be in a place in my life where I could afford to do an academic book, which pays nothing. During the last few years, with my husband getting his doctorate, I've been the breadwinner for our family, and so I've needed to choose projects that pay at least a little. Also, once you start making a little money by doing what you love, it's hard to go back to doing it for free! Getting paid to write is like a drug.

Tell us more about your writing and publishing projects.

I guess you could say my interests are wide-ranging. Some time ago I published *The Spiritual Traveler: Boston and New England*, a multifaith travel guide to the "sacred sites and peaceful places" of the region. That was a wonderfully interesting project, as New England is rich with history and religious diversity. I also worked on the introduction and annotations to *Mary Baker Eddy, Speaking for Herself,* a volume of Eddy's two autobiographies. What was most exciting about that book was that her second memoir had not been published before, so I was the first scholar and non-Christian Scientist to get a crack at it.

Two years ago I published a book called—don't laugh—*What Would Buffy Do? The Vampire Slayer as Spiritual Guide.* I wanted to write a book that continued the conversations I'd been having with several friends who are Buffy fans. Basically, we all sensed that this TV show engaged our deepest spiritual questions and that it resisted the glib answers that Hollywood seems most often to provide. It's a very ambiguous and angst-ridden but also profoundly moral show, which speaks to me. My next two book projects are both going to be about spirituality and popular culture.

More recently, I've worked on two books that attempt to explain our beautifully wacky religion to the larger world. Outing myself as a Mormon author wasn't something I took lightly, however. The publishing industry has a devilish way of pigeonholing writers, and I am interested in so many things besides Mormonism. But you know, Jan Shipps has been a wonderful mentor to me and served on my dissertation committee. When she inscribed my copy of her most recent book, she wrote about how I am supposed to be a bridge from Zion to the world, as she has been a bridge from the outside world to Zion. That meant so much to me that I jokingly refer to it as my "matriarchal blessing." I hope to live up to that.

Eric Samuelsen
Playwright

Considered by many as Mormonism's preeminent contemporary playwright, Eric Samuelsen earned his Ph.D. from Indiana University and is an associate professor of theater and film at Brigham Young University. He has won the Association for Mormon Letters award for drama three times, for Accommodations, Gadianton, *and* The Way We're Wired. *He's the author of a novel titled* Singled Out *and a forthcoming book of essays on Mormon culture. This interview is previously unpublished.*

What early experiences and influences shaped you to be a writer?

My mom was looking through some old boxes, and she came upon a play I must have written when I was about seven or eight. I'd totally forgotten about it, of course. So I guess I started fairly young. I do remember that when I was twelve I decided to write a novel. The main character was going to be a wolf, and it was set in northern Montana, a place I'd never been. But I did all sorts of research about wolves and Montana, and I wrote about twenty pages of the novel. The wolf was old and wise and just wanted to protect his cubs, but evil hunters were trying to kill him, and there were lots of adventures.

I certainly was always a great reader. My family used to tease me about it, how they'd take out the boat to go waterskiing and I'd be sitting in the cabin with my nose in a book. I mostly read action/adventure novels. I'd read all the C.S. Forester Hornblower novels by the time I was ten, and I read everything Alistair MacLean ever wrote. And then I got into Dickens for some reason, and I finished *David Copperfield* when I was about twelve or so. But I wasn't some highbrow intellectual kid. I also read all the Duane Decker baseball novels—he was sort of the Matt Christopher of the early sixties. I picked up a Duane Decker novel again a few years ago, and I couldn't believe how bad it was.

I acted in high school and majored in theater in college but didn't write any plays. But when I was on my mission, I told one of my companions that I was going to be a playwright, and I even made some notes for a play I was going to write when I got home. And I took Charles Whitman's playwriting class, and I did write the play I'd blocked out on my mission. It was the first draft of a play that I've been working on for thirty years, a play called *The Bottom of the Ninth*. It wasn't very good, and it still isn't, but I keep plugging away at it for some reason. Anyway, it had a couple of scenes that were quite strong, I thought, and he must have agreed, because he gave me a great opportunity.

It seems that the chair of the BYU theater department, Charles Metten, had an idea for a play about Liberty Jail, but he didn't want to write it. He asked Dr. Whitman to recommend a student to work on the play with, and Dr. Whitman recommended me. And so I wrote *Letter From a Prophet* from an outline Dr. Metten had provided. This was a great experience, because the story was already there and fairly sound, but I got to write the dialogue and create the characters. Dr. Metten directed the play, and it did fairly well. But the most important thing about that experience is how much I learned. Nothing in theater compares to the learning experience you get from seeing your play on its feet.

A couple of years later, I took an advanced class from Orson Scott Card, and for that class I wrote *Playing the Game*, about college football. He liked it, and BYU ended up producing it as well, and it went on to the Kennedy Center's American College Theater Festival. And then Murray Boren and I wrote *Emma*, an opera about Joseph Smith's martyrdom. He wrote the music and I wrote the libretto, and it got produced at BYU too and was even reviewed (very positively) in the *Opera News*. So I had three full-length plays produced at BYU and also four one-act plays, all of which was just a tremendous learning experience.

And then I went to grad school and stopped writing plays altogether. I didn't write plays—well, beyond a couple of short things—until I came back to BYU as an assistant professor, though I did scholarly work and some directing and acting. Then at BYU I wrote *Accommodations*, and I've been writing plays ever since.

How did you decide to write plays instead of stories or novels?

For me, it sort of went the other way around. I was an actor first, and on the side I wrote short stories. I was first and foremost a theater guy. Then I decided that the acting thing wasn't working out—there just didn't seem to be much clamor for undertalented 350-pound actors, and I decided to get into theater scholarly stuff. I became an Ibsen scholar, and I still kept directing plays, and every once in a while I'd audition for something and get lucky. So I was really fully immersed in theater.

Then one fine day, I got the idea to write *Accommodations*, and I showed it to my best playwright friend, Tim Slover, fully expecting that both of us would find the encounter sort of awkward, because I thought it wasn't very good. But he liked it, and we did it at BYU, and I've been writing plays ever since. I've written one novel and am about two-thirds through another one, but I see myself as a playwright first and foremost.

I think playwrights really need to be theater people. I'm not sure you need to have actually acted or anything—though most of the good ones have—but you need to know theater well enough to understand the strengths and weaknesses and possibilities of that particular art form. *Accommodations* is very much an Ibsenesque drawing room drama. Then I saw *Angels in America* and realized just how much you can bounce around in time and place; *Gadianton* followed.

What I love about theater is first of all, the fact that it's such a collaborative art form. I'm a gregarious person—I don't actually like the solitary aspect of writing much. I do it, but I really like hanging out with theater people—well, with anyone, really. When a play of mine is produced, I often come to rehearsals I don't necessarily need to go to, just so I can hang out with actors. I think actors are amazing people, so fearless and so vulnerable.

At the same time, you write in genres other than theater. Tell us more about your feelings regarding your other forms of writing.

I'll always consider theater my first love. Having said that, I do love writing fiction. I enjoy the opportunity to explore character so much more fully than I get to in theater.

Margaret Young told me once that she was surprised by my fiction, because there's so little dialogue. She figured that the fiction a playwright wrote would have more dialogue, since that's my forte. I love the rhythm and sound of good dialogue. I love listening in on conversations. I really do want to get dialogue right—I want it to sound like people talking. I can't really write anything at all unless I can get the characters talking to each other in my head.

But when I write fiction, I like the chance to create atmosphere and mood through description, and I like getting into the character's heads. I've got maybe ten short stories, all about this one ward in Utah, and I'll probably look for a publisher for them some day. *Dialogue* has already published the first one.

Essays are new for me, but basically they're a logical extension of two great conversations that I've been really blessed to be part of. First of all, I've been a long-time member of AML-List, and I've loved immersing myself in that terrific cultural conversation over the years. And second, my best friend and I get together every week or so and have these great talks about Mormonism and church history and the Bible. Our views are just barely unorthodox enough that I thought I'd write them down. My wife read them and said, "You should publish these," which I'm doing.

How would you place your playwriting work in context with what's already been done and what's currently being done in the Mormon culture? Do you have a sense of having broken new ground?

Well, that's a hard question. I don't know that I can assess my own place in Mormon culture. I do know that I'm one of a handful of writers who are trying to explore Mormon culture as it is, without really having much of an agenda. I write about Mormons because Mormon is what I know   those are the people I hang out with.

What I've been trying to do is just start a conversation with the Mormon audience. What are we really like? What do we really do? What sins are our favorites? What I'd love to do is be to Mormon drama what Levi Peterson is to Mormon fiction, but of course I'm very far from achieving it.

Which of your plays is your personal favorite? Which was hardest to write?

I don't have a favorite. I'm working on a play right now that's my favorite, because the main guy is driving me nuts—what does he want from her? *Accommodations* was hardest, because I really didn't know what I was doing. Or *The Seating of Senator Smoot* or *A Love Affair with Electrons*, because the research was so hard.

Which play do you think will best survive the test of time?

Probably *Gadianton*. It seems to be the play I'm most known for. It talks about issues that were really current when I wrote it. *The Way We're Wired*, though, was really embraced by the single adult community. I was certainly trying to treat

LDS singles respectfully, and the reaction to the play from that community suggests that I may have succeeded.

Most fiction is a combination of three elements: what the author has experienced, observed, and imagined. How do those three elements work together for you? Also, do you have an ideal reader/viewer in mind?

I mostly write about what I've observed. Very few of my plays deal with things I've personally experienced—I'm maybe a little bit like the dad in *Family*, but not really even he is all that autobiographical. I do try to pay very close attention to Mormon culture, though, and I try to get the details right.

As for an ideal reader, I was going to say my wife, but she knows me too well, and I know her too well. So my ideal reader/viewer is probably my sister-in-law. I have some fabulous sisters-in-law, and they're my ideal—smart, faithful, tough women.

Are there things you can do now that you couldn't have pulled off earlier?

I know how theater works as an art form much better than I did. And I'm much better as a writer of dialogue. And I'm a lot more unafraid. I hope to become even less afraid.

My newest play, *Miasma*, is really a breakthrough for me. I could never have written that play ten years ago—I was so much less willing to get inside the head of a guy I don't like. I wrote real villains back then—Fred in *Gadianton*, for example. *Gadianton* would be a better play if he were a more rounded character. I'm trying to overcome my tendency towards melodrama.

I need to set challenges for myself. My friend Bob Nelson, for example, is convinced that I can't write realism anymore—that I've regressed, because I'm so in love with asides and monologues. So I'm writing a realist play now, just to set myself that challenge.

Who are your main artistic influences?

Ibsen and Strindberg first—I love Strindberg's aesthetic restlessness, how willing he always was to take chances. I love David Mamet and Tom Stoppard and Tony Kushner.

As far as Mormon-related art, I love Neil LaBute, basically all his work. All of Margaret Young's work. All of Doug Thayer. All of Tim Slover. I love Levi Peterson. And I spend my days hoping I'm not disappointing Eugene England. When I get to the other side, my biggest fear is that Gene won't want to talk to me anymore—that he'll say, "You've squandered your talent. Go away." He wouldn't say, "Go away"—he was always too kind to do something like that. But I want him to be proud of me.

What is your greatest fear as a writer? Greatest pleasure? What do you see as your dominant themes?

My fear is that I'll be misunderstood. My greatest pleasure is when people tell me they saw one of my plays and talked to their friends about it for the next two days. As far as my major themes, here are some examples: Just when we think we've got someone figured out, they do something to surprise us. Everyone's capable of change. Be kind.

In your plays, your dialogue seems very natural and convincing. Tell us about the craft that goes into that and about your other writing habits.

Well, I really try to listen. I love standing in line to buy something; you can hear the most interesting conversations. I love eavesdropping on cell phone conversations. I just really try to listen.

From a craft standpoint, there are a few rules. First of all, never answer a question. If one character asks another character a question, the answer should be evasive or not to the point, because it builds suspense. Don't be afraid of non-sequiturs. That's the great lesson we all learn from Chekhov. If one of your characters says something you didn't expect him or her to say—well, go with the flow. Let that be what the scene's about, not what you preplanned. Finally, let people do what people do: lie and brag and intimidate through dialogue.

I write very, very fast. I can write a full-length play, first draft, in about three days. After that, I need a lot of sitting-around time. I let my subconscious do the heavy lifting. I also try to have what I call my fifteen-minute play going all the time. It's the play I work on in fifteen-minute increments, when I've got a few minutes between meetings or classes. I just open that file and write a half-page or so.

I have to have music playing in the background, and it has to be the right kind of music. One of my biggest challenges is finding exactly the right kind of music for whatever piece it is I'm working on. During *Miasma*, for example, I listened to a lot of Johnny Cash and Lou Reed. With *Family*, it was Bob Dylan and the late Beethoven string quartets.

I rewrite very substantially—I'll put a play through twenty drafts before we start rehearsals. And I never, ever use an outline. I just want to get the characters talking to each other; I want them to surprise me. I love a workshop environment. One of the great blessings of teaching is that my students respond to my work, because I'm writing right along with them. I listen to every opinion, but of course some I disregard.

Tell us more about your teaching profession.

Well, I love hanging out with college students. They keep me young, and they help me keep up with popular culture, and I love how smart they are, the good ones.

What I try to teach them is craftsmanship and structure, understanding that some of them are probably not going to progress much but that some are going to get better all the time, more interesting. It's fun. My advice to students is to write. Don't settle for easy answers. Be honest. Don't force the action.

Have your critics said anything that you'd like to summarize and respond to here?

One response to my work that drives me bats is when critics say my characters are stereotypical. I'm sensitive to this, because I often start with stereotypes. I think people often do that—they define themselves in certain ways: "I'm a dumb blonde, I'm a cowboy, I'm an intellectual." Then, when you get to know them, you discover they're nothing of the kind. So in *Family*, for example, Ashley has gotten a lot of mileage out of the dumb blonde stereotype. It works for her. It's also not who she is. So I start there, with conventional expectations, and then I try to show surprising—maybe even a little shocking—departures from it.

What are your views on Mormon cinema and the Mormon audience in general?

Aside from the Dutcher films, and to some extent *The Best Two Years*, the Mormon films haven't had the courage to really explore our culture. I think the writing has generally been bad, mostly because there's this constant fear: "I don't want to make the church look bad." And so we've made a bunch of films that end up making the church look shallow, stupid, and selfish.

As an audience, we're certainly in a conservative cultural moment. I think Mormon culture right now is very safe. When I talk to my friends—in my ward, say—they're worried about being damaged by pop culture, and so they define their cultural boundaries by "what probably won't hurt me." That seems to me absolutely antithetical to the plan of salvation. Let's face it, when we chose to come here, we were told, "It won't be safe. At times it's going to be awful. You're going to be in terrific pain at times. Sometimes it will be beautiful, sure, but at other times it will be horrible." And we all went, "Okay. Send me anyway."

When writing, do you ever say to yourself, "I need to include more explicitly Mormon stuff in this" or "I need to include less"?

I never think anything like that. None of those thoughts ever occur to me, not at all, not once. I think those are really bad thoughts. I think those thoughts are absolutely crippling our art. Those are marketing questions, not artistic questions, and if you're thinking "How can I market this?" then you're just flat out not an artist, and you're not a writer, and why are you wasting your life? I'm saying this strongly, I know, but this is really important to me.

I think that some people are going to stand before the bar of judgment, and the Lord will say to them, "I gave you some talents, and I put you in the way of some wonderful stories, and you didn't write from the heart because you didn't think it would play for the eighteen-to-thirty-five demographic, plus you thought it was too Mormon, so good luck in the telestial kingdom." I just want to create some characters and tell their story. I could care less if they're "too Mormon" or "not Mormon enough."

How do you balance portraying things realistically versus idealistically? What about potentially explicit things like sex and violence?

I love extended realism, and I love magical realism. But when I'm writing, I only have room in my head to think, "Is this story working? Are these characters real?"

First draft, I don't cut anything. After that, as I rewrite I'm afraid I do ask myself the audience question a little bit—I do pull back if I think the work's going to be seen by Mormons. Frankly, I'm a little calculating. I'm trying to get Mormon audiences to the point where we can actually stomach some serious dramatic fiction. I don't lie, but if I have to, I will pull punches slightly. Emphasis on *slightly*.

If I can't cut harsh language or sexual content without seriously damaging the play, then I'll finish the play the way it needs to be written and send it out with my fingers crossed to theaters where it can be appreciated.

What's your view of the fiction writer's role in building up Zion?

I think it's really important for us to have storytellers who can tell us true things about our own culture. I think Levi Peterson is a cultural treasure.

I wish most Mormons read more and better fiction, watched more and better movies, saw more and better plays. I think we'd have a better, truer, more compassionate culture. I think my role may be in part to nudge mainstream LDS culture along a bit.

Do you ever feel that you write divinely inspired work?

Certainly. But that shouldn't immunize it from criticism. I think that God uses us all as his instruments. And yes, I suppose I do think that someone as quirky as I am might have some small share of inspiration.

Have you sent out much for consideration by national agents and publishers?

Frankly, I have had some success under a pseudonym, but I'd rather keep my alter ego anonymous, for now.

Do you think this nation will ever have a Mormon Saul Bellow or Flannery O'Connor, someone winning a Pulitzer or National Book Award for fiction that deals with Mormon themes, settings, and characters?

Yes, I do. And I predict that when he or she does appear, most Mormons won't like the work. What will it take? Overcoming fear.

ROBERT FARRELL SMITH

Robert Farrell Smith
Novelist

Robert Farrell Smith's first humorous novel, Baptists at Our Barbecue, *was published by Aspen Books and later republished by Deseret Book and adapted into a commercial film for the LDS market. Several additional novels have followed, including the Trust Williams trilogy,* Captain Matrimony, *and* For Time and All Absurdity. *Smith lives with his wife and children in Albuquerque, New Mexico. The original version of this interview appeared in* Irreantum, *spring 2002.*

How would you describe your writing? Do you see yourself carving out a new niche in Mormon literature? What is your goal as a writer?

I would describe my writing as tall, with a nice face and an up-to-date wardrobe. It is also ultimately revealing in a contemporary, uplifting way. It is atmospheric. I think the focus is humor, but that wasn't necessarily what I started out to do. I wrote my first book just thinking it was good. It wasn't until I started showing it around that it became obvious it was that funny. I think people were laughing with me.

I don't suppose I'm carving out any new niche—it seems as if that would take effort—but I haven't seen much like my stuff out there. We seem to have two really strong styles in the LDS fiction market: one is historical fiction and the other is straight romance. So, in that sense my writing is going down a different path. Sure there is romance, but it's not so much soap opera as it is sitcom. It caters more to those who like comedy movies and humorous TV.

I suppose my goal would be to make so much money that I could go back and lavishly taunt those who may have given me grief in the past—that, and to further the work. I actually believe that the Mormon culture is a wonderful thing. We are so endearingly flawed that there is endless material. I love everything about us and our struggle to be the kind of people we believe our Heavenly Father wants us to be. I like to point out in a humorous way how each one of us seems to have a slightly different definition of just what He wants from us. It's amazing that we are even alive, more or less able to pick out our own outfits and do our own hair.

Which is your favorite among your books? Which is your least favorite?

How can I choose? It's like picking between eight awkward children. *Baptists at Our Barbecue* and *The Miracle of Forgetness* were the first in the birth order and consequently have the biggest birthmarks. The Trust trilogy popped out like a set of singing triplets that seemed to get me noticed and that everyone thought was neat. *Captain Matrimony* has earned me the most concerned stares, and *For Time and All Absurdity* had such a long pregnancy that I was more glad it came than happy to see it, despite the fact that it might be my favorite. So in conclusion, every one is a priceless literary gem that people would be foolish not to pick up, read, and then purchase more as gifts.

What prompted you to start writing, and how did you learn the craft?

I like that, "the craft." I have written my entire life. It was only when I decided to get serious that stuff started to fall together for me. I have said before that my third grade teacher's praise of a poem I wrote about gum has been as big a motivation to me as anything. I also remember my English teacher in Vienna shaking his head after reading my stuff and saying, "I'm just not sure what to think of this." That inspired me.

When I first bought the bookstore we used to own, I was amazed by the fiction that was available. By amazed, I mean more like when an asteroid is hurling directly toward you than when a spectacular comet is simply passing by. That's not to say that there weren't some good books out there or that I really am even one to judge. I just knew, however, that there was a place for contemporary humor that dealt with life in a way people could laugh at and relate to. Lucky for me that has proven true.

You ran an independent LDS bookstore for several years, and now you manage a Deseret Book store. What have those experiences taught you about the LDS reading audience, and how have those experiences affected your own work?

My wife and I owned a bookstore for about ten years before happily selling out. The experience has been great on all levels. Through all these years the most obvious thing to me, besides the fact that my friends and family like a discount, is that most of us Mormons really do like to read. We especially like to read what our neighbors have enjoyed, particularly when it comes to fiction. I don't suppose this is too different than the national market.

Nowadays most book releases are like a bell going off. We hear the ding and buy volume ten. And while I am certainly thankful for the faithful patrons who buy and stick with the multiple series of hot-selling books, I love the customers who want something slightly outside the approved pattern.

What, in your opinion, is and should be the role of Mormon literature—meaning created by or about Mormons—in Mormon life?

I think being Mormon is interesting, and not just to us. We're fascinating, kind of like the Amish people but with a lighter weight of clothes and big-screen TVs. We have a responsibility to let the world in on why we like being who we are. I can't imagine that in the not-too-distant future we won't become even more persuasive in the national market. We have a number of people who have already broken the ground and done amazing things for our literary credibility. I also think that it's possible to show the world our insides in an interesting and honest way that doesn't actually change our innocence or our peculiarity. Worldly fiction that has a Mormon character in it isn't necessarily Mormon fiction. We are different, and the result should reflect that.

Do you have an ideal reader in mind?

I think someone who is easily impressed and who likes to talk really loud about things they enjoy. Other than that I am always honored when readers pick out or appreciate things in my books that I figured only I would get. Humor is such a great thing to write because you can say as much or as little as you want while not letting on that you've really said anything. (I think that makes sense.) That's why I love it when those reading notice the dust between the cracks.

Tell us about your writing process. Any possibility of going full time?

I write all the time in hopes of the good stuff actually rising to the top. Despite the results so far, I'm going to stick with that system. I might think long and hard about a book, but rarely do I write anything down before I go at it. When I actually write, it comes pretty easy for me. My first drafts are usually a hundred pages longer than the actual copy I will send my publisher. I love to chop. Someone said something once about never loving your stuff so much you can't cut it, or something like that. That's really stuck with me.

I prefer writing a little every day, but at this point I usually put it off until I am so close to a deadline that I have to cram. Sometimes I miss having all the time I had to create my first book. I was at a book signing recently, and during an odd lull in people clamoring for me to sign, I was discussing with a couple of other authors how wonderful writing a first book is. I had all the time in the world for *Baptists*. I was able to mess around with it for much longer than I have been able to with my others. Of course, it is very nice to have a publisher and know that what I'm working on will probably see the light of day.

As for writing full time, I think that would be all right. Ultimately, however, it might simply give me more time to put it off.

What is your greatest fear as a writer? What is your greatest pleasure?

My greatest fear as a writer is having to fly to book signings and speaking engagements. Not that I mind the events, I'm just not a big fan of the plane. My greatest pleasure as a writer is definitely going to those aforementioned events and hanging out with folks I otherwise would have never probably known. It is so cool to meet strange people who know things about my books and characters. I really love the connection it gives me. Nothing is more surreal to me than having someone I just met give me an in-depth psychological evaluation of one of the characters I made up four years ago.

What kinds of things do you most like to read? What do you count as influences on your own work?

I'm easy. I'll read anything once. I love Nero Wolfe mysteries, not necessarily for the mysteries but for the atmosphere that Rex Stout creates. Archie Goodwin, to me, is the greatest literary character ever created. I seek out anything funny and talk about it for months afterward if it actually is. I am constantly praying and sporadically fasting for a better book than the one I just read, regardless of what it was. Nothing is so exciting as the possibility of finding an amazing read.

My world has been influenced by a lot of authors and things. Bill Peet, Roald Dahl, Rex Stout, soda, *The Simpsons*, Ben Folds, fast-food commercials, Archie comics, *Dandelion Wine*, that one book about that big fish, *Cold Sassy Tree*, Harper

Lee, Velcro, libraries, my parents, *Holes*, Adam Duritz, rain, sunshine, Dr. Seuss, people who play the piano, and anything shiny or that hums.

Where do you get your ideas? How much of your writing is autobiographical, how much is observation from real life, and how much is imagination?

"Where do you get your ideas?" is probably the most-asked question I get. It is also the hardest for me to answer. I used to think that everybody had these same kinds of things in their head. According to those who pity me, however, that is not necessarily true. In the beginning I would tell people that what I did for inspiration was eat a big bowl of bran flakes and then go lie out on the trampoline at dusk until creativity struck. But I discovered that most folks couldn't handle the truth.

I can't imagine writing a book that isn't at least fifteen percent autobiographical. I just can't seem to weed out more than that. Most of my writing, however, is from observation. I like the little things that add up to something huge. Usually I'll see or experience something and instantly think, "That could be funnier if . . ." I rarely know what the next page of my book will be until I write it. Not that the characters are alive and working independent of me, it's just that my mind is probably still preoccupied with the last meal I ate or the lyrics of some song I have forgotten.

What is it like to work with Deseret Book as an author? Have there been any occasions when your humor has gone too far for them?

The publishing department at Deseret Book has been supportive and interested in my work ever since *Baptists*. Before I actually published with them, everyone warned me that my writing would be too much for them and they would change everything. I have found that to be just the opposite. They have been incredibly willing to let me push and grow.

I think Deseret Book is very much in the mood to stretch. In fact, I think they are stretching. They have taken strong steps with their historical fiction and the quality of books they are putting out. They also seem committed to doing different and interesting things. Almost every idea I have gone to them with, they have said go for it without hesitation. I haven't come across a subject that I couldn't write about in some way.

There hasn't been much that any of my publishers have refused to print or wanted me to change, aside from some pretty embarrassing spelling errors. I remember when *Baptists* was first being edited, I had a scene where one of the characters was talking about using his bottle of consecrated oil to fry up chicken the night before. There was some concern over the idea, so I just changed it so the character was talking about using a bottle of oil he had been planning to consecrate to fry chicken. It's all in the details. Originally the bishop in *All Is Swell* struggled with a smoking addiction. My editor pointed out that usually people with that kind of addiction are not made bishop. So I just made him the second counselor instead. I have no problem changing ideas or situations as long as it improves the final package. In both of those cases it certainly didn't hurt.

Most every Mormon humorist at one time or another gets feedback that he or she is light-minded, irreverent, blasphemous, or otherwise out of line. Does having a church-owned publisher help deflect that kind of feedback?

I don't know how other Mormon writers feel, but my intentions have never been to offend. If I think something I wrote is going to actually hurt someone in a mean way, then I usually get rid of it or hide it in such a way that the kind of person who might be bothered would never even notice. That's not to say that my writing is watered down or that I pull punches. I just feel that I have accomplished nothing if I have simply turned people off. My goal is to turn them on and keep them tuned in while they experience things they might not normally get in Mormon fiction. That said, I still get called most of those things you've mentioned.

A woman was so offended that someone threw up in *Baptists at Our Barbecue* that she closed the book and never went on. A person in California was so bothered that Trust was falling in love while on his mission in *All Is Swell* that he sent me three letters to make sure I clearly understood how ticked he really was. I have had people at book signings whisper in my ear wondering if I really meant what they thought I meant by something I wrote. Usually I did mean it, and usually they are all right with that. A lot of people have told me they can't believe Deseret Book would publish that. Of course, they almost always say it as if they are impressed with both of us.

If someone actually is offended, it wasn't intended and there is really nothing I can do about it. I would be happy to tell them I'm sorry, but I would probably say it in such a way that they would doubt my sincerity. I don't think being a Mormon means you no longer can be creative or real. I haven't come across a subject that I couldn't write about in some way. My books talk about attraction, addiction, sin, repentance, murder, dishonesty, and blasphemy. They just do it in a way that produces a guilt-free happy ending.

What other kinds of feedback do you get from your readers? Do you know of any non-LDS readers?

I get great feedback from readers—apparently there are a lot of delusional people out there. I now have my habitual readers who don't let a book go by without telling me exactly how they feel. When *Baptists* first came out, it suffered from a number of spelling and punctuation errors. It seems like nothing incites a riot in the soul of a reader like a misplaced comma or a *their* when it should have been a *there*. Deseret Book put out a new edition, which excited me most because people would be able to pick on other things besides punctuation.

Baptists was a great first book because it gained me a small non-LDS audience. Most of them are Baptists and have stuck with my writing. They are very objective critics and great supports.

What new directions do you see your writing taking in the future?

Many different directions. In a number of ways I have always felt that what I have written so far is simply practice for the things I have been wanting to do. So, in the future I'll be writing vastly different stuff. Or maybe I will just try to spend some more time with my great kids, as well as my wife, Krista. Maybe I'll remodel our bathroom or fix that back fence. This, of course, is in no way a commitment to any of that.

DARRELL SPENCER

Darrell Spencer
Fiction Writer

Interviewed by Douglas Thayer

In addition to many stories in quarterlies, Darrell Spencer has published four collections—Bring Your Legs with You (*University of Pittsburgh Press, 2004*), Caution: Men in Trees (*University of Georgia Press, 2000*), Our Secret's Out (*University of Missouri Press, 1993*), *and* A Woman Packing a Pistol (*Dragon Gate Press, 1987*)—as well as a novel, One Mile Past Dangerous Curve (*University of Michigan Press, 2005*). Darrell's honors include the Drue Heinz Literature Prize and the Flannery O'Connor Award for Short Fiction, easily two of the most distinguished prizes for the short story offered in America. This interview originally appeared in Dialogue: A Journal of Mormon Thought, *39:1 (spring 2006).*

Interviewer Douglas Thayer has published several novels and short story collections, and he is a professor at Brigham Young University.

What got you started writing, the original impulse? Did you always think of yourself as a writer, or was it adult-onset?

Reading. That's the answer. Reading. Which I came to late. I didn't really start until I went to college. You don't count *Fielder from Nowhere, Hard Court Press*—the kind of books I read growing up. You hear about writers reading *Moby-Dick* when they were five years old, part of their journey through the local library, book by book, end to end, top to bottom. They discovered Kafka at age seven. Wrote novels before they were ten. Makes me feel stupid. I was collecting baseball cards and trying to figure out how to avoid getting spiked when some kid slid into third.

No, I did not think of myself as a writer. Me, a writer? The thought never occurred to me. What I wanted was to be trickier than Bob Cousy and play for the Boston Celtics, but I learned early and profoundly and without question that I didn't have the talent.

So I got to college, was thinking about law school, and then I read Faulkner. *As I Lay Dying*, first. That was a class assignment. Next, *Light in August* on my own. I bought all his books. *Absalom, Absalom!* He reset me, turned my world sideways. I read Fielding—what a swarm of words—and tried to imitate him. Used *sagacity* and *negotiant* and *victuals* in the opening paragraph of a seven-hundred-page novel I was going to write, but of course never did. I was twenty-one at the time. Even then it didn't occur to me that I could be writer. For people like me, that wasn't in the cards. What I needed was a job and a paycheck. Bread on the table. *Tom Jones* led me to what was then a contemporary novel, John Barth's *The Sot-Weed Factor*. Great fun is that book. I discovered the writers who were alive and writing and began reading them.

The impulse to tell stories must have been in me because I can recall only one assignment from high school. Mr. Butterfield asked us to write a short story. I was never a good student, not in high school, not in college, not until graduate school. But I worked hard on my short story. In the end, it was terrible. Shameful. Particularly when you think about what someone like Truman Capote was producing when he was a teenager. Lee Smith talks about one of her early college-day attempts to write fiction: in the final scene, a house has burned to the ground, and a family has died—I think it's Christmas Eve—and the only sound is a music box playing "Silent Night." She cites the story as an example of her early failures, as a story driven by its own melodrama, but I imagine it as better than mine. The short story I wrote for Mr. Butterfield was about a sixteen-year-old who has saved up and bought his first car. He's going on his first solo date. We follow him on his drive, during which he passes images of his younger self. I chose three images. Had to be three. There's significance in three, right? Three wishes. Three visitations. Three strikes and you're out. There's heft and every possibility of truth in three. At one point, he has to brake to avoid hitting a kid dribbling a basketball. He reaches his girl's house, rings the bell, and then glances down at his shoes. There is one spot of mud on the toe. Symbolism.

Profundity. What I knew back then about writing stories I had learned from literature classes, classes that teach us how to read texts and the world in sophisticated ways but that are not the best training ground for a writer. As I said, the story was terrible. I got a C-minus on it. But my point is that it mattered to me; it's the one thing in high school I cared about. I wanted to write a story that knocked Mr. Butterfield's socks off.

I have to mention John Berryman. There are incidents that take us on a 360-degree turnabout. You go in a door and out the same door, but you're different. My wife, Kate, and I were living in Las Vegas. I had given up on school. I was painting signs for a living, fourteen-by-forty-eight-foot billboards, doing show changes for Elvis, Wayne Newton, Buddy Hackett, putting highlights on the nose of the clown for Circus Circus, doing pictorials of the Coppertone dog. Kate and I went to the mall one night. She was checking on a book she had ordered, and I wandered over to the poetry section. No reason for it, but I picked up Berryman's *77 Dream Songs.* I had never heard of him, and I had never read anything like his poems, which were colloquial and rude and ill-bred, yet tight and rigorous in structure. Voices jigsawed together. Celebratory and mean-spirited. Retaliatory, yet full of love and joy. I am still, thirty years later, memorizing his poetry. Right now I'm working on his *Eleven Addresses to the Lord.* Berryman—eventually I would learn what a highly respected scholar he was—had no truck with decorum. The book was a carnival. Was like a mob. His poems are part of me.

The first serious thing I wrote—I was in graduate school by now, University of Nevada, Las Vegas—was an imitation of Berryman's *Homage to Mistress Bradstreet.* I was homaging Virginia Woolf. Not her fiction. I was reading her letters.

So the one-word answer to your question is *reading.*

I fell hard for words. Even how they sit on the page, which has to do with sign painting, I suppose. You eyeball lettering. It's an art. Fit and fix together. You have to know that O's dip below the bottom line and A's intrude upon and adjust in odd ways to the surrounding letters.

Do your remember diagramming sentences in grade school? I couldn't admit it to my basketball-playing pals, but I thoroughly enjoyed diagramming sentences. Miss Leach, sixth grade, John S. Park Elementary in Las Vegas. One sentence on the blackboard laid out like an overhead photograph of the city of itself. That, too, has something to do with my desire to write fiction.

How would you characterize your style? Some have called you a minimalist or said that, in some ways, you're like one. Are you? If so, why? What are the advantages?

A minimalist? No. Maybe the stories in my first book, *A Woman Packing a Pistol,* are somewhat minimalist. I'll confess to that, though I don't think of them in that way. I was reading Ivy Goodman, Mary Robison, and what people call early Raymond Carver.

Cheryll Glotelty, who teaches at the University of Nevada at Reno, contacted me because she wanted to include a story of mine in a Nevada literature anthology. I think it's titled *Home Means Nevada: Literature of the Silver State.* She sent me the headnote for my story. It began, "By writing experimental fiction, Darrell Spencer . . ." I phoned. Said, "Experimental?" All this in a friendly way. We talked, and then she wrote back. I need to mention that what she was including in the anthology was a short-short titled "My Home State of Nevada." She suggested "avant-garde," "postmodern." No. No. She sent me her brainstorming, talked about fiction that skirts the edges of realism, fiction that displaces reality and refuses to be taken literally.

I kept thinking, *They're stories; that's all. There is nothing avant-garde or experimental or postmodern about them. They're told in a straightforward and direct way. They're stories about folk walking about on the planet and trying to figure out how to live in particular ways.* I can't remember what we decided on. It'll be interesting to see what the headnote says when the book comes out.

I designed and taught a course in minimalism here at Ohio University. We read Amy Hempel, Ann Beattie, some Marc Richard, and Janet Kaufman. We read Carver and Mary Robison's *Why Did I Ever,* a novel that gathers on you like a breakdown.

Kim Herzinger edited an issue of the *Mississippi Review* that is devoted to minimalist fiction, a give and take, a few writers lamenting minimalist fiction's presence in the world and other writers celebrating its being here.

What you end up talking about in a class is contracted language that is blunt, clean, spare, sparse, exacting. Sometimes my language is contracted. I hope it's exacting. You talk about elliptical structure and form. Sometimes my work is elliptical. You talk about dislocation. You talk about silent surfaces. One class period I brought in an Ann Beattie story, a recent one, a nonminimalist piece. I had cut all the exposition from it—paragraph by paragraph, line by line. I asked the students to account for the action, to see if their exposition—why is the husband being rude to his wife?—matched the exposition in the original story. We also did a line-by-line comparison of Raymond Carver's "The Bath" and "A Small, Good Thing." What you learn is that what is not there on the page is present in the white space.

I admire minimalist fiction, but no, my work is not minimalist. If we were to run through a list of styles, I would say to each one, Yes and no. I don't mean to sound wishy-washy, but I don't know how to describe my style. Maximalist? Nah.

What do you strive for in your fiction? How do you want it to affect your readers? What should delight and please them, entertain them, in your work? Do you have a special audience in mind?

Barry Hannah says the brain got to sing. I can't sing. Not a lick. Or dance. Wouldn't you love to ballroom dance like the pros? Get dressed to the nines. All that footwork, the choreography of passion. Or hoof it. Tap dance. Foxtrot in shining shoes.

I can't sing and I can't dance, so I write. And what I strive for is that my work will sing and dance. I think of my fiction, each piece, whether it is a short story or a novel, as a repository of language. When I talk to friends about this, I find myself making a kind of bracketing shape with my hands, fingers curved as if I'm holding a small pot as an offering, or as if I'm stretching open a gunny sack. I hold my hands out in front me, like I'm struggling to contain something that doesn't want to be contained, and I say, I want to drop you in this bag, pocket, bucket, this pot—this repository. Jump in. Enjoy.

I like slang. Argot. Jargon. The colloquial. Vernacular. The demotic. I try to entice readers into an experience with a particular brand of language, such as, in a specific sense, the jargon of sign painting or roofing or, in a broader sense, the language of loss or grief or joy. Each piece contains, I hope, at least ten cats in a bag.

Almost every story I have written has begun with a line or phrase that I overheard or one that popped into my head. I'm writing one right now called "Can I Help Who's Next?" Nothing startling about that question, and, having eaten a lot of Subway sandwiches, I'm sure I've heard it dozens of times. Then one day I finally really heard the sandwich-maker say it. So I started a story. It seems to me that that question is a repository of language, that it contains all I need to know. It is as if once I write the words down, they gather to themselves all the other words I'll need to tell a story.

I'm also interested in story telling. I want to tell stories that break your heart. But my fiction is character driven. I don't see much plot in it. Plot doesn't interest me.

My work is, I hope, baggy. Off-shot. Disjointed. Unwieldy. I hope my stories, like John Berryman's poetry, won't hold still. Years ago I read an article about an architect named Gehry. The author said that Gehry did not accept the biblical idea that a house divided against itself cannot stand. Instead, Gehry believed that a house divided against itself would—I'm pretty sure this is the word the author used—*flourish*. Such a house will astonish us. I want my work to be divided against itself.

I hope each sentence I write sticks to the page and delights a reader, but not so you stop and take note or underline anything. There is a certain kind of delight we experience on the move. Are we back to dancing? Probably. But also I'm talking about the delight you feel when you strike a nail exactly as a nail ought to be struck. I hope my stories have some humor in them. I hope they don't come across as clever. That would make me very sad. I hope the characters entertain readers. And count. I hope the events and characters matter. Flannery O'Connor tells us that she loaned a few of her stories to a country woman who lived nearby. When the woman returned them, she said, "Well, them stories just gone and shown you how some folks *would* do." O'Connor adds that that is where you have to start, with "showing how some specific folks *will* do, *will* do in spite of everything." That knowledge drives my own work.

What are your themes, the things you are trying to say in your work? Or are you trying to say anything? Are there values you keep punching?

I'm a member of Chekhov's tribe as far as theme is concerned. I'm trying to take what Chekhov calls an intelligent attitude toward what I write about, but I'm not trying to convey a theme. I have no points to make or argue. No scores to settle. No axes to grind. Okay, one or two axes. Chekhov tells us that a fiction writer is not under obligation to solve a problem; an artist's only obligation is to state the problem correctly. *Obligation* is Chekhov's word.

We need something in this world that isn't trying to teach us lessons or get us to buy a product, that isn't self-helping us to death. All writing, fiction included, is, of course, loaded with bias and it certainly signifies—it distorts and deforms and jerry-builds—but fiction can draw us into a simulacrum of experience itself. We need that. We need work that isn't trying to tell us how to act.

William Gass says of his fiction that he wants to plant an object in the world. I think I'm close in quoting him: "I want to add something to the world which the world can ponder the same way it ponders the world." He makes it clear that he wants the object to be a beautiful object and that beauty is not to be subservient to truth.

There you have it. Beauty and truth: two cans of worms you don't want to open. Try talking intelligently about that pair, and you'll end up tripping over your own tongue. You'll end up deconstructing yourself word by word, talking and walking backwards, erasing yourself as you speak. Rewinding.

What I say to my students about beauty, about measuring one piece of writing against some standard, is that I'm going to ask Mikhail Baryshnikov to dance across the front of the classroom. Then I'll dance. And they'll notice a difference. Sure that comparison fails—culture is at the root of all judgment—but isn't that the pleasure of analogical thought: that it fails: that it celebrates, in the end, difference.

Gass and Chekhov both agree that part of the issue has to do with the way fiction works. Combine art and sermon? Chekhov asks. That would be pleasant, he says, but not possible because of what I believe he calls matters of technique.

Fiction speaks the voice of what—character, event, circumstance, situation—it depicts. Gass wants us to turn the moral issues and problems over to the rigors of philosophical and scientific thinking. He doesn't trust fiction. Fiction, for him, must not assert. I hear people say that fiction lies to tell the truth. I don't buy that. Fiction lies, and it distorts in order to depict and wonder. It wonders. The fictive experience can be—is?—as real as any other experience—as if there is any other kind.

I'm in these two camps, and Gass and Chekhov have said eloquently what I feel, so I thought I'd pass their words along. Nothing originates with me. Their views inform my sensibilities as a writer.

I want to add one more thought. I'm trying to explain what it is I'm after in my work. We know that all the stories we tell are texts that refer to other texts—story (small "s") refers to Story (big "S"). Call Story with the big "S" myth or collective unconscious or master narrative or arche or form. Call it whatever you want. What I'm saying relates—maybe only in my head—to what Vladimir Propp discovered when he analyzed folktales: that they're made up of functions. The second function of a folktale is what Propp calls the interdiction. Someone is warned not to do something. Don't go into the woods. You can hear some zealots: Don't go into the words. Don't go downstairs. Don't go to the far kingdom. When I was a kid, it was, Don't cross Oakey Boulevard. But, of course, the interdiction is violated so that the tale begins. Interdiction and violation, two members of Story, the one with the big "S." Or we can talk about Story with the big "S" in other terms: Greenhorn comes to town. Hero goes on quest. Someone is expelled from somewhere.

What I'm trying to say here is that I'm aware of all this as a writer, and there's one thought that drives me when I write: *Traduttore, traditore.* To translate is to be a traitor. To translate is to traduce. Recently I taught a class in form and theory here at Ohio University. It was guided by a phrase from Derrida's *The Retrait of Metaphor:* "a 'good' translation must always abuse." When I say that the small "s" story refers to the big "S" Story, I mean that it translates the master narrative, the myth, but does so, when it is well done, in an idiosyncratic way. I want my work to be a traitor to that big "S" Story; I want it to traduce that big "S" Story. Abuse it in some exacting and idiosyncratic way. John Caputo says to do so is to commit scandal, is to tell the story in a treacherous way.

If I have a theme, that's it.

I'm not saying I think about any of this when I write. I don't. You can't will any of this into being.

You've won both the Flannery O'Connor Award for Short Fiction and the Drue Heinz Literature Prize. How has winning those prestigious

short-story competitions affected you? Any other prizes or awards you plan to go for?

I feel lucky to have won the awards, and I'm grateful to the people who chose the books. The awards have affected me because they mean that two more of my books are now in print, are out there for people to read.

Virtually all of your success has been in the short story, but you recently published a novel with the University of Michigan Press. Why the switch, and what's the difference for you between writing stories and a novel? Do you see yourself leaving the short story to write novels? What advantage does the novel hold for you over the short story, if any?

The novel is titled *One Mile Past Dangerous Curve.* I haven't actually switched from short stories to novels, although the publication history makes it look as if there has been a changeover. All the time that I was writing stories, I was writing novels. Failed novels. Bad novels. I wrote two that I threw away. I have been revising a novel titled *Welcome to Wisdom, Utah* for almost ten years. Right now, I'm finishing up a book titled *So You Got Next to the Hammer.* It contains two novellas and five stories. The novellas are novels I cut and cut and cut. A few weeks ago I started a novel I'm calling *The Department of Big Thoughts.* It's about—is told by—one of the characters in my book *Bring Your Legs with You.* He's a roofer and a thinker. What he is is one more big-time talker on the planet. So I'm writing that novel, but at the same time I am writing short stories.

I write novels and stories in the same fashion. *One Mile Past Dangerous Curve* began with a sentence I overheard, a sentence that disappeared from the book a long time ago, a sentence that is no longer in play. The working title was *The Devil, You Say.* I plumbed those words for all I could get out of them. Stories require weeks of revision; the novel took years. But I think that's an obvious thing to say. I wish I could say something smart about the difference between the two forms. This is true for me: Language and character can carry a story. I tried to let character drive the novel, but I found that for each major revision I wrote I was restructuring in order to satisfy my desire and itch for plot. Maybe a better word is *event.* I was into a third or fourth draft when I realized that I was spending the first fifty or sixty pages caught up in a riff triggered by the opening paragraph. It hit me that I could move up one of the key events and that in doing so I would be upsetting the ground situation.

I don't think one form has an advantage over the other form. I acknowledge the major differences, but it's all writing and trying to create the immediacy that is essential to fiction. In practical terms, I like the short story because I can pretty much keep the whole piece in mind as I write. I can tweak the story at one point, knowing exactly what changes that will require three, six, nine pages later. I can make a change near the end, and I know where I have to go earlier in the story to make adjustments. It's difficult to keep an entire novel in mind. When I'm finished with a story, I hold an image of it in my mind. One story was held together by a picture of a woman sitting in a chair in her front yard. I wasn't able to do that with the novel. It's driven by an image, I think: bafflement. If that's an image. It can be. The sound of the word. But, again in practical terms, it was difficult to keep all of the characters and conflicts and situations in mind. For example, late in the publication process—I think we were in galleys—I was rereading a section where I had done some revision, and I discovered that a character was both in the house and still sitting outside the house on a redwood table. An egregious error, but there it was.

A novel, a story—each is written one sentence at a time. You write a sentence, and you listen, and the next sentence responds to it. They bump against each other. You like how they join each other, so you write the next one.

What are the major literary influences in your life as a writer? Which writers do you value most?

I'm going to start by sidestepping your questions somewhat. The major influence on my work is actually my wife's painting. I want to write fiction that is like her art. One of her paintings is the cover on *One Mile Past Dangerous Curve.* The people at Michigan were kicking around ideas for the cover, and I told them about the painting. I wish I could write the way she paints. Her work is referential, is representational, but the color, the texture, the shapes, the brush strokes—all the elements of her art resist lending themselves to picture. There is a remarkable give-and-take going on. I will badly recount this story, but Ernest Gombrich, in one of his books on art, tells us about a famous art critic describing an experience he had with a painting by Valázquez. The man kept walking up to the painting and then back away. Up and back. Up and back. He wanted to experience the moment when the paint and brush strokes transformed into a boat. The story goes something like that. Kate's work exploits that kind of tension, and I want to write stories that do so with language. Our friend, Wayne Dodd, bought one of Kate's paintings. I was talking to him about it one day, and he said, "Her work talks back to you." Yes. He was dead-on right. I want my fiction to talk back to you.

Now the literary influences. I've already mentioned Faulkner, who wasn't an influence as much as he was an impetus. I studied the canon in school, and I hope I learned from writers like Flannery O'Connor, Melville, Hawthorne, Gertrude Stein, Kate Chopin, James Baldwin, Ralph Ellison—the tradition, the masters. You know all the names. What I was doing was catching up and learning what art is. No one, at that time, was teaching Saul Bellow, but I found my way to him. *The Adventures of Augie March*—difficult to describe my response to that novel, what it meant to a young man trying to find his way into writing. No one was teaching Thomas Pynchon either, but I read him. Eudora Welty, Capote's *In Cold Blood*, F. Scott Fitzgerald. Well, the list seems endless, so I'll stop.

The writers whose work made me feel as if it was okay for me to write are contemporary writers. I'll name some names but first have to say that François Camoin was the writer whose presence and work influenced my own writing more than anyone else did. I once tried to figure out a way to describe François's fiction. When I think about his work, I always think *the sentences, the sentences, the sentences.* They are precise. Exact. Hard-cut. I told him I imagine him as Kurtz in *The Heart of Darkness*, only François is truly smart, and not mad, although his work can be scary. He has sounded the human heart. I see him making sentences in an unlit place, one small circle of light on the words he fiddles with. He shuffles them about. He rolls them like dice. Tosses them into the air. You see his hands—busy, busy, busy. Berryman begins the first of his *Eleven Addresses to the Lord* thus: "Master of beauty, craftsman of the snowflake." In that spirit, I think of François's sentences, his stories, his books. Isn't there a tale or myth about an artisan who forged a sword so brilliant and sharp it could cut air? It had to be put away by the gods, kept from the hand of humankind. The universe was at risk. François's sentences—there you go.

And you, Doug—your fiction, which was important for me to read, also taught me to pay attention to sentences. Not one word wasted. Another good friend at BYU, Bruce Jorgensen, once wrote out a quote from Chekhov for me. It still sits on my desk. Chekhov was writing to a friend of his; the two of them were discussing fiction writing, and Chekhov wrote back: "Your laziness stands out between the lines of every story. You don't work on your sentences. You must, you know. That's what makes it art." My wife says Bruce's own writing is full of heart. It is. Truly. And there is not one lazy sentence in it.

It's inevitable that I will forget some influences if I try to name names, but I would rather be accused of forgetting than risk not paying tribute. These are the writers whose work makes me want to write; I can't read anything they've written but that I want to get up, go to my desk, and write. Stanley Elkin, Grace Paley, Harold Brodkey, Barry Hannah, Amy Hempel, Mary Robison, Frederick Barthelme, Lee K. Abbott, Kate Haake, Debra Monroe. There are dozens whose work taught me—William Gass, John Barth, Alice Munro—and whose work I greatly admire, whose work is the good news, if only people would read it.

Earning a doctorate seems to damage some fiction writers, distracts them from what they want most to do. But that didn't happen to you. What was your University of Utah doctorate like? Do you think of it as making you a better writer, or not? Was it a good experience?

Good things happened to me at the University of Utah. It was a terrific program then, and it still is. I met working writers. Leonard Michaels came in for a residency. I drove William Gass around in a snow storm, which led to a story

I wrote called "I Could of Killed Bill Gass." I tossed that one away a long time ago. It was important for me to meet writers. Not because of what they said to me about my work, but because their being what they were made writing fiction seem a possibility. Legitimatized it for me.

The scholarly work at the University of Utah was as important to me as the fiction-writing workshops. In fact, in certain ways it was what I really needed. I became interested in narrative theory, and I read what I could get my hands on—Gérard Genette, Shlomith Rimmon-Kenan, Seymour Chatman. The list is long. Roland Barthes and Jacques Derrida. I wasn't reading theory in order to learn how to write. I was intrigued. Think how it might affect a writer to have running through his veins Heidegger's idea that truth is untruth, that the work of the work of art is to enact the eternal strife between concealing and unconcealing, that when the artist lights up a space, that lighting itself darkens the edges. Here's one that I will never forget: "The truth of things lies in the event of their *thinging*." Ha. Don't you hope your own writing *things*?

All this has to do with writing fiction, but I am not in any way suggesting that I think about any of it when I am writing a story. You can't impose strife on your work; you can't will *thinging* into a piece about a kid growing up in Pahrump, Nevada.

But the concepts bounce about in your mind, and they can't help but influence your work. You asked about style earlier. I don't know what my style is, but I do know that it is what it is—not directly, but because the idea sits on my heart—partly because of my understanding that the life of a metaphor lies in the fact that it practices (Derrida's notion) difference not in similarity.

The University of Utah also placed me within a community of writers. There may have been competition there, but I didn't feel it. Or it worked in beneficial ways. I made friends, writers who have gone on to great success, who have kept in touch, whose work I turn to when I need to be reminded that what we do can matter.

Certainly a degree in writing, whether it's a Ph.D. or an M.F.A., is not what everyone needs. I can see how a degree might slow a writer down. But you're learning. How can learning hurt a writer? I hear people say that writing programs produce a sameness in the fiction. That's hooey. I would bet that you could list a bunch of fine, fine writers, and ask those critics—assuming they don't know beforehand—who had M.F.A.s and Ph.D.s and who didn't, and the critics wouldn't be able to guess based only on the work. The only danger might be that a young writer isn't ready to accept workshop criticism that is helpful and ignore workshop criticism that isn't.

What were your BYU years like? You were known as a brilliant writer and teacher, yet you left. Can you say something about that?

Here's what I'll remember most about BYU: pals and a horde of young writers whose work was impressive and who have gone on to have great successes. There was a period of about five years when every graduate workshop I taught had two or three writers whose work was the kind that makes you sit back and say, "Here's the real thing." You simply try to get out of their way. These remarkable young writers kept coming year after year. Several of them went on to the University of Utah. Here I really don't want to mention names because I'll forget someone, and I don't want to do that. But they're writing and publishing novels; they're writing movies.

At BYU, Bruce Jorgensen and I found one excuse or another to walk to the bookstore three or four times a week. I miss those days, our talks. Bruce is wise and kind and generous and funny—and he is one smart man. He introduced me to writers I needed to read. He was good company, and we all need that. He, as they say on the playground, schooled me. I'm grateful to him for his friendship.

So many brilliant teachers at BYU. That was nice of you to say I was known as one of them, but I wasn't a brilliant teacher. I cared about what I was doing, but *cared* is one of those words like *sincere*. Sincere folk can be frightening and destructive in five or six different ways.

I chose to leave BYU. I needed to leave because I was uncomfortable teaching there. Felt that I was living a lie. By leaving I was trying to act with some integrity.

What kind of writing schedule do you have? Do you work at writing every day? Are you a morning person? What kind of distractions can't you tolerate? What does it take to get you started?

What I'll describe here is only an ideal, is what happens when all is going well, when the corn is as high as an elephant's eye. I'm not a morning person, but that's when I write. Teaching—the reading, the preparation, the responding to manuscripts, the classroom discussions and workshops—fills up a day, usually seven days a week. When I was younger, I often worked at teaching until one in the morning.

So, the ideal: During the afternoon and evening, I complete all the preparation for teaching so that, when the morning comes, I'm ready to write. I try to leave my desk clean. I often put my manuscript in the center of it. I get up, write for a couple of hours, go for a run—thinking about what I'm writing—return and do some more writing. At night, after I've finished preparing for classes, I read over what I wrote in the morning, scribbling on the manuscript. That means that when I wake up I've already begun the writing process: I need to type in the revisions I've made, so I'm already at work. The writing has already begun. There is momentum.

When the world is right, I work on short stories during the week and the novels on the weekend. Of course, that means I'll be thinking about the novel all week long, making notes, writing down possible changes, asking questions.

The one lesson I have learned again and again and again: Get yourself to the place where you write. Put some words down. Don't let anyone sit on your shoulder and say, "That's bad. That's not working. That's dumb." Write. Write poorly. Write well. Write. Something will come of your putting the words together. Italo Calvino calls it combinatorial play.

The only distraction I could not deal with was our dog Willie. No dog has ever barked like Willie. It was a matter of his timing. I would be working, and he would ask to go out, so I would open the door to the backyard. About the time I started to think it was going to be okay, about the time I was writing well, he'd bark. Once. Twice. At nothing. He might be staring at the fence. He might be studying the sky. He had his own rhythm, which was really no rhythm. Three barks. Sometimes, one. And I waited. Surely the one will be followed by more. No? Start to work. Then a seven-bark riff.

What does the future hold for you in terms of writing? What are you working on now, and what future projects do you have in mind?

I mentioned earlier that I'm polishing up a story collection titled *So You Got Next to the Hammer* and a novel titled *Welcome to Wisdom, Utah.* The collection opens with a novella, the title work, and closes with a novella I'm calling *They Had Their Man for Breakfast.* Sort of bookend novellas. The second one is a cut-down version of a novel I wrote about Las Vegas. It has to do with growing up there in the 1960s. The book will contain four or five short stories and three short shorts. There's a certain kind of symmetry to it, but not to any purpose I can think of.

I'm excited about the novel I recently started, *The Department of Big Thoughts.* I mentioned that it is told by one of the characters in *Bring Your Legs with You.* The narrator of the novel is also the narrator of a story, "How Are You Going to Play This?" His name is Mac, but the other roofers have nicknamed him Spinoza. He talks big talk now and then. The book begins the day his girlfriend leaves him. He's in his late forties, and she's younger, probably in her thirties. The novel is set in Las Vegas.

Should take three or four years to finish. I probably ought to focus only on it, but I can't stop writing stories.

Las Vegas appears repeatedly in your writing. Why? What meaning does Las Vegas have for you, and the American West in general? Do you

view yourself as a Western writer, and if so why? How important is it to live, write, and teach in the West?

I wasn't born in Las Vegas, but I grew up there. I was a baby when my family moved there. So it's my context. Las Vegas frames the world for me. I'm not talking about Las Vegas as it now exists. Growing up, I didn't think Las Vegas was unusual. It defined reality for me. A Salt Lake City magazine asked me to write a piece about night, so I wrote about the showgirls coming to the grocery store where I worked when I was a kid. They came in full costume, complete with boas. I thought that was normal. Once I was talking to François Camoin about eating breakfast at Circus Circus while the aerialists above were swinging from trapeze to trapeze, doing their stunts. He said, "No wonder you write the way you do."

A Western writer? No. Not really. I'm not trying to say something about living in the West. That assumes a sense for the big picture, which I don't have.

I've been in Ohio for seven years now. I don't live here the way I lived in the West. That's a fact. After I was hired, I came to Athens to look for a house. I was on the porch of the one I eventually bought, and I said to the realtor, "I guess we'll need to put in a sprinkling system." She led me over to a spot out front and said, "You have drains in the lawn here." I asked her where our property ended and the neighbor's began. She said, "Your yard is where you mow to." Winter came, and the sun retired. Next to the walkway to our place, there was a lamp that was light sensitive; it turned on at night and off when sunlight hit it. It stayed on for three weeks straight, day and night. The local newspaper advised us, after our first winter here, to walk slowly around the house and inspect for damage.

It's a different world. We experienced our first ice storm. It knocked out the power. There was a fireplace in the dining room, so we put our bed in there. No heat, no light for three days. I learned how to build a fire. You need kindling, Kate told me. I thought, *Kindling?* I'd heard the word but didn't know what kindling was. A colleague loaned us firewood. In Ohio, I saw fireflies for the first time.

When we lived in the West, we didn't let the bed coverings touch the floor. Scorpions might climb up. As if you could stop them. You saw them high up on the ceilings.

Athens, Ohio, is built on clay. It shifts. The walls of your house crack. You adjust. You live in a certain way.

I don't know if all of this comes through in stories. Where I live in Ohio is truly beautiful. Trees. Rivers. Those colorful small towns you see in black-and-white movies starring Spencer Tracy. I found a narrative point of view for *One Mile Past Dangerous Curve* that allowed the novel to both appreciate and wonder at the world here. The minute I found that voice the book took off.

But I'm not answering the question. Las Vegas—the wide, hot streets I grew up on. We did actually fry eggs on them. We counted the number of steps it took to scoot across them in our bare feet. The desert I wandered in, the unreal round moons that sat on the city, Fremont Street. To this day I'm cursing the man who covered Fremont Street and turned it into the Fremont Experience or whatever it is they call it; he should be tarred, feathered, and ridden out of town.

I rode my bicycle all over the city. No fear. It was a safe place. Wide open. I think there were about 200,000 residents when I was in high school. There were the Strip people and townies. My friends' dads ran casinos. They comped us tickets. I got to see the Rat Pack. My sister's friend dragged her out to a motel on the Strip, knocked on the door, and Elvis answered. This was his first try at Las Vegas. They sat and talked.

There's a frankness about Las Vegas. It's tacky, and it knows it's tacky. I recently wrote a review of a book written by Marc Cooper. Its title is *The Last Honest Place in America: Paradise and Perdition in the New Las Vegas.* What Cooper argues is that the city is honest about the fact that it wants your money. It's upfront about what it is all about. I'll go back to that word *frankness.* I want to capture that in my fiction.

You don't want to get me started on how important it is for me to live, write, and teach in the West. I'll end up begging for someone out there to hire me. I enjoy my job here at Ohio University. My colleagues are smart and funny and cultured. I've worked with students whose work dazzles me. Made pals.

But I do need the West. I miss the sky. I miss the way the day whitens in Nevada. I desperately miss driving through the desert.

Any advice for the young fiction writer on how to get started, what to avoid, and what to seek? How helpful is an M.F.A. for the beginning writer? Does it serve an essential purpose if one doesn't want to teach?

My advice is clichéd: read and write.

Don't write in a void. Find the fiction that cares about itself and read it. There are writers who will make you want to write. Find them.

M.F.A. programs, Ph.D. programs—essential purpose? What if, instead of sitting in your house writing, you're sitting in a workshop and some writer says exactly what you need to hear? Sure, a program can help. But *essential?* I can't answer that question.

For me, yes. I needed the University of Utah's program. I was otherwise too ignorant. If nothing else, the program saved me ten years.

You've never viewed yourself as a Mormon writer, but does your Mormonism signify in your writing in some ways?

I was born into a Mormon family. There was a time when my father entered wholeheartedly into the religion. So I grew up as a Mormon. It has to inform my writing, but I don't think about it when I'm writing. Our growing up is present in whatever we write.

I don't really write about Mormons, though there are Mormons in some of my stories. I don't think about Mormon themes. I'm not interested in the religion as a subject.

John Bennion wrote an article about a few writers whose work in some way deals with Mormonism, the reference to which I unfortunately no longer remember. He spent some time talking about one of my stories—"The Glue that Binds Us," from *Our Secret's Out,* my second collection. The story is about a man who has married a Mormon woman. They've returned to Salt Lake City for a short visit. John compares the story to what he calls conventional Mormon texts, and he points out that what the story resists is any kind of easy connection between signified and signifier. John argues well—I'm a reader here, not the writer—and soundly that the story doesn't so much undermine Mormon thought and culture as it simply won't settle into the kind of thinking or worldview that Mormons and most Mormon fiction easily accept. It doesn't attack Mormonism, but it won't let Mormonism capture the narrative. John is kind to point out that my work does not make judgments or pronouncements. I like to think that Mormons are present in the story the way they are present in the world.

ANITA STANSFIELD

Anita Stansfield
Novelist

Interviewed by Annette Lyon

    Anita Stansfield began writing at age sixteen and published her first novel sixteen years later. Released in 1994, First Love and Forever *launched her career as perhaps the best-selling LDS author of romantic fiction, and since then she has published more than twenty books. In addition, she has been published in* Cosmopolitan *magazine and has written many novels for the worldwide market. She lives in Alpine, Utah, with her husband and children. The original version of this interview appeared in* Irreantum, *summer 2003.*

    Interviewer Annette Lyon writes LDS romance novels, several of which have been published by Covenant Communications.

You are one of the few LDS authors who can make a living at it. How difficult is writing full time?

Writing on deadline has definitely been more difficult than simply writing because I want to. Either way, writing along with being a mother is a distinct challenge. I learned many years ago that I just had to expect interruptions and deal with them, or I would never get anything written. I wrote equivalent to a full-time job for many years before I was published, so in some ways nothing has changed except that I have to do it.

Many consider you the trailblazer for LDS romantic fiction. When *First Love and Forever* came out, did you have a sense of breaking new ground?

Actually, I did. When I decided to write an LDS novel with a relationship at the heart of it, I found very little to go on as far as books and writers already established. In talking with women who had once been avid readers of LDS romances, I learned that most of them had quit reading such books because they were too idealistic, fluffy, et cetera.

So publishers had, for the most part, quit publishing them. I decided to write books that dealt with real-life issues that could be solved through accurate psychology and gospel principles. I think when my LDS characters are faced with tough issues, readers immediately relate to them, as opposed to reading about trite and meaningless romance. I believe that women have an innate desire for romance in their life, and clean romance novels are a way for women to fill that in a positive way. But when it's fluffy and meaningless, it feels like simply a waste of time.

By the way, I have been pleasantly surprised by the number of men who read my books. I believe that having strong and relatable male protagonists and realistic plot lines has contributed to this.

First Love and Forever was shopped around to many publishers before ending up at Covenant. What was that process like?

Frustrating! As you know, the number of LDS publishers is limited, and I wanted a company that was stable and capable of putting out a quality product. I had learned from years of writing, however, that rejection is part of the game and that if you believe in something, you have to keep going. In the end, timing had everything to do with it. Covenant at one time had rejected the project, but several months later I resubmitted it, and they bought it.

Trace how your writing inclination developed and how you first became a published writer.

I began writing at the age of sixteen, with my focus on historical romantic fiction that I was trying to sell to the national market. My goals stemmed a great deal from my frustration in reading. Every romantic novel I picked up was either trashy and obscene or fluffy and trite. Either way, it was an insult to a woman's intelligence. I set out to write books that had a relationship at the heart but had powerful characters, deep, intricate plots, and real-life issues, even if the story had larger-than-life circumstances.

After writing several such books without success in getting published, I felt an inclination to move to the LDS market, with strong feelings that my experience in learning how to write a strong novel could serve the market well. I actually wrote for sixteen years before I was published, and the rejections were innumerable. I still intend to see my non-LDS work put out into the world, and my goals are focused in that direction. But it takes time and diligence, and I'm too busy right now just meeting the deadlines.

You have said that you "guarantee a happy ending." What challenges do you face in creating realistic and believable situations while still keeping that promise? Have you been criticized that there is something unrealistic about always having a happy ending?

My first response to people who cynically tell me there are no happy endings in this life is, "If you're standing there talking to me, it isn't over yet."

As LDS people, we believe that we will achieve the rewards in the next life that we earn in this one. That is the ultimate happy ending. Life is tough, and we often don't get what we bargain for in this world, but we should have a perfect brightness of hope in working past our struggles, making our lives the best we can, and aspiring for eternal blessings.

The concept of "happy endings" gives the reader hope. I believe that in spite of life's challenges, we as human beings are capable of making life good if we can get past our baggage and get a grip. Opposition and trials happen, but you can look around yourself and see a huge difference in the way people handle those trials.

Also, I might have a happy ending in one book, but in the sequel those characters are confronted with new challenges—as it is in real life. Therefore, a happy ending is relative in regard to certain segments of life, rather than assuming they lived happily ever after without facing another challenge.

I feel that for a book to be satisfying, you have to feel completely content and hopeful at the end. But be careful when you open the next one!

Describe your writing process and habits.

I try to write every day but Sunday, but there are days when it simply doesn't happen, due to the other demands of life. Normally I follow a household routine in the morning, making certain the minimum is in order, getting the laundry started, and seeing to any pressing matters with business or family. Then I just write while I deal with interruptions and do what has to be done.

If I'm on a deadline or I'm in a creative mode, I will write every minute I can, but it's difficult to say how many hours I'm getting in. Ideally I would like to be able to write without any distraction and in orderly surroundings. The reality is that I am a mother, and my family is most important to me. My office is cluttered with bills, schoolwork, et cetera. I use a laptop to write, and it's not used by anyone else in the family for homework, Internet, et cetera. I sometimes have to take the laptop and go hide because my office has become the heart of the home, somehow. It's crazy, but I love my five children!

As far as the writing itself, I'm very unscientific. I don't outline. I just write. When ideas are coming faster than I can put them down, I open a new window on the computer and write notes to describe the scenes or circumstances I am seeing, often with snatches of dialogue or scene fragments. Eventually I have to put those in order, and I will follow that as I complete the story, but that has its challenges. Right now I have a seventy-two-page file of notes and scene fragments in no particular order, and I have to rearrange the entire thing before I can go on. It's a mess.

But I always put my priority on creativity. I never try to create and edit at the same time. They are two different processes and should be treated as such; otherwise, creativity is stifled. On research, I am a storyteller first, and I do research as necessary to make the story accurate. The bulk of my research is in psychology, and I often search for people who have experienced what I'm writing about. They aren't going to give me textbook answers. Their experiences come from the heart and soul, and that is what will touch the readers.

My older work required many more drafts. Some of my books have been seriously reworked several times. Now, I am able to write a book fairly close to submission quality right out of my head. Once the first draft is done, I can just go back through it once and turn it in, although the first draft may have required a lot of reworking of certain areas as the plot developed. But it's taken more than twenty years of practice to be able to do that. I've learned that you can't be afraid of revision; revision makes for some of the best books.

Most fiction is a combination of the author's experiences, observations, and imagination. How do those three elements work together for you?

I wouldn't describe my work as autobiographical at all, beyond the point of "If I were going through this, I would probably handle it this way." My story ideas just come to me, very obviously a gift of inspiration. If I don't get the inspiration, I can't write about it. I am definitely a very observant person. While my plots and characters are fiction, the circumstances and situations are definitely based on real life, with snatches of different things I've observed. I might take a snippet from a movie, a book, a song, what I saw in the mall, what someone told me in an airport, et cetera. Putting it all together makes a new creation.

What have you learned about marketing yourself as a writer? What other things have you consciously done to maintain a full-time writing career?

Through my first several releases, I put in a lot of legwork. I did many, many book signings, called newspapers, begged for interviews, et cetera. Signings were slow and boring, but the store managers and employees put a face with the books, and the advertising-related sales were beneficial. Eventually it reached a point where the books were selling whether I went to stores or not, so I stayed home to write. Now I do a lot of Relief Society meetings and firesides, which gives me the opportunity to share my testimony through relating my experiences, and it sells books indirectly.

I think one of the main keys to maintaining a career is to not allow the quality of your work to diminish. This is a challenge with deadlines amidst life's challenges, and I know that some of my works definitely have more quality than others, but I do try to be conscious of satisfying the reader as a story evolves. If the reader starts to feel that you're resting on your laurels, he or she will stop reading.

What's your view of the fiction writer's role in the building up of Zion?

I know that this is a God-given gift, and I feel a definite responsibility to use it the way He would have me use it. I don't question the source of my inspiration; I'm simply grateful for it. The good thing about being LDS is that we have the light and knowledge that allows us to understand the source of such gifts and how to keep our lives in balance as we use them. My foundation in the gospel keeps me from going over the edge creatively. You don't have to look very far in history to see how creative people had very destructive lives.

I believe we are accountable for what we write and the impact for good or ill that it may have on those who read it. If my books strengthen testimonies or bear simple, quiet testimony of God's existence, then I'm on the right track. Even in my books that have no LDS elements, the characters believe in God, they acknowledge His hand in their lives, they pray, and if they sin they suffer consequences. These principles are woven delicately in a way that's not contrived. That's bearing testimony of my beliefs without shoving it down the readers' throats.

Which of your titles are you most proud of? Which of your novels has been the hardest to write?

What I am most proud of is not published yet. Of the books published, it's hard to say. They're like my children. You love them all for different strengths, and you're aware of their different weaknesses. As far as which was hardest, my answer is equally vague. Some were difficult because of the subject matter, some because of the grueling time and/or research involved. Some books were extremely easy. However, looking back, the easy ones don't stick with me as well. A difficult writing experience creates a more lasting impression for the writer as well as the reader.

Do you dabble in other forms aside from novels? Are there any other forms you would like to try your hand at?

Novel writing is definitely my niche, and relationship fiction is my passion! I have written many personal essays, but it's more out of a need to share my experiences than actually liking it. Many people are unaware of my book *Reflections*, which is nonfiction. In it I share many experiences of motherhood, writing, and struggling to succeed.

What is your greatest fear as a writer? Your greatest pleasure?

I can't say that I have a fear as a writer. I trust in the Lord to just make it work and keep me going. I have concerns, and those are all related to the publishing business and the politics involved, which have been my greatest source of difficulty, but if you want your work to get out there, you just have to deal with such things.

My greatest pleasure? That's easy! There is nothing like just getting lost in the writing of a new story. To feel that creative energy consume me and carry me on a new adventure is simply an incomparable experience!

What works of Mormon literature have you personally most enjoyed? What works of general literature?

I'm ashamed to admit that I'm not much of a reader. I know that's unusual for a writer. Frankly, I did most of my writing while being a mother, and I just didn't have the time to both read and write. The good thing about that is perhaps that my work is more original in not being influenced by other writings. In my youth I read some, which initially spurred me to write something better. The books that stand out as leaving a deep impression were *Gone With the Wind* and *The Scarlet Pimpernel.*

What have been some highlights and lowlights of reader and critical responses to your works?

For the most part, response has been very positive. I can't count the times I've been told, either in person or through a letter, how my books have changed lives for the better and helped people deal with the struggles in their lives. I feel great joy about such responses, because I think that's what it's all about.

On the negative side, there is always someone who is unhappy with me. I've received occasional letters conveying the idea that "we shouldn't talk about such things, or we shouldn't talk about them that way." These have been difficult for me, and I have faced them prayerfully. (I'm getting really personal now.) In my heart, while knowing I am far from perfect, I feel very strongly about addressing the issues that I have and in the way that I have. I believe that the many who will benefit far outweigh the few who are offended. I believe a reader's offense is more about his or her personal struggles than it is about the books. I also understand that you can't make everybody happy.

In writing about relationships, I feel that it's necessary to address human intimacy related to some issues—breast cancer and rape, to name a couple. Some people feel that we shouldn't talk about it at all, even though I have made every effort to discuss it appropriately. I received one letter that accused me of writing pornography, and in the same batch of mail I got a letter from a woman—in reference to the very same book—thanking me for writing a clean historical romance that her teenagers could read. It's a matter of perspective.

After the controversy over alleged immoral sexual content in Richard Paul Evans's novel, Deseret Book pulled some of your titles off the shelves as well. What was your reaction to that news?

This is a touchy subject, and I've been asked to be discreet. I must say that I am all for a standard. Personally, I am easily offended by sex and violence and the way it is portrayed so commonly in this world. My concern comes in the way that this particular standard appears to have been drawn rather vaguely. I've heard of a number of incidents where books have been pulled for vague implications, and meanwhile I've heard that characters committing sin is allowed as long as it's portrayed appropriately and consequences are carried through.

Yet, some of my work that was pulled seems to be based on that very thing, which leaves me confused. I am concerned for struggling people who have been validated by my books and how they might feel to have those books banned. I am concerned with the way the vagueness of this has incited fanatics. The same kind of people who have accused me of writing pornography may see this as free license to be judgmental of many things they don't understand.

In talking with Rick [Richard Paul Evans], I was appalled to hear that people were actually sending him hate mail and saying horrible things. At the same time, of course, I related to his situation because similar things have happened to me. I am not going to be judgmental of Deseret Book, their policies or reasoning. They have the right as a business to do what they feel they have to do.

Jerry Johnston handled this issue well in the *Deseret News* when he did a column on the topic after he interviewed me. I agree with his stand. Deseret Book and I are two separate entities just trying to do the right thing, even if we're going about it in different ways. We need to have mutual respect and press forward.

According to a newspaper article, you were asked to remove a line from one of your books about a new husband on his honeymoon laughing and kicking the door closed. Did Covenant make the request? What was the rationale?

The article you're referring to was done by the Associated Press and went all over the country. I've had sightings of it in several states. Again, this is touchy. It's always tough doing an hour-long interview with someone who is gifted at getting you talking and then to see what they actually end up quoting. The quote was an insignificant part of a long conversation.

Covenant has definitely cracked down on any reference to intimacy. We have batted the issue back and forth and have come to an agreeable point where I can address the issues I feel I need to write about without upsetting anyone. The line in question came up at a time when the pendulum had swung to an extreme; it has now achieved more balance, which is evident in more recent publications I've done.

Do you ever feel inspired in your writing?

I think I've already addressed that, but to clarify: yes! In spite of all I have learned about the act of writing well, I count on that inspiration to get my ideas and see them through. I feel that my life has to be prioritized correctly in order to keep that conduit open. My house is livable but far from orderly. I don't cook much, but my family members know I'm there for them if they need me. If I'm looking out for what's important, then I feel better about expecting that inspiration to come when I need it.

Do you struggle with "putting words in God's mouth" when it comes to answering your characters' prayers, interpreting scripture, portraying miracles, and so forth? What other spiritual challenges have you come across in your writing?

I just try to follow the Spirit on that. I've studied spiritual and doctrinal matters enough that I have a feel for what's appropriate. Sometimes I have to call two or three bishops and ask a question and go with what's doctrinally accurate. When I pray for guidance in handling the issues correctly and try to live right—far from perfect, mind you—I simply hope that God will use me as an appropriate instrument to handle such things the right way. I can relate to the writers of the Book of Mormon in their making it clear that any mistakes are their mistakes, not God's.

My greatest challenge spiritually came in a book that is yet unpublished. It is far into a series, and while its characters become Mormons and migrate to Utah in the 1870s, it is not written for a Mormon market. As I explored Mormonism in that time period, I found it necessary to look at many issues that are difficult—most specifically, polygamy. In the end I felt that it was handled appropriately in a way that can help people understand the righteous issues and separate them from the fanaticism that we are reputed for. I was able to explore the emotional aspects of the issue from the minds of fictional characters confronted with it and how they gained a testimony of it when it is sanctioned by God and handled righteously.

What is your best advice for aspiring fiction writers?

Follow your heart, trust in the Lord who put those feelings into your heart and those stories into your head, and never, never, never give up! Practice and hard work make a big difference. I think the best way to keep improving is just to keep writing, keep letting people read it, keep listening to what they have to say, and sort out their opinions from what you believe in your heart. Practice. Practice. Practice. You don't hear a concert pianist play and assume this is the first time they've sat down at the piano. It's the same for a good writer.

DOUGLAS THAYER

Douglas Thayer
Fiction Writer

Considered one of the founding fathers of modern Mormon literature, Doug-
las Thayer earned his M.A. at Stanford and his M.F.A. in fiction writing at the
University of Iowa. As a professor at Brigham Young University, he has taught lit-
erature, composition, and creative-writing classes, in addition to writing his own
fiction. A Utah native, Thayer has received several regional awards for his short
stories and novels. The original version of this interview appeared in Irreantum,
autumn 2002.

To start off, please give us an overview of your published works.

I published *Under the Cottonwoods*, a collection of Mormon stories, in 1977;
Summer Fire, a novel, in 1983; and *Mr. Wahlquist in Yellowstone*, a collection of non-
Mormon stories, in 1989. My most recent novel, *The Conversion of Jeff Williams*,
came out with Signature Books in 2003. I've published stories in magazines and

journals, most of them included in the collections. I don't have any particular favorites in my work, although I think that *Harris*, an unpublished novel I finished last year, might be the best thing I've written. Anyone who wants an overview of my work might try *Cottonwoods* and a recent story in *Dialogue* called "Wolves."

What do your stories tend to be about? What do you see as your major themes?

I write about wilderness and contemporary man's largely unsuccessful attempts to understand it and gain some kind of spiritual attachment to it. But mostly I write about righteous, or near righteous, contemporary Mormons trying to live their somewhat conflicted lives as they seek their salvation, or whatever else they might be after. I'm not interested in writing about evil people, but about good people and their inevitable joys and sorrows.

What prompted you to start writing? How did you learn the craft?

I started to write because I kept getting a lot of ideas for stories. I felt that if I didn't write, I would regret it someday. I also felt that I *should* write, that it was one of my tasks in life. I don't know why.

I learned to write by teaching the short story and taking every story apart piece by piece to learn how it worked. I also learned by writing sometimes thirty or more drafts of my first stories—I'm down to about fifteen now—and getting good readers to read my manuscripts and make suggestions, most of which I took. The M.F.A. also helped. If I have talent, it's in my ability to write and rewrite until I get what I think I want, although I have also been accused of writing all the life out of my fiction.

What are your goals, motivations, and desires as a writer? Your greatest reward as a writer? Your greatest fear? Do you ever feel inspired in a spiritual way with regards to your writing?

My intention—I don't like the word *goal*—is to write serious Mormon fiction that intelligent readers will enjoy and learn from. My reward is to write something I know is good, that works, and to have readers tell me they like my stuff. I don't have any fears, great or otherwise. I am, though, a little concerned that I will die, have a stroke, or go senile before I finish some of the stuff I'm working on now. I don't feel spiritually inspired, although there are moments of clarity and insight that come after about the tenth draft—but they have to be earned. Writing is mostly hard work. But I do believe it is my lot in life to write, that it's important for me to write, that I would somehow be *shirking*—a word my mother used to use—if I didn't.

Most fiction is a combination of three elements: what the author has experienced, observed, and imagined. How do those three elements work together for you?

My ideas come to me out of my experience and out of what I read. Journals, diaries, memoirs, gossip columns, family stories, sacrament and testimony meetings, and just watching and listening to people are good sources of material. I'm not sure how the sources work together. As far as I can tell, they all get mixed up in my mind somehow, and then I find what I need or it just surfaces in some odd way. Not much is autobiographical that I'm aware of, although my wife, Donlu, is somewhat afraid that I will inadvertently spill my personal beans, to our mutual chagrin.

Does your mission experience in Germany turn up much in your fiction?

It's in a couple of short stories. It's very much in *Harris*, which runs from 1945 to 1953. Serving 1947 to 1948 in the army of occupation in Germany also provided background. Because I returned from my mission fifty years ago, I have had time to gain a little perspective, and I've also had several children complete missions, which helps the perspective. Missions are also important in *The Conversion of Jeff Williams*, although not my mission as such.

Tell us about your writing habits.

I try to write two hours a day, at least. I take the first two hours of my working day. They are mine. If teaching gets heavy, I stop writing and take care of teaching. I need absolute quiet to write. Fortunately I have a study in the BYU library with cinder-block walls. When I write a draft, I take notes as changes come to me, print the draft, and write the notes in the margin where I think I want to put them. If the notes are many—for a novel, I might have a hundred or more after an early draft—I write them on three-by-five cards, categorize them, put them in a box, and then add them to the margins of the new draft. I typically single-space and reduce two pages to a sheet of paper so I can spread out the draft of an entire novel on tables in the library to enter my notes (I don't write long novels). In this way, I get a sense of the balance of the story or novel, of the parts and how they fit together.

What works of Mormon literature have you personally most enjoyed? What works of general literature have most influenced you? Do other cultural influences besides fiction—such as music—play into your creativity?

The Mormon books I have most enjoyed include Levi Peterson's *The Backslider*, Virginia Sorensen's *Where Nothing Is Long Ago*, John S. Harris's *Barbed Wire*,

Marilyn Brown's *The Earth Keepers*, Orson Scott Card's *Ender's Game,* Annie Clark Tanner's *A Mormon Mother*, Don Marshall's *Rummage Sale*, and Dean Hughes's *Children of the Promise* series. I also enjoy Gene England's personal essays, Ed Geary's *Goodbye to Poplar Haven,* Brigham Young's sermons, and an array of other poems, personal essays, and stories by individual Mormon authors.

Looking beyond Mormon literature, I don't know about particular works that have influenced me, but certain writers have: Ernest Hemingway, William Faulkner, Flannery O'Connor, James Joyce, John Steinbeck, Eudora Welty, J.D. Salinger, James Thurber, E.B. White, D.H. Lawrence, and Leslie Norris.

I've always wanted to sing, play the piano, dance, and paint brilliantly but never have, alas. This yearning may have affected my writing in some way—I don't know. I like poetry; I think a good story is in some ways poetic. I like paintings that are full of color and passion and would like to think that some of my stuff shares these two qualities, at least at times.

How does teaching writing and literature affect you as a writer? What are your observations and advice related to students of creative writing? Is the proliferation of college creative writing programs good or bad?

As I said earlier, teaching the short story taught me something about writing fiction. If nothing else, it taught me what the typical college student could understand in a short story and what he or she liked. Teaching distracts me from writing and tires me out at times, but I learn a lot from my students, particularly those in freshman English.

As far as creative writing students go, the vast majority of them don't have the endurance and work ethic it takes to be a writer. M.F.A. programs are okay if the student wants to teach, but unfortunately by the time the typical student has the M.F.A., he or she has been in college for six or seven years, which can be disastrous in terms of a wider experience. What experiences have they had, outside of school, worth writing about? Instead of getting the M.F.A. and teaching, I much prefer that a student become a lawyer, doctor, corporate CEO, engineer, plumber, high school teacher, soldier, or mother of ten kids and write from that experience and perspective. In fact, it might be well not to let anyone under thirty or thirty-five take an M.F.A.

An M.F.A. certainly isn't necessary to become a writer, although far too many students think that it is. The best way to learn to write is to write, learn to read as a writer, get somebody who knows how to read and comment on your stuff, develop your capacity for honesty, and consistently and persistently send your stuff out to publishers.

What have you learned about marketing yourself as a writer and approaching different publishers?

I haven't tried to market myself much. Without *Dialogue*, Signature Books, and Peregrine Smith Books, I would have been dead as a writer. I owe them a lot. Deseret Book doesn't publish the kind of stuff I write, although I've tried them. I've tried national book publishers and have published two or three stories in national quarterlies, but not Mormon stuff. As far as I can tell, the national market isn't enthusiastic about Mormon fiction, but I've always assumed that if a novel or story is good enough, it will get published somewhere, whatever the subject or setting. But obviously a Mormon writer doesn't have to write about Mormons. He or she can write out of the Mormonness without a hint that is what's going on.

I want to publish for a Mormon audience, however small. I think about one-half of one percent of the English-speaking population of the church would be interested in reading a book-length piece of serious or literary Mormon fiction. That's about 25,000 readers. But then you have the big problem of distribution. There is no way that I know of to tell these readers what's available and get it to them. Web pages and online sales may help in time, but I don't see much happening right now.

What have been some highlights and lowlights of reader and critical responses to your works?

Mormon reviewers and critics have, for the most part, been good to me—Jerry Johnston, Gene England, Bruce Jorgensen, and Richard Cracroft, to name four. I have no complaint. It's all been pretty even, no low or high spots.

What do you think of *Only Once*, the film adaptation of your story "Greg" and your wife's story "Kelly"?

I found the title very odd. The film doesn't bear a lot of resemblance to the two stories, except maybe thematically. The film was produced for a Christian market, not a Mormon market, which makes it essentially non-Mormon. Donlu and I didn't write the screenplay.

What are your observations about the historical development and current state of Mormon literature?

I don't have any particular observations on the development and current state of Mormon literature. It's not something I think much about. I don't feel that Mormons as a whole are much interested in serious literature or that they are very interested in reading generally. Like the rest of the country, they're more interested in TV, movies, and electronic games. Mormons aren't, as far as I can tell, seriously interested in the knowing and feeling that come through becoming an intelligent reader of fine literature.

Yet, I think that Mormons, particularly Mormon men, are lonely and that serious literature could help heal some of that loneliness by showing that we are all in most ways the same and help us understand and connect with each other more. It might also help convince us that each of us is a unique individual and that we might want to value that uniqueness more. What is the point of heaven or salvation if we are all the same? How incredibly boring the eternities will be. However, Mormons don't like conflicts with unhappy endings, and they don't like writers who turn over rocks.

What serious Mormon writers and readers need is a press that publishes book-length fiction, poetry, biography, autobiography, and memoir—maybe even creative nonfiction, although I haven't really figured out what that is yet, but I may in time. The press would have to be run as nonprofit, I expect, but it would still need to be professional and pay its bills. Such a press would probably need an endowment of some sort. Certainly there must be a literate Mormon millionaire out there somewhere who seeks a kind of immortality in this life. The press would need to offer substantial prizes—$5,000 is probably a substantial prize—and publication for winners of annual contests in the various types of book-length literature.

Since you're one of the founders of modern Mormon short fiction, what do you think of the genre? Are the kids getting out of hand?

No, I don't think the kids are getting out of hand, if you mean that young Mormon writers are somehow saying things they shouldn't or writing about forbidden topics. Mormons typically don't get much out of hand, young or old, writers or plumbers. From what I've seen of new short fiction, I'd say the stories often seem too dashed off to me. They need to be more worked on, more polished. The one or two editors I talk to who publish stories say they seldom get a first-rate publishable story. The last contest I read for sent me eighteen or twenty stories, the best from all the stories submitted. I found one, maybe two, that I thought were publishable.

I'd say a story ought to go through ten or fifteen drafts over a period of a couple of years before it's probably ready. You keep maybe half a dozen stories going at the same time. You write a draft, put the story away for a month or so, maybe six, while you work on other stories, and then come back to it. This way you get perspective, and you also have time to think about your stories. There are, of course, many ways to go about writing a short story. My way is only one. From what I've seen of the students in our creative writing program here, I think we have a lot of fine young writers coming along. They certainly have ability; I don't know about their capacity to endure or if they have something to write about. But I'm hopeful. Write more; talk about writing less.

What do you think of modern fiction in general?

Finding first-rate novels and short stories isn't easy. You have to hunt for them. Too much suffering, despair, angst, failure, self-pity, self-hatred, pop psychology, and faithlessness for me—plus an abandonment of plot, theme, responsible characters, and significant resolutions.

Is it a worthwhile goal to get Mormon characters and themes before a national audience? Do you think this nation will ever have a Mormon Saul Bellow or Flannery O'Connor, someone winning a Pulitzer or National Book Award for literature that deals with Mormon themes, settings, and characters?

Yes, I think it's worthwhile, very worthwhile. Mormon writers have a great story to tell, perhaps even a unique story, one centered on virtue, faith, families, hope, and charity, with all their attendant difficulties and conflicts. I'd like to see a Mormon Flannery O'Connor—she didn't write much about Catholics, although her faith in the Atonement informs every story—and I think it's possible. Perhaps there's a Mormon Saul Bellow out there somewhere, but if so he or she is going to have to be very humorous, sophisticated, intelligent, and believing. I think the time may come when a Mormon novel or collection of short stories will win a national prize. Why not?

Why the long period of time without much published work? What's ahead for you?

I got started writing two novels and a collection of short stories more or less simultaneously, and it took a long time. I published one of the novels, *The Conversion of Jeff Williams* with Signature, as I mentioned earlier; the other, *A Good Man*, sits in my desk drawer and probably needs to be heavily revised, along with a rewritten gentile version of *Summer Fire*, now called *Fire Season*, and a novella version of the "Red-Tailed Hawk." I finished the collection of stories—five of the nine published in *Dialogue*—but haven't submitted it to anybody. I also finished *Harris* and got it out.

Right now I'm working on some stories and a memoir about growing up with my hooligan friends in Provo in the thirties and forties, so I haven't been sitting on my literary duff much. I plan to get everything all finished and published—I may have to start my own press to do it—if I'm spared, which I hope to be.

BRADY UDALL

Brady Udall
Fiction Writer

In addition to his celebrated novel The Miracle Life of Edgar Mint, *Brady Udall is the author of a story collection titled* Letting Loose the Hounds. *Born and raised in the Indian country of northeastern Arizona, Udall is a graduate of the Iowa Writer's Workshop, a James Michener Fellow, and a winner of the* Playboy *fiction contest. His stories have been published in* GQ, Story, *and* The Paris Review, *among other places. He has taught literature and creative writing at Southern Illinois University, the University of Montana, and elsewhere. The original version of this interview appeared in* Irreantum, *winter 2001–02.*

What early experiences and influences shaped you to be a writer?

I grew up in a little town in Arizona where there was a lot of manual labor to be done—hauling hay, chopping wood, irrigating, herding cows. I decided very early on that these were things I didn't want to pursue on a professional basis. I didn't want to be a lawyer or a doctor or, heaven forbid, a schoolteacher, so writing seemed to be the natural choice.

Most fiction is a combination of three elements: what the author has experienced, observed, and imagined. How do those three elements work together for you?

All three work in a way that's fairly inexplicable, but I will say this—I don't think anybody respects a good imagination nowadays. We live in the age of the memoir, and a lot of fiction seems to be nothing more than thinly veiled autobiography. This seems absolutely screwy to me. Why stick to the truth when there is such a wealth of untruth to choose from?

Which do you prefer writing, short stories or novels?

Right now, novels. I like the big ol' challenge of it. It's like going on an expedition—there's a lot of advance planning to be done, maps to read, supplies to gather. A short story is like going on a day trip. They both offer very different kinds of pleasures.

Do you have any rituals or conditions for a good writing session?

I write from around midnight to four or five A.M. I cannot write before midnight. Even if it's 11:48 and I've got nothing better to do, I'll sit around until the clock strikes twelve before I sit down at my desk. It's not superstition; it's ritual. Writing at 2:00 in the afternoon just feels wrong to me.

What have you learned about marketing yourself as a writer and approaching different publishers? What is your best advice for aspiring fiction writers?

I've never really marketed myself or approached any publishers. I've always had the same editor and agent, two lovely people who are passionate about what they do. I've lucked out in this, as I have in many other things. The only advice I have to aspiring writers is this: do what you want, don't listen to me or anybody else. And don't take yourself so seriously. Writing fiction is not a holy activity, but to be successful you'll have to work as if it is.

Tell us about reader response to your two books. What are sales to date for each? How do you feel about your critics?

I honestly don't know what the sales figures are. The first book, a story collection, sold well as far as collections go. The novel is doing well, as far as I gather. I had a friend of mine build a website for the novel, and it's been a great way of communicating with readers. I get two or three e-mails a day from readers, and it's a wonderful thing to know that your work is having an effect. I've had responses from priests, pastors, eighty-nine-year-old grannies, twelve-year-old girls, friends I haven't heard from in ten years.

As for critics, I'm not sure what to make of them. They've been great across the board for *Edgar Mint*, but I don't trust any of it. I've noticed that almost without fail the book the critic is reviewing is not the same book I wrote. That's okay—art is bound to be perceived in the most particular of ways—but it makes the whole review process rather confusing.

Tell us about your teaching profession and how it plays into your career.

I get satisfaction out of teaching, and it actually contributes to my writing. I've found that I can't sit home all day and write; I need to get out and do things and have a life. So teaching helps in that respect. I have my day job, and what I do after hours becomes something of an illicit pleasure instead of a chore.

Which authors do you draw the most from, and what kinds of fiction do you like to read?

I love comic writers: Twain, O'Connor, Rushdie, Barthelme, Grass. As far as I'm concerned, a book that can't make me laugh at least once every thirty pages isn't worth the paper it's printed on. I guess I don't like literature or art of any kind that takes itself too seriously. I don't like Hemingway or Virginia Woolf. I don't like books or movies or plays that have an axe to grind.

I hear writers say they don't like fiction that aspires to teach or has a lesson for the reader, but then they'll turn around and say that they, on the other hand, want to make the reader uncomfortable or challenge the reader with their own fiction. What's the difference? Either way, you're trying to teach the reader some kind of lesson. I don't want to teach the reader a lesson of any kind. I simply want them to have a hair-raising, heart-thumping, mind-numbing, soul-tearing experience. I think I would prefer it if they didn't think at all.

Let's discuss your use of Mormon elements and how your Mormon background is reflected in your fiction.

Mormon stuff gets into my work because I'm a Mormon. I was raised Mormon, I go to Mormon church on Sunday. I'm proud to be a Mormon. I'm fairly active, I do my best, but I also have some difficulties with aspects—both theological and cultural—of the church. Other than that, there are no real considerations or motivations about how Mormon material enters my writing.

I'll grab hold of whatever is useful. Because it's close at hand, Mormon material gets thrown into my stories along with everything else I can get my mitts on. I don't have any special message to offer the world about what the Mormon experience is like—I have only the individual experiences of my characters, some of whom happen to be Mormon.

What do you imagine Heavenly Father and the Savior think of your fiction? Do you see yourself as part of a Mormon literary community?

I don't imagine that Heavenly Father or Jesus think anything whatsoever of my fiction. For me, writing is not really a spiritual activity, though at times it does approach the kind of transcendence that can be experienced in Zen meditation.

As for the Mormon literary community, I don't really see myself as part of it, mostly because I'm not really sure what it is. There are a number of good writers out there who happen to be Mormon or who write about the Mormon culture in some way or another. I'd consider it an honor to be counted among them.

You've mentioned the strong influence of former Brigham Young University professor Darrell Spencer, who subsequently took up a post at Ohio University. How do you feel about your undergraduate Brigham Young University experience?

I learned just about everything I needed to know about writing from Darrell. He's easily the best writing teacher I've ever come across. I'm sure he's been sorely missed at BYU, but there are still very good teachers there—John Bennion and Bruce Jorgensen, to name a couple.

I don't really know what the political climate at BYU is like these days, but I doubt it's very conducive to a good writing education. Writers—and scientists and philosophers and mathematicians and theologians, for that matter—need freedom to explore and redefine their respective disciplines, to ask hard questions, to challenge. BYU simply doesn't afford that kind of freedom.

Have you read much stuff written by Mormon authors or published by Mormon presses? What's your impression of the Mormon reading audience?

I've read Walter Kirn, Paul Rawlins, Brian Evenson. But I don't really see these people as Mormon writers. They're writers who are Mormons or who write about the Mormon experience in some significant way. I don't want to offend anybody with this, but I think writing books of fiction that are aimed solely at a Mormon audience is a fool's errand. This is a gross generalization, but I'll make it anyway: Mormons don't read. Go into a typical Mormon home, and what will you find on the bookshelf? The standard works, maybe a volume or two of church-sanctioned reading material.

As far as I can tell, the only way to write a book of fiction that Mormons will universally embrace is to cut out anything that might be remotely offensive to any sensibility, to stay within strict guidelines of cultural acceptability, to teach an unambiguous moral lesson, and to make sure that everything comes out all right for everybody in the end. In other words, the only way to write a book that would be widely accepted by the Mormon reading audience would be to write, as my son might put it, a piece of ca-ca.

What will it take to get more Mormon characters and themes before a national audience? People seem to relish reading about Asians, Jews, Catholics—why not Mormons more often?

The only way to produce work that a national audience will care about is to produce more and better writers. I can count on one hand the number of Mormon writers with a national reputation. This is not because the world at large misunderstands us; it's simply because we, as a culture and people, don't produce a large number of individuals who are capable or willing to take the big risk, to challenge their own beliefs and the beliefs of others, to put their own culture under the microscope.

I think the biggest problem with Mormon culture is that we're so darned worried about what people think of us. We want to be liked! We want to be accepted! We want people to see us as happy and clean and moral and hard-working, and any kind of depiction that goes contrary to that, especially if it is created by one of our own, is considered an affront. We're taught from day one that we're examples to the world and must act accordingly. I don't think it's overstating it to say that, in Mormon culture, it's often more important to be a good example than to be a good person. Asians, Jews, Catholics—they've been around much longer than we have, and they've learned to confront their own demons and to laugh at their own foibles. We haven't yet.

In your novel, the character Edgar Mint does not appear to think about his ethnicity very much, and it is not a large part of his self-identification. You seem to downplay any major differences between Anglos and Native Americans. Do you think the place of race and ethnicity in the formation of identity is overemphasized in American culture? How about the place of religion in the formation of identity?

We are obsessed with race and ethnicity, heavens yes. And I don't think there's anybody who thinks this is a healthy development. The only way to put an end to it is to stop talking about it. Ignore it. Generally that's what I prefer to do. Religion obviously plays a large role in many lives, but I don't think that's something being strongly addressed in the fiction of the moment.

Much of today's literary fiction seems to avoid emotion, preferring cool, detached observations. Your work, on the other hand, is drenched in strong emotions.

Fiction is an emotional art. No two ways about it. Our great works of fiction are works of the heart, not the intellect. If I want to give my intellect a workout, I'll read philosophy or science. If I want an emotional experience—and I include the kind of emotional experience that is had primarily through the music of language—I'll read a novel.

Why is most of your fiction written in the first person?

I've written in third person, but I prefer first. I like the fact that with first person you not only get a story but a storyteller as well. It is generally more intimate. When you're dealing with emotions, intimacy seems like a good thing to have.

R.E.M. lead singer Michael Stipe's film company has taken out an option on *Edgar Mint*. How do you feel about your work being made into a film?

I don't really have much hope that it would ever be made into a film. One Hollywood guy called me and asked me if I thought Lou Diamond Phillips would make a good Edgar. I explained that Edgar is a child for ninety-nine percent of the novel, not a full-grown man, and the guy said, "Things can be changed, don't worry about that." I've had friends who've written scripts and worked on movies, and almost all their stories are ones of torture and pain. I think I'll stick to teaching at the university.

You've revealed that your next novel will be centered on a modern polygamous family. Can you tell us more about your future plans and projects?

That's basically it. I'm also working on some humorous essays—I guess they're just funny stories that are presumably true. At least I hope they're funny.

ROBERT VAN WAGONER

Robert Van Wagoner
Fiction Writer

Robert Hodgson Van Wagoner has received best short fiction awards from Caro-lina Quarterly, Shenandoah, Sunstone, *and* Weber Studies, *and he has been published in* The Best of Writers at Work, In Our Lovely Deseret, *and other anthologies. For his novel* Dancing Naked *(Signature, 1999), he received a publication prize from the Utah Arts Council and was given the Utah Book Award by the Utah Center for the Book, an affiliate of the Library of Congress's Center for the Book. He has been a resident artist with the Utah and Wyoming Arts in Education programs and a faculty member at Writers at Work, the Southern Utah University Writers' Conference, and others. He lives with his family in Washington State. The original version of this interview appeared in* Irreantum, *autumn 2000.*

Tell us about your beginnings as a writer.

I had no experience writing fiction until my senior year in college, when I wrote my first short story. A really bad short story. I was finishing up a double major in English and psychology at the time and hadn't yet decided which field to pursue professionally. I had every intention of going to graduate school—contingent, of course, on figuring out what I wanted to do with my life—but when I wrote that bad short story something clicked. The process compelled me, made me alive the way only rich and complex experience can. My wife, Cheri, and I were in our first year of marriage, and she, like me, was finishing her degree, tying up a secondary education certification. By the time we graduated, I'd managed a few stories more promising than the first and I'd had one accepted for publication in Weber State University's student literary journal, *Metaphor*. I also had an idea for a novel and was intrigued by the idea of actually trying to write it.

Together, Cheri and I came to the decision that I would take a year to figure out what I wanted to do about graduate school while trying my hand at the novel. We were used to being poor, and a first-year teacher's salary looked pretty good to us by then. Yikes, were we naive! So I did. I took a year and wrote a fatally flawed and never-published novel, followed by a series of pretty good short stories, most of which I sold in a relatively short period of time. Post graduation, my first published short story, "Love in a Unit," appeared in *Carolina Quarterly*. I'd been writing "full time" for about two years by then and had just begun the novel that eventually became *Dancing Naked*. Obviously, my "one year" turned into a bad habit.

What writing influences you most? Do other cultural influences besides fiction—such as music—play into your creativity?

I'm a fairly eclectic reader and am most influenced by whatever I'm reading at the moment. Consequently I've become more discerning about what I read, partly because I'm not terribly fast and don't have much time for books I don't find compelling on multiple levels. Language has become increasingly important to me. I look for fiction, particularly, in which the language is textured and carefully balanced against other literary elements, such as character and setting and conflict. I am drawn to language that is sonically evocative, lyrical, yet understated. It's tough to do, though I hope someday to be able to do it myself.

As far as other artistic influences—I was born and raised in the home of the painter Richard J. Van Wagoner. I grew up watching him paint in his studio and otherwise taking the arts for granted. I was very lucky that way. Early on, music was my discipline of choice, and I pursued it seriously for many years. I was even a music major at BYU for three semesters before my mission to Norway. Now, I'm mostly a connoisseur, though I include both the visual arts and music in my writing process. In my studio, I require certain pieces of my father's work, and when I'm revising, I almost always listen to music: blues, straight-ahead jazz, and classical, especially.

Though you wrote it at a relatively young age, *Dancing Naked* is for many readers unusually convincing in its depiction of grief, middle-aged marriage, intergenerational conflict, and lifelong friendship. Most fiction is a combination of what the author has experienced, observed, and imagined. How did those three elements work together as you wrote *Dancing Naked*?

I was born and raised in an active LDS family, and I was a believer. A fervent believer. I've thought a good deal about how this has informed my art. During my early years of religious disaffection, I tried to convince myself that my art and my twenty-five years of fervent belief should remain separate. It was a thin and dangerous self-deception, and I was forced to play the contortionist for a time.

I was angry. I felt as though I'd been betrayed and felt myself to be complicit in that betrayal. I was determined to excise my Mormonness, which of course was impossible, short of lobotomy.

So in many ways, *Dancing Naked* was the child of that painful struggle. I was still active in the church during the time frame of those first few drafts, and I was much too close to both the church and the work to recognize how profoundly my interior battles were affecting the novel's aesthetic and ideology. Ironically, I did not mention Mormonism once in those early drafts, an omission that bespeaks my years as a contortionist. The Mormonism was there, however, as it is in all my writing, whether I mention Mormonism or not. Every thought I think, every act I commit, every line I write, is fundamentally informed by my making. I am Mormon. It took me many years, but I finally understood that I had to stop knifing away at the unexcisable. I had to embrace who and what I was. When I finally accepted that I was forever Mormon, whether I believed in the theology or not, my art began to succeed in a whole new way.

The problem during those many years was conceptually simple, as most important problems are: How could I reconcile the dark issues I found most artistically compelling with my Mormon making, about which I was so conflicted? I was too conflicted, in fact, to see the obvious—that good art is never really about reconciliation but about the tensions and energies and consequences at play when one tries to reconcile the (often) irreconcilable. Frankly, there is so little in life that's truly reconcilable. And let me tell you, reconciling the irreconcilable is hard work. With *Dancing Naked*, it took me nine years and about sixty drafts to realize it could not—and should not—even be done.

Which brings me more directly to the experience/observation/imagination part of the question. At the time I conceived *Dancing Naked*, I was intrigued by the way authority—be it personal or institutional—trains each new generation to accept and perpetuate certain attitudes, particularly intolerance. Moreover, I was interested in exploring what I perceived to be the high price such perpetuation exacts on the perpetuator. When I wrote the novel's early drafts, I did not know that my younger brother was gay, but I already strongly believed homophobia to be one of the few remaining bastions of socially sanctioned hatred. (My brother came out to me shortly after he'd read one of those early drafts.) I did not want a gay protagonist, because I did not believe I was qualified to write about a homosexual's interior life, in much the same way I am not qualified to write from a black protagonist's point of view. I did, however, know something about homophobia, having grown up a bit homophobic myself. And I knew something about sexual repression. And about authority. What would happen, I wondered, if a sexually repressed homophobe from an authoritarian background were forced, in the wake of a child's death, to face that child's sexuality?

I did not base *Dancing Naked* on any personal experience, though I had witnessed in my twenty-five years plenty of unsavory homophobic episodes. My parents are loving, wonderful people, with no resemblance whatsoever to any of the parents in *Dancing Naked*. When my brother came out, they accepted him even before they understood his sexuality.

So, rather than a story of authorial experience, *Dancing Naked* became the product of imagined characters placed in ferocious conflict, then strained—along with my raw and bleeding hide—through a very personal aesthetic and ideological evolution. Simply, I started with that father-son conflict mentioned before and let the characters take over. I had no idea how the novel would progress, how it would resolve. I seldom know such things about my stories and novels. E.L. Doctorow once said something like, "Writing a story is like driving at night with the headlights on. You may only be able to see a few feet ahead of you, but you can drive that way all night, and get home." Makes sense to me.

You said you felt your writing improved when you accepted you were forever Mormon, whether you believed in the theology or not. Could you expand on this? Maybe it would be easier to grasp in relation to nationality or ethnicity, but it's harder to imagine a Baptist saying, "I don't believe in the tenets of Christianity, but I consider myself a Born-Again Christian, because that's the tradition I grew up in." What is it about Mormon culture that allows you to say the same thing, and how do you feel it nurtures your writing?

For my first twenty-five years, Mormonism was my way of life, and the Mormon culture—its geography and demographics (both interior and exterior)—was my country. I did not often travel beyond its borders. Mormonism was so pervasive in my early life that I had little time for—and, frankly, little knowledge of—the bigger world. I accepted the old Mormon saw, to be "in the world, but not of the world," which effectively filled me with suspicion and fear of anything outside my Mormon range of experience. Without effort or self-analysis, I spent my time with Mormons, participating almost exclusively in activities administered or sanctioned by Mormon organizational and cultural forces.

Mormons organize and insulate themselves against perceived threats, which demonstrates the premium we place on community and cultural identity. Mormons and the Mormon doctrines seem easily threatened, however—threatened by criticism, by beliefs and behaviors different from our own, by doubts and contradictions, by changes and legal challenges to doctrinal or cultural tenants—and this, in my case, helped generate an intensity of experience that constitutionally and permanently shaped me. With all due respect to more traditional ethnic identities, Mormonism became my ethnicity. It played that large a role in my life, plays it still. Just because I ceased believing in the doctrines does not mean I suddenly reshaped myself or assumed a different identity. I process information much as I used to, only now I have a much broader range of experience to draw from. My personal and artistic conclusions represent that growth.

As a writer, then, I tackle ideas using all the tools I own. I'm in an interesting position, knowing personally what it means to be a fervent believer and an ardent nonbeliever. It was an important moment in my development when I realized both my belief and my nonbelief pivoted on my Mormonness, that same fundamental identity. Once I accepted this, I was strangely free to identify with the individual and cultural struggles inherent in being a Mormon who believes and a Mormon who doesn't. I was suddenly able to empathize, not just sympathize, to feel compassion, not just tolerance (or intolerance). I was able to do these things, and in ways, with a creative range I'd not experienced as a fervent believer and, later, as an angry nonbeliever. The synthesis of my disparate parts became, largely, my muse. I am a much better writer in the aggregate, and I have many more things to write about.

For all *Dancing Naked*'s angst and darkness, it has a surprisingly happy, resolved ending. What if the novel had ended on page 345, without the last chapter and epilogue? Tell us about how and why you developed the novel's denouement.

I'm not sure I would agree that the ending is either happy or resolved, though I do agree that it's hopeful. One alternative resolution, the one you suggest by your reference to page 345, would obviously have been worse for everyone—except, of course, for Blake and Father, though even there Terry's ultimate demise would have come at the expense of their memory. Still, I accepted the possibility that such an ending might be necessary, though I admit I was pleased that the narrative's momentum carried everyone through.

So how and why did I develop the novel's denouement? I didn't really; I left it up to Terry and Rayne, who'd led the way all along. John Gardner in *The Art of Fiction* discusses a concept he calls profluence, which I've subsumed and bastardized in order to understand my own creative processes. (I looked for my copy just now and can't find it, so you'll have to forgive me for dealing mostly with my own take on the concept, which was nonetheless inspired by his.) In essence, profluence is the physical act of plotting, and it occurs in real life and good literature. For my own needs, I think of profluence as the chemical reactions that take place when real characters authentically interact with real conflict. In my work, that chemical reaction fuels the narrative's forward movement. Characters are real people, with real personalities, real strengths, real flaws. We writers so want to interfere—and, yes, we must occasionally do so—though sometimes we interfere in ways inconsistent with the story's authenticity and honesty. That's a fatal mistake, for without authenticity and honesty, all natural chemical reactions cease, and the forward movement stops, and unless we beg our characters' pardon and return them their heads, we are left to drag and push our poor, manipulated stories to their sorry, failed endings. I know. I've done it plenty of times.

Let me put it this way: Despite himself, Terry is a good man. I love the guy. As evidence of his strength, read to page 364. I am very proud of him.

Comparing the chapter of *Dancing Naked* excerpted in *In Our Lovely Deseret*, you—or a Signature editor—toned down the description of the gay pornography found at Blake's death scene. How much explicit material was similarly edited, and what were the motives? How much rewriting did you do after acceptance for publication?

I did quite a bit of rewriting after *Dancing Naked* was accepted for publication. It had been some time since I'd worked on the manuscript, and, based on Signature's comments and on my own neurotic proclivities, I worked very hard to get everything right. Though, of course, I never get everything right. In terms of toning down, Signature and I negotiated and compromised—both of us. Every writer overreaches at times, and a good editor (which I had) is often able to see things the author can't or won't. When I say good editor, I'm speaking to a kind of selflessness. A good editor understands the author's intent and suppresses his or her personal agenda for the sake of clarifying the author's meaning. For this to work, both the author and the editor must always remember that it's about the work, and nothing else. Anyway, when I thought a specific word or image didn't particularly matter to the overall impact of the narrative, I conceded and toned it down, so long as the change didn't compromise my intent. By doing this, I was able to stand firm and keep what I felt strongly about, which in a couple of cases meant some risk for everyone. Nothing essential was toned down.

You've said you didn't initially include any Mormon elements in your novel, though it was always set in Salt Lake City. The Mormon additions you later made seem mostly related to the main character's macho, authoritative father, and Terry's rejecting of him and, in an interrelated process, of Mormonism. Is the father—or Terry himself— any kind of metaphor for Mormonism? Is there anything you find

**redeeming about the culture or religion that would ever find its way
into your work?**

As I said before, Mormonism is always present in my work. In the case of
Dancing Naked, I didn't add much new material but rather called things by their
real names. It was a very easy thing to do, and the changes tightened and justi-
fied the motivations considerably. As far as Father or Terry standing metaphori-
cally for the church, I'd have to leave that to the reader. I will say, however, that
the novel is not about Mormonism, not in the least. It's about human beings,
some of whom happen to come from a Mormon background, who find themselves wrestling with human conflicts. No matter how hard we imagine or
pretend, real Mormons in real crisis seldom look like the cover of the *Ensign*. In
their dire and private hours, Mormons look like everyone else. Likewise, Mormonism does not have a corner on intolerance, or on crisis of faith, or on sexual
repression. No matter how much we want to be "peculiar," we're far from it.

It's simple: I'm Mormon, and Mormonism is my experience. My goal has
always been to deal with universal human issues through the specifics of the
culture I know. Readers may not always recognize themselves in my characters,
but when I'm doing my job well, those same readers have a hard time denying
the characters' authenticity. Just because a reader does not like my depiction of
something, that dislike, whatever its source, does not alter the depiction's accuracy and truth.

The final part of your question reveals an interesting bias on your part and assumes a bias in my work as well. What do you consider redeeming? How should
such a thing be defined? Like I said, some readers are troubled by my stories'
depiction of Mormonism and its culture; others are relieved and grateful to find
themselves among characters and issues they understand and recognize. *Dancing
Naked* is a story of redemption, I suppose. In the end, even Father is redeemed to
some extent.

I've finished a collection of short fiction, most likely to be titled *Strong Like
Water*. Eight stories, some of them connected, all of them with Mormon characters. Again, I find every story redemptive on some level. Almost every character
is a good person, struggling with his or her own problems. Once again, none
of the stories are about Mormonism, while all are fundamentally Mormon.
However, whether the Mormon culture or religion is redeemed or redeeming
in my work does not much matter to me. Writing about what I know, getting it
right—those are the things I care about.

Do you like writing? Tell us more about your writing habits.

Like is not a term I much understand when it comes to writing. Well, maybe
I should say that I like to have written well, but I find the process very difficult
and painful, even in the good times.

I am, however, physically and emotionally better when I'm working. I have long periods when I'm not cutting new material, and not necessarily because I'm busy rewriting or promoting my work. I feel weak and lifeless during those periods. I am inclined to depression and anxiety. If I will force myself to read, though, I find over time that the intellectual stimulation pulls me back, until pretty soon I'm churning through books at a pretty good pace. My best ideas—and the desire to write about them—almost always come when I'm actively reading.

I seldom use notes, never an outline, at least not so far. Accuracy is important, so I research when necessary. I write many, many drafts, and sometimes those drafts include large and radical changes.

What have you learned about marketing yourself as a writer and approaching different publishers? Trace for us your experiences with national publishers and how you ended up at Signature. How is your agent currently doing handling your prospects, such as paperback rights to *Dancing Naked*? Are you trying to go national as opposed to regional?

I dislike the practical and financial parts of marketing, but I enjoy meeting people and discussing ideas. I was very glad when I linked up with my agent. I was going through a nasty negotiation with a university press that had accepted *Dancing Naked*, and my agent helped me through it. I ultimately withdrew the book because the publisher was not handling the negotiations to my liking. They were very angry when I pulled the manuscript.

After resolving that nasty episode, Jenny Bent, my agent, shopped the manuscript for a time, and though we were not able to sell it on the national market, the book made it to the boardrooms of three large houses. Ultimately, all three publishers rejected the work because it was "too dark and literary" for a first novel by an unknown writer and because they were afraid Terry was too unsympathetic. We did, however, make some friends and fans among the senior editors at those houses, and we agreed to give them a first look at my next work.

Having said this, I am very pleased with my Signature experience. I was treated fairly and with respect, and they made a beautiful book. My intended audience is literary, be it regional, national, or international. Naturally, I prefer national because it means more people are reading my work. Though I have not had much national publicity, my readership is slowly creeping toward both coasts, and publications like *Bloomsbury Review, Publishers Weekly, Gay Today, Midwest Book Review,* and *Feminist Bookstore News* reviewed *Dancing Naked* favorably and in some cases multiple times. Signature is not a large house, but it is becoming increasingly respected nationally, and for good cause. Trite but true, bigger is not always better, and though like most writers I hope to have a large, national readership someday, I would be pleased to see Signature as part of that equation, supposing they would have me again.

You've won some awards and grants. What other things have you done to carve out and maintain a full-time writing career—in other words, how do you support your wife and children?

I don't financially support my wife and family. Cheri has been the family's primary breadwinner since we graduated from college. However, some years ago we purchased some reasonably priced rental properties. We did this by selling our home and using the equity for a down payment. Such ventures do not always work, but in our case it proved to be a good investment. Anyway, I managed the properties part time, doing most of the remodeling and upkeep, and now the investment provides a small income, which has helped a great deal. Additionally, I sell stories now and then, have royalties coming in, and am paid for many of the literary events I participate in. I teach at writing workshops when I'm asked, and I even substitute-teach when things get tight financially. Cheri and I take this writing thing very seriously and do what we must in order to ensure the next project. Obviously, I'd never have made it anywhere without Cheri.

Awards and grants have made a big difference in my career. Besides affirming my efforts in what is a difficult and lonely profession, they have provided good publicity, recognition from editors and agents, and cold cash. I was contacted by five agents because of short story awards. Jenny Bent was one of those agents. I have been asked to participate in events for which a certain amount of award status was prerequisite to the invitation. Then there are the less tangible benefits, such as confidence and motivation. No matter how much I want to rely on writing's intrinsic rewards, I need some extrinsic validation every now and then too. And grants—before my sons were in school, grants bought me some time to write. I was the primary caregiver during those years, and with the money I was able to bring in a nanny for a few hours each day while I wrote. I liked having the boys at home with me while I worked, and a nanny made that possible.

Please comment on the story that was nominated for the Pushcart Prize. What did it mean to you to have it nominated? Did the nomination open any doors for you? Would it help Mormon writers if LDS-related publications regularly submitted the best work they publish?

I've had two stories nominated for Pushcarts, neither of which won. Both nominations pleased me greatly and, if not directly, indirectly opened certain doors. Every agent soliciting my work has commented on the nominations. No matter how much we wish it were otherwise, writing is a political profession. The bigger and better the vita, the easier it is to get a good reading from editors and agents. Without doubt, *Sunstone, Dialogue, Exponent II, Irreantum,* and any other Mormon periodical publishing literary work should submit the very best to the appropriate competitions. The very best, however, must be defined by the highest literary standards, and nothing else.

How do you think the contemporary literary establishment views writers with any kind of religious affiliation?

It's tough to generalize, because there is no one contemporary literary establishment, really, and a writer's religious affiliation can manifest itself in so many ways. Still, I think I know what you're getting at. For me, the most important word in your question is *literary*, which to me suggests an aesthetic sensibility that precludes dogma and propaganda. Some writers have a tough time making distinctions between what's aesthetic and what's pretty or reassuring. Great art rarely assures us that all is well, and it never prescribes the one true answer that will solve the world's problems. Not that I've seen, anyway. Circular, self-referential arguments cannot withstand question or scrutiny, yet so much religious fiction is just that—circular, self-referential, indefensible. Thus, religious fiction rarely rises to literary levels. Nobody wants another person's faith crammed down her throat. Serious readers don't want all the answers—sometimes they don't want any answers. Still, some writers with religious affiliation write and publish great, well-received literature all the time.

Do you think this nation will ever have a Mormon Saul Bellow or Flannery O'Connor, someone winning a Pulitzer or National Book Award for fiction that deals with Mormon themes, settings, and characters? What will it take for Mormon literature to assume a place in the culture the way that Irish, Native American, and Jewish literature have since World War II?

Yes, I do think the nation will have its Mormon Bellows and O'Connors, perhaps writers of even greater importance, though it seems likely to me that those Mormon writers (and their works) will not, at least initially, be embraced by the institutional church, nor by the more orthodox factions of our small but growing literary establishment. Which, of course, won't matter one bit, because the artifact will not need the church's endorsement or approval to define it as Mormon or successful or anything else. The works' quality and accuracy will transcend the inevitable socio-political smallness, the fears engendered when power and control are forever lost. Already, there are a few Mormons writing promising fiction, and there are certainly more to come. It's just a matter of time. And growth. And courage.

My friend Margaret Rostkowski, author of *After the Dancing Days, The Best of Friends,* and *Moon Dancer,* once said she believed loss to be the soul of great literature. I have thought a lot about her observation and have come, over time, to believe she is largely right. Loss, however, presents some interesting problems for Mormons. Mormonism, as a theology and a culture, exists—at least in theory—to neutralize loss, which is perhaps why so many Mormon writers treat loss as a tragedy and strive to overcome it by applying church-approved and faith-based solutions to their fictional conflicts. The irony in all of this is that loss, deep and permanent loss, is sometimes the only way to salvation. What happens when a Mormon protagonist finds hope—or yet more dangerous, salvation—by losing her faith, or her church, or her chastity, or her community? What if she loses her god and, in the process, finds some other belief that makes her whole? What if she actively participates in the mercy killing of her old and suffering parent? What if she chooses abortion, and that choice ends up bringing life and salvation to many? What if she embraces her homosexuality and finds peace and spirituality and love? These things and many more like them happen all the time. They happen to everyone, including Mormons—even earnest, faithful Mormons. Yet how many Mormon writers are willing to wrestle with such issues, knowing that so many Mormon readers and leaders could never read their stories without thinking it all tragic, perhaps more than tragic, because the struggle appears to embrace the greatest of all Mormon losses—separation from the Mormon god and the Mormon concept of eternal family?

You asked what I think it will take for literature written by and about Mormons to assume a significant place in American letters. A writer of such a work must be willing to wrestle honestly and authentically with the human condition, not simply the Mormon condition. By necessity, the art that writer makes will explore and document that struggle with finesse, beauty, insight, and compassion. Finally, the work and its maker will have to overcome fear, her own and that of others, because such an enterprise will be terribly dangerous and painful and permanent. But it will happen. Sooner or later, it will happen.

Tell us more about the response to *Dancing Naked*, including sales figures. What sort of reader feedback are you personally receiving? How has the response met, exceeded, or failed to meet your hopes? Have there been any misunderstandings by critics that you'd like to respond to here?

As far as I know, we made it to a fourth print run. I don't know how that translates into actual numbers, though the print runs were not large: one thousand and change each, I believe. All the reviews I saw were favorable, and a few were quite extraordinary. I love personal feedback, and most of that has been favorable as well. People who don't like a work seldom call the author to complain, though, so who knows? As far as expectations go, I try to avoid them so I won't be disappointed—though who can really do that? The reviews have been great, but there are never enough. The sales have been good, even brisk at times, but I'll never sell enough copies. *Dancing Naked* has launched my career, but thankfully there's much, much more to be done. No misunderstandings so far. I put it all out there in my work. In the end, each piece has to live or die on its own.

You've been working on a novel about Mormon missionaries. How will that book compare with *Dancing Naked*? How will the Mormon elements be handled? What audience and publisher are you shooting for?

The Hammerfest Fraternity is its working title, and yes, it does deal with Mormon missionaries in Hammerfest, Norway, high in the Arctic Circle. In a previous life, it was a novella. I fleshed it into a pretty long novel a few years ago, but I've never been satisfied with its shape and language. At the moment, the manuscript's on ice. I may come back to it someday—then again, I may not.

In the meantime, I've been working on a new novel, a literary mystery entitled *Cautionary Tales*. The narrative circles around the disappearance of a five-year-old Mormon boy from an Ogden, Utah, neighborhood. Shown through the eyes of four characters, the mystery unfolds over a three-day period. The child's disappearance and the mystery are the vehicles that carry the narrative into the psychological territory I am forever drawn to. It's a far more ambitious novel than *Dancing Naked*. And, if possible, it's a darker, more troubling work. The first draft came in at over one thousand pages. The draft my agent has is half that length. As for the Mormon elements, *Cautionary Tales* is more fundamentally Mormon in its characters, environs, and subject matter than *Dancing Naked*. It's an intense, compulsive narrative, and as such it presented me with some wonderful problems to solve. Page-turners often devolve into melodrama—especially when they deal with a child—so I worked very hard to achieve character complexity and an understated, transparent rendering. Its language, of necessity, is less lyrical than the language I employed in *Dancing Naked*. Despite what I said earlier when you asked if I like to write, I guess I'd have to admit that *Cautionary Tales* was a gas to write—well, when it wasn't miserable, that is. I'd be tickled to see a national publisher release it and a national audience read it.

Rick Walton
Children's Book Writer

Interviewed by John Bennion,
Cheri Earl, and Carol Lynch Williams

Children's writer Rick Walton has published more than seventy books with national and LDS publishers, including picture books, riddle books, activity books, mini-mysteries, and a collection of poetry. Many of his picture books tie into language-arts themes, such as Pig Pigger Piggest, *which teaches use of comparative adjectives. His books have been featured on* Reading Rainbow *and* CBS's This Morning. *Walton lives in Provo, Utah, with his wife and five children. The original version of this interview appeared in* Irreantum, *winter 2002–03.*

Interviewer John Bennion is a professor at Brigham Young University and the author of a novel, a collection of stories, and other works. Interviewer Cheri Earl teaches writing at Brigham Young University. Interviewer Carol Lynch Williams has written several nationally published novels for young-adult readers.

John: **Which is more important: to have written or to have made money writing?**

To have written.

Cheri: **Liar. Why do you say it's more important to have written?**

The reason I'm a writer is that I like to write; I'm obsessive about writing. Ever since I was a teenager, I've written incessantly, just for the sheer creative thrill. And I do it all the time. I spent the morning today writing stuff that will just go on my website and will not be published except there.

Carol: **What percentage of your writing is just for fun, and what percentage is to make a living? Or is there overlap in the two?**

Well, some overlap. The writing itself—hopefully the writing to make a living, too—is fun. That's not always true, but I would guess that about seventy percent of what I do is just for fun.

Carol: **So what's the difference between what you've written just for fun and what you actually publish?**

Nobody else wants to read what I write just for fun.

Cheri: **That's true! Take *Rolfe the Exploding Elephant*.**

That's a great story.

John: **Then there's that one about the talking dog who joins a circus on another planet.**

Yes, the story of Bob and Louie. Oddly enough, I'm rewriting that because a publisher wants to see it again. It turns out that they are the American branch of the publisher who first did Harry Potter, so who knows? Maybe they recognize great genius.

John: **When I first read the Bob and Louie story, I didn't know what to say. I might as well have been reading *Finnigan's Wake* for all the sense I could make out of it. Either *Finnigan's Wake* or the monologue of a schizophrenic person.**

Actually, I shouldn't say that nobody wants to read what I've written just for fun, because I actually get all sorts of strange e-mails responding to a variety of things that I have on my website. Somebody had, just a couple of days ago, a couple of words that he thought I should add to one of my word lists.

Carol: **What words?**

I'm not going to tell you. I said to him, "I know I'm missing a lot of words on my list. I do that on purpose because children read these lists."

Cheri: **Was he from Britain?**

Actually, I think he was, based on the words.

Cheri: **There you go.**
John: **You used to work full time?**

Um, not for very long. I've never held a job for more than a year.

John: **So, from the very beginning, you've been a full-time writer.**

No, there were times when I was pursuing other careers: teaching school, working in the arts, an M.B.A. program, law school, an English master's degree—all these different things.

Cheri: **The law-school thing was so he could represent himself in court. Why didn't you stick with it?**

I came to my senses, realized that I was not law-school material.

Carol: **So what is picture-book writer material? What makes you a good picture-book writer?**

I have a short attention span.

Cheri: **Let me ask the question a different way. What makes a good picture book?**

There are a lot of things that go into a good picture book. It has to be simple and understandable by a child. It has to appeal on more than one level because nine or ten adults are going to have to pass off on the book before it ever gets to a kid. There's a great deal of rhythm in a picture book; there's a conciseness of language. There's a tremendous visual nature to picture books; the text has to evoke visual images in order for the illustrator to be able to do something with the text. There's a certain directness and unity to a picture book that doesn't allow for diversions or fleshing out in the same way that you would with a story or a novel.

And one of the things that's important too is that a picture-book manuscript needs to be fresh; it's got to be something that's not run-of-the-mill or something that has been done a hundred times. Unless it is something unique, the editors have all seen it before—many times—and will just pass on it.

John: **What has been your most successful book, in terms of either reviewers or number of books sold?**

So far, *So Many Bunnies* has sold about 300,000 copies in various editions.

Carol: **Is that all the bunny books together or just *So Many Bunnies*?**

Just *So Many Bunnies*.

Cheri: **How about *Bunnies Gone Mad*? Are you working on that?**

Bunnies Gone Mad is still in concept phase. Same with *Bunnies Gone Bad*, *Bunny Love*, and *Massacre Bunnies* . . .

John: **Bunny Lust.**

Yes, that's where all the bunnies come from, after all; that's the reality.

Carol: **Bunny Girl.**

Yes. And others. Just yesterday I got the first copy of my book *Bunnies on the Go*, which is bunnies traveling. The sequel is going to be *Road-kill Bunnies*.

Carol: **Okay, we need to get serious again. Here's my question. Everybody in the world who wants to be a children's writer thinks they can write a picture book. And we know most of us fail miserably. What made you decide to write picture books?**

What I said earlier about having a short attention span was only half a joke. I do much better writing short things, such as short poems, games, activities. I write a lot of riddles that are short. I can't write longer stories, but I can write minute mysteries. Anything that's short and I can wrap my mind around all at once, I can do. Also, I think that, probably, I ended up doing picture books because I have a strong music background, and the sense of rhythm I got from being a musician helped me.

Cheri: **But that doesn't mean everybody who plays the piano can write fiction.**

No, it doesn't.

Cheri: **Dean Hughes said one time that he gets asked this question by writers and people in academia and, you know, just people in general: "When are you going to graduate to adult writing?" Do you get that same question, and, if so, how do you respond to that?**

I get the question very seldom. My books are for such a young audience, usually, that I think people just assume I will never graduate to adult writing. Dean writes those middle-grade and young-adult novels that if they were just twice as long and more fleshed out, they might actually start looking like adult novels. And he did graduate to adult novels.

John: **He did.**

But the question about graduating to adult fiction doesn't bother me, because I don't care what anybody thinks about children's literature. In fact, I prefer children's literature to be a well-kept secret. I don't want children's writers to be famous.

Carol: **Just rich.**

Just rich. Children's writers should all be making tons of money, and nobody should know who they are.

Cheri: **Why?**

Because I don't wanna be like Shania Twain and have to leave the country because I get hounded everywhere because I'm too famous.

Cheri: **In large part it seems that you write because you have fun at it and you make money at it.**

Yes. I write to make money so that I have time to write for fun.

John: **Do you often think about what effect your books can have on the world?**

There are times when I get the feeling that my writing should save the world, and a quick reality check beats that back into submission.

John: **Why?**

Because the reality is that there are people who write beautiful, inspirational works, and I'm not one of those people. Whenever I try to write inspirational, it ends up being just a bit sappy. I don't want to write sappy. I think that some of my books have educational elements. Some of them teach language-arts concepts.

In fact, at the Randall Museum in San Francisco they introduced me as the king of language-arts picture books. Of course, they probably got that title from my publisher, who has a vested interest in that title. Overall, I'm happy if my books just make somebody have fun for a few moments. That's what I want to get out of a book. I just want to have fun for a while. I don't always want to be inspired.

John: **You're presuming that in order to have an ethical effect, a book has to be preachy about it.**

No, I'm not, actually. I'm saying that, in order to have an ethical effect, it shouldn't be preachy, it should be inspirational—which is different. And I have trouble writing inspirational without being preachy, so I don't want to do that.

John: **I still think—maybe I'm wrong—that even *Pig Pigger Piggest* and *Once There Was a Bull . . . frog* and all of those have kind of a—I don't know how to describe it—but the creatures in them, at bottom, are kind hearted. And they treat each other with a kind of dignity, and I don't know if you notice that or not.**

Only because my wicked characters don't get through the editorial process. I do have one book coming out called *The Remarkable Friendship of Mr. Rat and Mr. Cat*. It's kind of a watered-down Itchy and Scratchy or Tom and Jerry, that kind of thing. But it does show great friendship. You're limited with a picture book on what you can do, because there are a lot of gatekeepers with children's literature, and the younger the literature, the more gatekeepers there are, and the more strict they are on what you can do.

John: **I'm not talking about something that's kept from being in the books. I'm talking about what's in there because you're who you are. For example, take the bullfrog. He's just a cheerful guy and has all these adventures and . . .**
Carol: **John, you're waxing literary here.**

I'm just trying to tell a fun story. Actually, I'm appalled at what some of my characters do. You talk about Bullfrog being a decent character, but in the sequel, *Bullfrog Pops*, he goes on an eating rampage through a town, robbing, stealing, vandalizing, all sorts of things.

John: **But he's so happy doing it.**

I know, but I can think of a lot of people on death row who are very happy doing what they were doing.

Cheri: **So you're saying that Bullfrog is a psychopathic character?**

He's an out-of-control, maniacal eater.

Cheri: **So, when you go off on these wild, crazy *Rolfe the Exploding Elephant* kinds of tangents, what kind of an audience do you have in mind?**

Me.

Carol: **You've always told me that you want to write wacky stuff, and you want to find an editor who likes wacky stuff. What kind of wacky stuff are you talking about, for one thing, and why do you want to write it?**

It's just the kind of humor that I like, and I don't think there's enough of it out there.

Cheri: **Well, define "wacky stuff."**

Roald Dahl, Monty Python, John Scieska, Daniel Pinkwater; the edgier British humor.

Carol: **Those are your models?**

Yeah, those are the kinds of things I like. Woody Allen.

Cheri: **Ew.**

Supposedly, Roald Dahl wasn't a particularly likeable character. And Shel Silverstein either. If he were still alive, I'd definitely keep my kids away from him.

Cheri: **Satan's minion.**

Absolutely.

John: **What other authors do you like?**

I like writers who make me laugh; and it's not always easy to make me laugh. I like Dave Barry. Anybody who's really funny. I like the Lemony Snicket books. Those are funny. I thought they'd get old for me, but they haven't gotten old yet.

Carol: **Do you think you could do a series like that?**

Maybe I could, theoretically. I've got some ideas. I have an idea for a novel that I think I could do. It's about the last trip we took to San Francisco.

Cheri: **But you're not going to share that with us, are you?**

Of course not.

Carol: **How many manuscripts do you send out?**

It's hard to say. Most of mine I don't even send to my agent. Most of mine are sent to whichever editor I think it is good for. I basically have a policy of keeping all my editors overwhelmed. They all have manuscripts that they are considering right now.

Carol: **How many manuscripts each?**

Probably one to four.

John: **This is on kind of a different tangent, but why are there so few LDS picture books?**

In the local market?

John: **Yeah.**

Two reasons. And they're related. I think there's room for a good LDS picture-book market, but picture books are very expensive to produce and to buy. Publishers are hesitant to get into that because they can lose a lot of money on it. But, there also has not been the same perceived need in the LDS market for children's books as in the areas of YA and adult fiction, because, frankly, most children's books on the national market are quite appropriate for LDS children. The older readers get, the edgier the national market gets. The gap grows between what the LDS market wants and what the national market is providing, so there's more of a need for the LDS market to produce something that is unique.

Still, I think there are a lot of things that the LDS market can do with picture books. I'd like to see them create picture books that inspire the national market. I think the LDS market should be producing Max Lucado books, only do it much better.

Carol: **But don't you think local publishers are trying to do that right now and just doing a poor job of it?**

No. No, I don't think so. They're trying to market gift books for the LDS market, so they're looking for specifically LDS themes rather than general concepts that would appeal to a broad national market.

Carol: **I noticed that at the beginning of your career, you were doing more picture books for the local market, the LDS market. Why have you shied away from that?**

They don't publish the kinds of picture books that I do, so I've just had more satisfaction publishing for the national market. I'm not opposed to doing more picture books for the LDS market if I came up with the right idea and if the publishers were amenable to it. I'm interested in doing whatever I can to help the LDS market grow, but as for writing the books myself, I just don't feel that's the thing I should be doing.

Cheri: **Do you think it's possible in the LDS market to have picture books that are really picture books for children and not picture books for adults? What we see coming out are—**

Adult allegory types of books.

Carol: **Do you think there's a way to write these good LDS children's picture books that would work?**

I think there are. For example, every once in a while there's a story in the *Friend* that's kid-friendly and could be adapted into a picture book. There are books on the national market, too, that have messages that appeal to both children and adults, and they're well written. One book, for example, is the book called *The Other Side* by Jacqueline Woodson. It's a great book, and it has a great message for kids, but it has a depth to it that only adults can understand.

So, I think this kind of book could be successful in both markets. I think it wouldn't be a bad thing for people who want to write picture books for the LDS market to study the national-market books that are presenting valuable messages in a kid-friendly fashion and then try to duplicate that.

Carol: **I have a question about your writing culture. Can you talk about the writing culture that you belong to? The community of writers that you belong to?**

The culture. There's a very active and growing children's writing culture in Utah, and it's been exciting. There are a lot of good conferences. The Utah children's writers e-mail list has well over two hundred people, and it's very active.

Participants announce publications and other successes all the time. These are not LDS lists, but the reality is that most people on the lists are LDS. They are a good way to help the community network and grow. We have parties, retreats.

Carol: **There are some people who do not have writers groups. Do you think you need one?**

For my writing, in a minor degree, it's helped. Mostly, it's helped keep me sane because, as a writer, I have a very isolated life. It's me and my one-year-old home all day. So, about the only people I really know are other writers, and they're the only people I have any contact with.

Cheri: **Okay, everybody wants to be a picture-book writer. So, what are your best points to give them?**

And everybody asks me about it. So, to the three people in the universe who haven't heard my answer, here it is. It's the same thing as if you want to write anything. The main problem that I find with people who want to write picture books is that they don't do their homework. They come to picture-book writing because they think it's easy, and so they just sit down and jot off a story and then think they can sell it. It might be a perfectly fine story, and they might have had fun writing it, and their kids might love it—and those are all legitimate reasons for writing—but you've got to know what the market is accepting, and you've got to know the rules of the market. If you're going to break those rules, you've got to know why you're going to break them.

The only way to do all this is to do a lot reading of the kind of thing you want to write, network, talk to people, read books on the subject, get on the Internet, do some research on the subject. I have a lot of research on my website at www.rickwalton.com. This site, by the way, was chosen as one of the top-ten author sites in the country by the New York City Young Writers. They said it was the funniest website they had seen. It's been nice because my website has opened up friendships with other children's writers. I've made friends with the Albanian Aesop, a poet in Albania who's published like fifty books of fables and verse that are quite fun. I was corresponding for a while with a children's author in Iran, and we exchanged books. Authors in Brazil and other countries. It's been fun to get to know people that way.

Carol: **What's the most important thing you teach your students in creative-writing workshops?**

I think the best thing I teach them is that there's a variety of ways to come up with ideas. Most of the time when I'm talking to a group, and I ask how many of them have an easy time coming up with ideas, maybe ten to twenty percent of them will raise their hands, which means that eighty to ninety percent of them have trouble coming up with ideas. So, one of the things I do is teach them lots of easy ways to come up with lots of ideas, and it seems to open up possibilities for a lot of the writers. I also teach them the realities of the market and the importance of networking and doing their research.

Carol: You're teaching them marketing. Is that the first thing people should learn when they want to be writers?

No, and that's a staged question, clearly, because you know better. One of the reasons I wanted to teach at BYU is I wanted to teach a group of writers in a longer setting than the workshops that I had been doing. I wanted to take them from the very beginning all the way to the submission process. But, the first thing we teach them is what makes a good picture book, and we teach them about coming up with good ideas, then we do writing and a lot of critiquing, and it's not until they have some manuscripts and we have gone through the critiquing process that I talk about the marketing process.

Cheri: So, marketing is one of the last things you do.

Marketing is—should be—one of the last things. As a matter of fact, one of my mistakes early on was putting too much stress on the marketing before I had enough good manuscripts. I find this to be one of the major mistakes of beginning writers. Look at any writing conference. The marketing sessions are always cram-packed. Everybody's trying to find the easy way to get their manuscript published.

The easiest way to get your manuscript published—well, besides marrying a doting editor or having lots and lots of money and publishing it yourself—is to focus on the product. I see a lot of children's writers who spend a lot of time— some are fairly successful—focusing on the marketing. They travel a lot, they do lots of public appearances, signings and things like that, lots of marketing tricks. Of course, you need to do a certain amount of that, but my sense is that you're a lot better off if you spend most of your energy on the writing. If you do this, then the marketing, to a degree, will take care of itself.

Most long-term successful writers are successful in the long term because they focused on the writing. There are a lot of people who are successful in the short term who are focused on marketing. They disappear quickly because they don't have anything to feed their long-term career.

Carol: If you couldn't be a writer anymore, what would you do?

I'd probably be a travel agent or a tour guide because I love to travel. Or I'd be a kept man, a stay-at-home househusband. I don't know what I'm qualified to do. One of the reasons I'm a writer is because I've tried every other job there is and bombed out miserably.

TERRY TEMPEST WILLIAMS

Terry Tempest Williams
Creative Nonfiction Writer

Interviewed by Jana Bouck Remy

Described by some as a literary environmental activist, Terry Tempest Williams is perhaps best known for her book Refuge: An Unnatural History of Family and Place. *Her other books include* Red: Patience and Passion in the Desert, An Unspoken Hunger, Desert Quartet: An Erotic Landscape, *two children's books, and additional titles. Her work has been widely anthologized, having appeared in* The New Yorker, The Nation, Outside, Audubon, Orion, The Iowa Review, *and* The New England Review, *among other national and international publications. The original version of this interview appeared in* Irreantum, *summer 2002.*

Interviewer Jana Bouck Remy is a writer and editor who lives in Irvine, California.

How did you find the courage to write so candidly about your family's experiences in *Refuge*? Was the writing process a healing experience

for you? As you travel and meet other women with similar experiences, how do you reach out and comfort them?

In writing *Refuge*, I wanted to honor the memory of my mother, Diane Dixon Tempest, and my grandmother, Kathryn Blackett Tempest. I knew the first requirement in creating this memoir would be to try and tell the truth as I saw it, felt it, and remembered it, in respect to the integrity of their lives. They were women of tremendous courage. I had to try and find that same kind of courage on the page, even if it meant risking my own comfort level within the boundaries of emotional and cultural landscapes.

I kept thinking of a passage in one of Emily Dickinson's letters. She writes, "Life is a spell so exquisite, everything conspires to break it." How can we not respond? I had to believe that in writing about the death of a loved one, that which is most personal is most general. And so in a very real sense, "nakedness was my shield," to quote a Buddhist koan. With the publication of *Refuge*, that turned out to be true.

Many people responded to our family's story because they too had gone through the process of cancer with someone close to them. I could see both the grief and compassion in their eyes. We are told a story, and then we tell our own. We are bound by our vulnerability as human beings. To make this connection on the page or in the world is its own form of comfort. It makes us feel less lonely, knowing that a shared grief is grief endured.

I read that your book tour for *Red: Passion and Patience in the Desert* became a series of "vigils" to honor the thousands killed on September 11, 2001. What were some highlights of that experience?

The publication date of *Red* was, in fact, September 11, 2001. I was in Washington, D.C., for the opening of the Nature Conservancy's photographic exhibit entitled *In Response to Place*. I had written the foreword to the book published simultaneously with the exhibit. The photographers and I were at the Corcoran Museum of Art that morning—scheduled for a press conference at 10:00 A.M.—when we received the news that the World Trade Center had been hit by planes and that the Pentagon had just been struck.

We were directly across from the White House. The security guard basically said, "We have reason to believe the White House is next. Run." Chills shot through us all as we vacated the museum. It was chaos outside. Gridlock. People running across the White House lawn with their cell phones to their ears. The next thing I recall is seven of us crammed into a cab. The driver turned around very matter-of-factly and said, "And just where would you all like to go?" It was at that moment I realized there's no place to go; we are here.

We ended up in the lobby of the Mayflower Hotel and watched the horror on television with all other Americans, not being able to distinguish which sirens were on the TV and which were outside on the streets of Washington. Within minutes, Washington, D.C., became a police state.

Stories. We all have our stories. But the terror of that day, that week in D.C., not being able to get home, still registers in my bones. This was the beginning of the book tour for *Red*. My publisher wanted to know if I wanted to cancel the six-week tour. I said I simply wanted to be of use, that perhaps this was the fate of *Red*, to take these words and find a context for where we found ourselves now as a nation.

Much of *Red* focuses on issues of democracy and why America's redrock wilderness matters to the soul of this country. Pantheon was very supportive. The reading scheduled that Friday in Washington, D.C., at [the bookstore] Politics and Prose became a vigil. The booksellers were wonderful. Together, we tried to create an atmosphere of safety where people felt comfortable to speak. Over two hundred people gathered together. Candles were lit as we sat in silence. I read a short passage and then turned the microphone in the other direction, and we all listened to people share their thoughts and feelings. Stories. It was incredibly moving.

I remember that a cab driver from Afghanistan came in with the person he was driving to the bookstore. "I am afraid," he said. "There is a hole in my heart. We all share this same wound."

For the remainder of my book tour, I tried to be sensitive to where I was and what the situation required. It literally changed day to day, place to place. Many times, the planes were empty, the security severe. The time from September 11 to October 6 seemed like a grace period when we faced our vulnerability and love of country together. It felt like as Americans we were truly contemplating what mattered in our lives. It was a time of pondering the questions together with great compassion.

When the United States began bombing Afghanistan on October 7, something shifted. The conversations became something different. "You are either with us or against us." The rhetoric of war replaced the thoughtful deliberations. And then with the anthrax scares, fear entered the public discourse once again. I tried to read passages from *Red* that offered some kind of solace in the name of the natural world and all that endures in wildness. I also tried to read passages that focused on the power of democracy, that to question even in times of war is another form of patriotism.

This was a very tender time, a very intense time. There were many days and nights when I was both exhausted and scared, but I found great strength in the people I met, in the power of community. Perhaps the most meaningful encounter was in Boulder, Colorado, where Hopi elders were in attendance at a particular gathering. They spoke of what we might do to help bring about the transition from the Fourth World to the Fifth World. It was a gift to hear native wisdom at a time when there was so much hysteria in the media flying about.

In *Leap*, you make some pretty clear connections between environmental ethics and artistic ethics. Could you speak to how that ought to affect LDS writers and their attempts to write about their faith?

*Ought*s and *should*s always make me nervous. I think each writer finds his or her own path within the questions that propel him or her to write. In *Refuge*, the question I was holding was "How do we find refuge in change?" With *Leap*—which I view as a sequel to *Refuge* in many ways—the question keeping me up at night was "What do I believe?"

As explored in *Leap*, the medieval triptych *The Garden of Delights*, painted by Hieronymus Bosch, inspired me, allowed me to see various patterns and connections within my own religion and homeland. The painting became a meditation. Each panel began a different conversation. I recognized that wildness exists in both art and landscape and that the work of both the artist and the activist draws on spiritual beliefs; call it inspiration, motivation. And it is deeply personal.

My father will give anyone who has finished *Leap* a prize. When I asked him what he thought of the book, he said, "I'm stuck in hell, and I don't want to talk about it!" I know it's a difficult and strange book, but it is the book I had to write. Hélène Cixous says, "The only book worth writing is the book that threatens to kill us." I believe her.

There was one very gratifying moment that I will share with you. You never know if a reader will understand what you are attempting to do, especially if you are experimenting with form, which I was in *Leap*. Shortly before Elder Hugh Pinnock died, my father and I went to visit him. He was a childhood friend of my father and a very close friend to our family.

When we arrived, he invited us into their living room. On his table was a copy of *Leap*, with dozens of marked pages and passages. For over two hours, he asked me questions and gave me his impressions of the book. It was an exhilarating discussion on religious ideology, concepts, and principles that ranged from personal visions to authority to the Creation and how an ethic of place might be realized within the church. He truly understood the spirit of the book, particularly the notion of restoration, whether it is the restoration of a painting, a landscape, a body, or the restoration of the gospel of The Church of Jesus Christ of Latter-day Saints. He gave me an extraordinary gift through his faith and belief in the creative process, which is a spiritual process.

Each of us must follow our own creative hunger in our own way, with our own gifts. I believe this is a matter of conscience and consequence. *Leap* brought me to a place of peace out of a place of struggle.

Some theorists have suggested that the body is perhaps a better source of language and understanding than the mind. What do you

think about these ideas, and how do you think an LDS writer could use them to overcome something like the use of religious clichés or institutional thinking?

The body does not lie. Therefore, if we write out of the body, we are writing out of the truth of our lives. This creates a language that is organic and whole. Original. We listen to what is coursing through our veins, what is held within our hearts, what is registered in our bones. Call it cellular knowledge, something akin to instinct. It is here, perhaps, where we write muscular prose that lifts our ideas to both a higher and deeper place where the full range of our intelligence can be found. If we are simply writing out of our heads, there is no weight to our words. They become abstractions that dissipate into the air. This is the realm of rhetoric. The body is the realm of the story. And it is in story that we bypass rhetoric and pierce the heart. We feel it first and understand it later. Memory resides in the body. Memorization resides in the mind.

I think we fall into religious clichés when we become afraid of the deep reflective work that organic writing requires. Clichés follow answers and almost always lead us to sentimentality. Nothing surprises or delights. Original prose that breathes and bleeds follows the questions, the mysteries, the place where we dare to say, "I don't know where I am going on the page." It is the place of discovery and revelation. This is where we can begin to trust the body. The body carries the physical reality of our spirits like a river. Institutional thinking is fearful of rivers because rivers inevitably follow their own path, and that channel may change from day to day, even though the muscle of the river, the property of water remains consistent, life-sustaining, fierce, and compassionate, at once. To write out of the body is to write ourselves into a freedom. It is here we can let go of fear and trust the joy that is held in each movement of the hand, word by word by word.

Is there an antagonism in the church toward the tag "environmentalist"? If so, why is that? And do you think it has had an effect on many LDS writers' choices to skirt environmental topics in their writing?

Maybe I am in denial, but I don't believe there is antagonism in the church toward environmentalists. If we read Genesis about the power and beauty of Creation, if we read about the obligation and responsibility of stewardship toward the land, if we think about what community really means in the broadest sense—I think you can find all these ideas and tenets, if you will, rooted deeply within the principles of the gospel.

True, there may be individuals within the church who do not respond to ecological concerns or who may view environmentalists with suspicion of one kind or another. I certainly have encountered that kind of hostility. But that belongs to the realm of politics, not religion. And for the most part, I do believe there is a desire to move toward more respectful conversation and dialogue between differing parties. In the end, I believe there is more that brings us together than separates us. As writers, one of our challenges is how to create narratives that open hearts rather than close them. How to write in a language that can be heard.

There is a very strong movement in this country centering around the greening of Christianity. I think we are finding it within Mormonism as well. I think it is about seeing the world whole, even holy, not compartmentalizing spiritual concerns here or environmental concerns over there. We are talking about the dignity and sacredness of life.

Why are there not more LDS writers writing about the environment or practicing what is called "nature writing"?

Again, I think it is choosing to compartmentalize literature into various genres, categories, and self-imposed distinctions. We don't have to do that. Some of our strongest LDS writers are creating beautiful, complex characters in tangible landscapes that we can see and hear, taste and feel. Levi Peterson is a writer of place. His characters wear the character of the landscape they inhabit. Certainly Eugene England was a writer of place whose evocations of the natural world were rooted in the sacred whether he was fly-fishing or hiking in the Wasatch Mountains. I think of Marilyn Arnold's work, particularly her novels; they are filled with a love of the land, particularly the subtleties and erosional power of the desert. Susan Howe's poetry is infused with the lyricism and hope of nature. Emma Lou Thayne's poetry and prose is a celebration of Creation in every line or sentence. Her voice is a voice of praise, and it is grounded in her passionate familial embrace of Mount Aire, Sun Valley, or Bear Lake. We may not think of these writers as nature writers, but they are writers whose work carries its own sense of wildness. Orson Scott Card is another example. His novels create other worlds with their own natural histories.

Has the publication of the anthology *New Genesis: A Mormon Reader on Land and Community* effected change related to the church and environmental issues?

I honestly don't know. What pleases me is that it has been used as a text in various classes and departments at Brigham Young University, which means it is creating a discussion around environmental issues and the church. This is all we were hoping for with *New Genesis*: to create conversation. I also know it is being used in book groups and study groups. When we conceived of this idea, Bill Smart and Gibbs Smith and I wanted to dispel the stereotype that only Democrats and non-Mormons cared about the environment. We didn't believe that. We wanted to bring together a diverse group of LDS people who love the land. We wanted to show that this is a bipartisan issue that transcends party lines. And we wanted to ask the question, How has the natural world influenced your testimony of the gospel and, conversely, how has the gospel influenced your view of nature? Again, we felt the most powerful way we could engage in this kind of dialogue would be through personal stories. I love the stories that are held in that collection, from "The Natural History of a Quilt" by Martha Young Moench to the story told by world-renowned biologist Clayton White of going to see peregrine falcons on top of a hospital in New York City and walking through an AIDS ward before he could find his way to the birds, to Hugh Nibley's treatise on air pollution.

We have received some very moving letters from readers saying that the essays in this anthology provided them with "cover," that they could bring forth their views on conservation issues more freely without ridicule. And other readers have said they have appreciated the scriptural references that support a stewardship toward the earth within church doctrine. It gives us a sense of history, a people in place, something we can build on in creating an ethic of place.

In _Leap_, you discuss your relocation to southern Utah. How has this move affected your spirit and your writing? What advice do you have for someone contemplating a similar change, whether geographical or occupational?

Moving to the redrock country of southern Utah has been a great gift for both Brooke and me. It is a much slower pace. We live in a landscape where rocks tell time differently. Time and space. In the desert, there is space. Space is the twin sister of time. If we have open space, then we have time to breathe, to dream, to dare, to create, to play, to pray, to move freely, so freely. This is a landscape of the imagination. You can hear yourself think in the desert. I have become completely addicted to stillness. I am not so easily seduced by speed. I find I just can't move so quickly in the world. It's the silence. This deep, resonant silence. Very humbling.

I love living in an erosional landscape where the lesson of the day is change. It encourages our own changes. I love the extremes of the desert, the intense heat and the intense cold. The wind. There is a reason this country looks the way it does. Wind is the architect of beauty, movement in the midst of peace. This is what I seek as a writer. Art is created through the collision of ideas, forces that shape, sculpt, and define thought. There is a physicality to beauty, to any creative process. The wind reminds me of spirit—what we feel, what has the power to change stone, yet we cannot see.

Living in these redrocks and near the Colorado River has brought the necessity of wildness and why wilderness matters out of the abstract into the real. It terrifies me to think what would have happened to us if we hadn't moved. Movement. Yes, it takes courage to leave the known for the unknown, especially when you are comfortable and established. But both Brooke and I love taking risks, to make ourselves a bit uncomfortable, to see the world with beginner's eyes. This is how we grow. And if we are growing as human beings, then our writing is growing alongside us.

Brooke and I did not plan this—it just happened, or rather we allowed it to happen. When the opportunity or possibility presented itself, we took it. We didn't really think about the security we were leaving behind, certainly not the practicality of what this move would mean. We honestly didn't have a clue how radically our lives would change. We were rooted in Salt Lake City. We had a voice. Here, we will forever be newcomers. I am just beginning to learn the language of what it means to live in rural Utah. But it felt right. Maybe it goes back to what the body knows, that cellular knowledge that carries its own wisdom.

We are in the middle of our lives; why not shake things up a bit? Every morning that I wake up here in this beautiful valley, I think to myself, *I don't have enough time to see all I want to see here, to learn all I want to learn.* And I love the diversity of our neighbors. It's a real community, rural and raw. We are in the process of defining together what it means to weave together a village adjacent to wilderness, how to extend our notion of community to include all life forms: plants, animals, rocks, rivers, and human beings.

It's very different living in the desert versus visiting it. There is an intensity here that can be very difficult. You are exposed in an exposed landscape. Nothing hidden. It's good to get away at times. And then there is always the blissful return to silence, that ringing silence. This is the source and inspiration of my writing.

How do you feel that your Mormonness is reflected in your writing? Have you ever encountered problems with your editors about the Mormon elements of your books? On the other hand, are LDS readers uncomfortable with the unorthodox behaviors you describe in your books?

Mormonism is one of the lenses I see the world through. We cannot escape our conditioning. Why would we want to? I grew up in a Mormon household where that was the focus of our lives. It was the fabric that held everything else together.

I think it's still so much a part of me. I cannot separate out the various strands again; it's my connective tissue. Given that, there are other lenses that I see the world through as well, and that creates an artistic tension in my work.

I have worked with the same editor for over fifteen years, beginning with *Refuge.* He is extraordinary in his support of the Mormon elements of my work. In both *Refuge* and *Leap,* he advocated for more material regarding the church, to always go deeper and further than I may have felt comfortable. We don't see how interesting and peculiar our religion is; so much is taken for granted, a given.

I remember distinctly with *Refuge* in one of the later drafts, he said, "Write against your instincts. . . . When you feel you have said too much about the church or your feelings, say more, go deeper, take us further into the ideas." He was right. But I can tell you that it was not easy. It is never easy to push against the rigidity of the status quo, but in the end, I believe it's about your own integrity. Again, telling the truth as you feel it. One of the curious situations I have found myself in as a writer is that outside of Utah, I am seen as Mormon, whereas inside Utah I am seen as an edge walker, an unorthodox Mormon. What that says to me is that we just have to write out of the center of our own lives.

I love what the writer Clarice Lispector says: "I now know what I want to stand still in the middle of the sea." If you worry about what other people are going to think about you, you better just put down your pencil for good. Writing will always offend someone and provoke powerful emotions. It can also inspire. I believe writing has the capacity to save our lives, both as writers and as readers.

Regarding LDS readers being uncomfortable with the unorthodox behaviors in my books—this makes me smile; it sounds like some kind of aberrant sexual behavior—there's no question some people have been offended. I can think of the scene where Brooke and I break open a bottle of champagne on the edge of Great Salt Lake. I realized that would bother some people, but I also realized that at that particular moment, it was a gesture within our own marriage to celebrate that which was ours. It was what we did. It would be a lie to pretend Brooke and I are devout, practicing Mormons; we are not. But there are many aspects of our religion that we cherish and hold on to. Must it always be all or nothing? I think life is a continual accommodation and adjustment of our beliefs, if we are honest.

There have been so many offensive moments in my books for some LDS readers, now that you bring it up, that there are too many to list, from criticizing Mormon crafts like glass grapes to the fact that Brooke and I don't have children to theological complaints centered around my asking the question "If there is a Godhead, where is the Motherbody?" These critiques don't bother me. I think it is good to have these kinds of discussions. I certainly don't have any answers.

I think of the passage in *Leap* when Brooke and I choose to burn up our marriage certificate. Again, it was a gesture on behalf of renewal. Anyone who has been married for a long time understands the need to rewrite the script one wrote in one's youth. For us it was about growth, daring to ask some tough questions about what we want in our life together now in our forties, which is very different from our needs in our twenties. It is allowing each other to bow to not only our own potential but also the potential of the marriage. I think it is about stepping back and taking a deep breath and saying, "What is working here, and what is not?"

I have to say, on the other hand, I have also had very beautiful and poignant letters from LDS readers who are very supportive, who have found strength and recognition within my books that gave them the courage to continue on their own individual path within the context of the church. I believe it is healthy to have diversity within our beliefs and interpretations. To me, that is the sign of a gracious, compassionate, and expansive theology. I believe there is room within The Church of Jesus Christ of Latter-day Saints for all of us.

Some Mormon authors believe that inspiration plays a part in their artistic creation. Do you ever feel that what you are writing is inspired?

I do not feel my writing is inspired by God, if that is what you mean. I do feel, however, that any serious, deliberate act of writing is inspired by the burning white heat of our desires, our questions, our passions. And there are many sources of inspiration.

What works of Mormon literature have you personally most enjoyed?

To tell you the truth, I am not exactly sure what constitutes Mormon literature. Again, I'm uncomfortable with these distinctions. I loved *The Giant Joshua* by Maurine Whipple. I loved the biography of Annie Clark Tanner, *A Mormon Mother*. Judith Freeman has written some powerful novels with insight into the culture, such as *The Chinchilla Farm* and *Red Water*. Freeman's voice has a literary elegance. Laurel Ulrich is an exquisite writer of great depth and perception. Dorothy Solomon is a voice of grace, integrity, and wisdom. I admire her writing tremendously.

I have appreciated Levi Peterson's voice in his short stories, the humanity of his characters. Certainly, Emma Lou Thayne's poetry is a compassionate embrace of tolerance and peace. I think Carol Lynn Pearson's poems are full of courage and insight. I also appreciate the writing of Walter Kirn, Orson Scott Card, Linda Sillitoe, Marilyn Arnold, and Lyman Hafen. Eugene England gave us all courage and inspiration to continue on the path of individual truth while still standing tall within the faith. In working with students around the country, I am seeing some brave and beautiful narratives written by younger Mormon women, Louisa Bennion from Spring City, Utah, among them. But to limit any one of these writers to "Mormon literature" is to diminish the fullness of their work as writers.

Tell us about your writing habits.

I do not write every day. I write to the questions and issues before me. I write to deadlines. I write out of my passions. And I write to make peace with my own contradictory nature. For me, writing is a spiritual practice. A small bowl of water sits on my desk, a reminder that even if nothing is happening on the page, something is happening in the room—evaporation. And I always light a candle when I begin to write, a reminder that I have now entered another realm, call it the realm of the spirit. I am mindful that when one writes, one leaves this world and enters another.

My books are collages made from journals, research, and personal experience. I love the images rendered in journal entries, the immediacy that is captured on the page, the handwritten notes. I love the depth of ideas and perspective that research brings to a story, be it biological or anthropological studies or the insights brought to the page through the scholarly work of art historians. When I go into a library, I feel like I am a sleuth looking to solve a mystery. I am completely inspired by the pursuit of knowledge through various references. I read newspapers voraciously. I love what newspapers say about contemporary culture. And then, you go back to your own perceptions, your own words, and weigh them against all you have brought together. I am interested in the kaleidoscope of ideas, how you bring many strands of thought into a book and weave them together as one piece of coherent fabric, while at the same time trying to create beautiful language in the service of the story. This is the blood work of the writer.

Writing is also about a life engaged. And so, for me, community work, working in the schools or with grassroots conservation organizations is another critical component of my life as a writer. I cannot separate the writing life from a spiritual life, from a life as a teacher or activist or my life intertwined with family and the responsibilities we carry within our own homes. Writing is daring to feel what nurtures and breaks our hearts. Bearing witness is its own form of advocacy. It is a dance with pain and beauty.

What are your favorites among your works? Which one has been the hardest to write?

I suppose that is like asking a mother which one of her children is her favorite. I couldn't say. Each book was conceived through its own question. Each book sent me on my own pilgrimage. Each book brought about its own sense of inquiry and liberation. Each book wedged its own struggle inside my heart and then released me into another peace of mind. Each book has its own fingerprint and character and audience. Each book has a life of its own, apart from me.

How did you become a writer? In what ways do you think you've developed as a writer during the course of your career? Are there things you can do now that you don't think you could have pulled off successfully when you were first starting to write? What do you do to keep developing as a writer?

These are tough questions. How does anyone "become" a writer? You just write. I have always written, always kept a journal, always loved to read. Perhaps as writers, we are really storytellers, finding that golden thread that connects us to the past, present, and future at once. I love language and landscape. For me, writing is the correspondence between these two passions.

It is difficult to ever see yourself. I don't know how I've developed or grown as a writer. I hope I am continuing to take risks on the page. I hope I am continuing to ask the hard questions of myself. If we are attentive to the world and to those around us, I believe we will be attentive on the page. Writing is about presence. I want to be fully present wherever I am, alive to the pulse just beneath the skin. I want to dare to speak "the language women speak when there is no one around to correct us."

What's ahead for you?

I honestly have no idea what's ahead, what's coming up for me. I find that very exciting. I am not working on anything in particular. I have made a conscious decision to retreat and focus on home. We are restoring the place where we live with native plants so it blends more naturally into the juniper and sagebrush flats. I am reading a great deal of poetry. It is time for me to lay low and listen.

For now, I just want to walk in the desert.

DAVE WOLVERTON

Dave Wolverton
Novelist

Educated at Brigham Young University, Dave Wolverton received the International Writers of the Future Gold Award in 1987, the highest honor available to an amateur writer of science fiction and fantasy. Within two weeks he was offered a three-novel contract with Bantam Books. He first made the New York Times *bestseller list at number seven with his novel* Star Wars: The Courtship of Princess Leia. *Writing as David Farland, he has become well known for his Runelords series. In addition, he has been involved in designing intellectual properties for multimedia, stories that can be transferred from books to movies, television, comics, video games, and other mediums. The original version of this interview appeared in* Irreantum, *winter 2000–01.*

You've written a variety of different types of stories within science fiction and fantasy, from quasi-military science fiction to swashbuckler novels, "soft" science fiction in *Serpent Catch* and *Path of the Hero*, juveniles, Star

Wars stories, and fantasy with your books published under the name David Farland. What do you think are some of the advantages of writing across such a wide range? Are there some disadvantages?

You forgot to mention a few. I've also written literary short stories, comedy in the novel *A Very Strange Trip*, and some young adult horror with the Mummy series. I also write in a number of mediums: I design and script video games, am working on some movie scripts, have written poetry and music lyrics, and so on. And of course I write for people of all ages. I have a children's picture book I've been half-heartedly trying to market and have written many middle-grade books and young adult novels.

Of course, the primary disadvantage to writing so broadly is that it can make it hard to develop an audience. If I had written just cyberpunk military SF, I might have a staunch following of hard-core fans. Instead, it seems to me that people are discovering me all over the place. Many months I get fan mail on every adult book I've written.

On the other hand, I think that writing broadly has its advantages. The works of Orson Scott Card and Zenna Henderson are more powerful precisely because you never know what direction one of their stories might twist. Their work might be funny one moment, horrific the next, heart-warming a third. I love that kind of surprise, the suspense that comes from not knowing what to expect.

So I like to write different pieces to fit my mood, and I want to be versatile. But with me, I suspect that it goes even deeper. I've had hard-core science fiction fans ask, "Why don't you write more books like *On My Way to Paradise*, instead of that fantasy or those kids' books?'" The answer is simple: Everyone is entitled to read great fiction.

Readers have commented on the strong moral element in many of your books. How do you feel that your Mormonness is reflected in your fiction?

I try to write what feels true and right and good to me. I tend to think of the action, the world, the characters—and in some cases the magic systems—as metaphors that help me explore a theme. I'd like to put the emphasis on *explore*, because I don't approach my tale with the idea that I have a message to cram down the throat of the world.

Instead, the tale normally focuses on some moral issue, and during the months or years that I spend writing, I find myself meditating on that issue time and time again. The result is that I find I can't plot a novel until I understand how the action can be successfully resolved within the confines of the controlling metaphors. And almost without fail I finally come to understand what it is I want to say and how the story should resolve while I'm contemplating the scriptures.

A friend once told me he had a dream in which someone told him all my books tend to simply rehash the plan of salvation. In a sense, I think he may be right. My best stories are like vast, complex parables or allegories that hopefully will help you understand life even when you're in the act of trying to escape from the daily pressures of the world.

At the same time, I realize now that in all of my hundreds of pieces of writing, I've never written about a Mormon character. I don't think it is because of an act of cowardice on my part. I'm glad to be Mormon, and I am glad to tell others about it. I think, rather, that the reason is twofold.

First, I try to write for a wide audience. My audience isn't the five million Mormons who speak English. The pool includes all seven billion people living today and hundreds of billions more who have yet to be born.

Beyond that, I don't write about Mormons partly due to the fact that I'm a convert to the church. I joined at age sixteen, and I have never really felt as if I were culturally a Mormon. Perhaps I should explain that. Whether you are aware of it or not, to some degree young converts are ostracized from the church. Some parents are leery about letting their daughters date recent converts, and so on. You will, of course, hear children comparing how long their families have been in the church, and even adults do it. For example, in an issue of *Irreantum* I noted that Terry Tempest Williams is a "fifth-generation" Mormon. Why was that pointed out? Is it a matter of pride or a marketing ploy? I served a mission. I've been a member for twenty-six years. Does the fact that she's a fifth-generation Mormon mean she's more of a Mormon than I am?

It may surprise you, but I think the answer is yes.

In order for us to attain Zion, we have to create a Zion society that is vastly different from the society we now live in. We have to learn to see the world and think about it and feel about it differently from what we now do. We have to purge ourselves from the violence, greed, lust, and laziness that are intrinsic to modern American culture. It is a work that will be accomplished not in decades but over a period of generations. I think there is a valid reason why so few of our General Authorities are converts.

In observing members of the church, I've felt a sense of want. I've wished that I were born in the church, that I had the kind of family that held family home evening and family prayer. As a young member of the church, I was keenly aware that my family life was nothing like that of most other members. My grandfather ran away from home when he was thirteen and joined the mob, and for much of his life he ran whorehouses and gambling casinos and worked as a smuggler. The advice he gave me to live by was not the kind of thing you normally got in family home evening. For example, when I was eleven he told me, "Never commit a crime with an accomplice. He'll always rat you out." Or, "Remember that the sole purpose of a life of crime should be to maximize your potential income while minimizing the risk of incarceration; and always remember that the risk of incarceration for a crime rises in proportion to the level of violence in the crime."

My father ran away from home when he was thirteen. He managed to avoid a life of crime, but his parenting skills left much to be desired. As a child, I always felt I was on unstable ground. My father was extremely violent and abusive. As a five-year-old child I was convinced that either he would kill one of us kids or we'd have to kill him in self-defense. I often wished my mother would find the courage to leave him.

So I've got a dark past. I have a strong testimony and love for the church. I've served a mission, taught seminary, and so on, but I've never felt I completely belong because I was not raised in this culture.

I was surprised to read Richard Dutcher's interview in *Irreantum*, because he obviously does feel acculturated, even though he also was raised in less-than-perfect circumstances. It may be the age at which he was brought into the church. He joined at age eight. Psychologists say most kids begin developing their self-identity, forming their worldview, at around age ten or eleven. By then I had certainly realized I didn't belong to any group I could see, and I've always maintained a strong sense of individuality.

A lot of Mormon writers seem to be attracted to science fiction and fantasy. What do you think are some of the reasons for that?

I could name a dozen contributing factors, but in the end I think they're attracted primarily because science fiction and fantasy are literatures that allow you to express moral themes. I first fell in love with science fiction while reading C. S. Lewis's *Perelandra*, and soon after that I discovered fantasy with *Lord of the Rings*. Both authors were deeply moral people, and I think genre bestsellers today remain so. Look at authors like Terry Brooks, Anne McCaffrey, and Stephen Donaldson; all of them are wonderful, deeply moral people.

On the other hand, I really believe that if you tried to write an LDS brand of moral fiction in the literary field, selling to magazines like *The New Yorker*, you wouldn't find any buyers. The editors in those fields have been trained to believe that moral literature is somehow tainted or suspect.

Ever since your days at BYU, you've been actively involved in a community of Mormon science fiction and fantasy writers and fans. How do you think that involvement has affected your writing? You've also been involved in several writers' groups. Could you describe what a writers' group, at its best, can do for a writer? How can you tell if the writing group you're in is a good one—at least, for you?

To some degree we're all products of our environment. I've learned a lot from all of the people I've worked with and hope they're better off for knowing me.

I suspect the ideal writers' group would be small—four or five people at the maximum—so you could get through a critique session in an hour or two. Your companions would be people who care passionately about what they write, and they would be committed to become the best artists of their generation. These people wouldn't just read books on writing; they would invest time to discover things that no one else has yet learned. Beyond that, they wouldn't just study the craft of writing but would discuss issues of career management.

If your writing group doesn't fit that mold, then you should see if you can change it or change to another group. But there are two kinds of writers' groups you definitely ought to get out of. The first one is the group where destructive personalities are involved, where writers constantly belittle one another. If you really feel people are picking on you, get out. The other destructive group is the one where no one is a real writer, where people go month after month without finishing a story but still come to weekly meetings to talk about writing.

Some of your earliest story publications were mainstream stories in *Inscape*, BYU's student mainstream literary magazine. At one time you were working on a mainstream novel. Do you think you're ever likely to return to writing mainstream fiction?

You used two terms in the same sentence, mainstream and literary. I don't think of them as the same. Literary stories are written for a small audience that is trained to criticize your work according to a certain set of conventions. On the other hand, the mainstream audience is the huge mass of uneducated readers who consume stories for pleasure.

When I was in college, I did write some literary pieces and even won a few awards, but the stories felt false to my sensibilities. I soon began to realize that I didn't just dislike literary fiction; I found it morally repulsive. The reason was that as I studied, I recognized that in order to publish one had to toe the line when it came to a number of literary proscriptions, literary rules. Many of these rules were first devised to promote literatures that are contrary to my own worldview.

Let me give you an example. When I was reading heavily in *The New Yorker*, *Atlantic Monthly*, and smaller reviews during the mid-eighties, it soon became apparent that the editors rarely published formal stories—stories having a beginning, middle, and end, along with some internal coherence. Now, this proscription against formal stories arose in an intellectual climate influenced by Social Darwinists, existentialists, and the secularism of post-structuralist thought. Critics pointed out that since, in their view, there is no creator—since life is really just a meaningless, random series of events that our minds struggle to make sense of—then it is wrong to write formal stories, to create a series of events designed to lead to a certain emotional, intellectual, or moral conclusion.

Well, in certain critics' eyes, this proscription seems reasonable. If you don't believe in God and if the purpose of your work is to depict the universe as you perceive it to be, then it makes sense that you shouldn't write formal stories.

Seeing this, literary writers began to abandon form in the 1920s. They either wrote slice-of-life pieces in the style of Virginia Woolf; or they truncated stories, cutting off the beginning and ending to create a slice-of-life effect, as Hemingway did in "A Clean, Well-Lighted Place"; or they sought other means to purposely obfuscate the form and meaning in their stories, such as leaving the ending unresolved.

Of course, this abandonment of form didn't take place all at once. It has gone in and out of style over and over again in the past eighty years, but when I was writing literary fiction, form was definitely out.

The problem is, I'm not a Darwinist. I know for a fact there is a God and our lives have meaning and purpose. I believe that there is an order to the universe, that we perceive stories because we live in a world of cause and effect, and that the Lord expects us to learn from our experiences. So I bridled at the proscription against form. It seemed obvious to me that form is a useful tool and that one can write a formal story so beautifully that the form is difficult to see for the casual reader.

I also dismissed the entire realist movement because it was obvious to me that the father of modern American realism, William Dean Howells, was merely a socialist who used his position as the editor of the most prestigious magazine of his time in order to reward others for writing his kind of economic fiction. I'm not a socialist. I'm not a capitalist, either. I'm a consecrationalist.

I dismissed impressionism because it was designed to appeal only to intellectual elitists, not to communicate with real readers. Indeed, for a while it seemed to me that this appeal to elitism was the primary motivation for the emphasis on style in the literary markets. Almost without fail, literary writers would purposely try to elevate their fiction so that it could not be understood and appreciated by the average man, woman, and child.

Now, let me make this point: I find elitism to be reprehensible in any form. People who imagine they are better than others simply because they wear the right clothes, or have more money, or more talent, or are stronger are just plain wrong. An invalid drooling in a nursing home is a child of God, with the divine potential to father worlds. The welfare mother down the street is a glorious being.

We have been smart enough to outlaw certain forms of elitism. We don't allow kids to pummel one another in the streets in order to prove who is better. We don't allow multimillionaires to use their wealth to bludgeon the poor into submission to prove that they are better. Yet intellectual elitism runs unchecked in intellectual circles. Critics pummel one another with words, trying to prove their arguments in order to gain prestige and money. They try to ruin one another's careers and sully one another's reputations. I've seen critics and college professors shouting at one another and calling each other idiots, each claiming to have an IQ higher than the fellow sitting next to him.

I found this intellectual barbarism to be so prevalent in literary circles that I just didn't want to have anything to do with literary writing anymore. I don't feel a driving need to prove I'm smarter or more talented than anyone else. I write for other reasons. I want to write stories that move, enlighten, and entertain my readers. Sometimes I want to write stories because the words themselves seem to crave release.

And I believe that when one is purposely obfuscating the meaning of a tale in order to exclude those who aren't trained to read it, it's reprehensible. When one is writing artsy stories—overly stylized tales—in order to receive the praise of critics or win the Nobel Prize and thereby receive monetary reward, it's a shame.

So, at age twenty-five I decided to have nothing to do with literary fiction.

Over the years my views on literary fiction have softened somewhat. Certainly, intelligent people have the right to communicate at their own level. Yet I wonder why any writer who is trying to make a living feels he has to exclude ninety-nine percent of humankind from his audience. Why not write on multiple levels, in the manner of Frost and Shakespeare, so that the masses can enjoy it too?

As for the emphasis on style, I'm convinced that more than just elitism is at work. The emphasis on style is a matter of survival for literary writers. For any story to feel safe to an audience and therefore become accessible, there must be a fantastical element to it. If, as is so often done in literary fiction, your characters are restricted to common sorts of folks, and if your setting is restricted to a contemporary setting, and if your conflicts are restricted to the common types of conflicts that your readers will face, then the only fantastical element left to play with is the style in which you depict the tale. In such cases, the author's flair and personality becomes a primary draw to the tale—otherwise, no sane reader would suffer through the story.

Because of these and other observations, I decided to quit writing for the literati. I enjoy beautifully told tales as well as anyone, but I don't go looking for them in *The New Yorker*. Eventually I decided I had to try to strip away all of the false precepts I was learning in college and figure out how to write in ways that really can touch common people—while holding to those principles that worked. To a large degree I had to unlearn how to write.

I discovered I'm a formalist and I'm a fantasist. Beyond that I'm trying to develop my own philosophies, trying to discover for myself how to create more powerful stories.

For your fantasy *Runelords* series, you adopted the pen name of David Farland. What were your reasons for doing that? Has it been successful in accomplishing what you had hoped for?

Scott Card once raved about my third novel in his "Books to Look For" section of *The Magazine of Fantasy and Science Fiction*. At the end of the review, he said, "Make sure that you look down on the bottom shelf, where Wolverton's work is wont to be." When I read that line, I recalled that years ago the Campbell Soup Company had commissioned a study in which they found that ninety-two percent of shoppers wouldn't stoop over at the grocery store to pick up their favorite can of soup from the bottom shelf.

So I began to study the shelf life of novels by such fine writers as Roger Zelazny and Gene Wolf, and I noticed that the chains didn't reorder those authors' works very well. I decided that having a last name that begins with the letters T through W has prematurely ended many an author's career. So I decided to change my name.

I had a friend named Greg McFarland, and I thought his last name would make a wonderful pen name—except that it would put me on the shelf along with McCaffrey, McKillip, and all the other Mc's. But then I remembered an old friend named Jennifer Farland and decided to simply use Farland.

It has worked out very well. My first two Farland novels earned more than all my other books combined. In the United Kingdom, back in Tolkien country, my early sales record far outstripped that of Robert Jordan, and I've been touted there as the "new king of fantasy."

But I'm not sure it has to do entirely with the name change. I'm also writing to a wider readership, and I feel more morally centered in fantasy than I did in science fiction. I think readers notice it too. It makes sense that if you write better books, you'll sell more copies. Here's the opening from a review: "It seems that about once a decade a writer of traditional fantasy arrives on the scene who stands head and shoulders above the competition. Steven Donaldson and Robert Jordan come to mind. Last year, David Farland joined that elite order with *The Runelords*. The second volume, *Brotherhood of the Wolf*, will serve to cement his reputation."[1] As I say, I feel more at home in this genre, and the critics are taking notice.

There's a lot of violence in some of your work. Are there people you would steer away from reading your fiction?

No. I don't want to offend anyone, but I'm reminded of an incident one Christmas. I was in the store shopping, and a woman who'd had *The Runelords* recommended to her stopped me. She was very sensitive to violence. While trembling and with tears in her eyes, she told me it had been hard for her to read my novel because certain passages were emotionally overwhelming. I really thought she would reprimand me. She then added, "Yet I've never read a novel that had more beauty and truth in it. It's one of the few books that I won't read just once. I plan to read it again and again."

So, I don't want to steer anyone away from that book. I write about violence because I have a violent past. I write about it because I know it intimately, and I hate it.

But lately I've been giving a lot of thought to what constitutes a moral hero, and I realize I want to write a story that isn't so shocking. I suspect in the near future I'll be writing some gentler, kinder fiction.

What kinds of responses have you encountered from readers who discovered you are LDS?

Nothing spectacular. No one has thrown eggs. One or two fans have begun investigating the church after learning that I was LDS, nothing more.

What kinds of responses have you encountered from church members who discovered you were a science fiction and fantasy writer?

It depends. If they like the genre, they're excited. Otherwise they think I'm probably some kook who wears Spock ears in the bathtub.

You were coordinating judge of L. Ron Hubbard's Writers of the Future contest for several years. What do you think are some of the major mistakes beginning writers make that prevent them from being published—or if they are published, from finding enthusiastic readers?

The single biggest problem is that most new writers don't want to invest the time it takes to develop a writing talent. They don't want to read, they don't want to study, and they don't want to practice. I don't know of another art form—other than possibly film-making—where people approach the work with such gonzo expectations.

Within the Mormon literary community, do you think science fiction and fantasy receive the recognition and respect they deserve?

Why does that question bother me so much? Why does it make me mad?

It's because you're asking the wrong question. The question shouldn't be, "Do we receive the recognition and respect we deserve?" It should be, "Are you confused enough and worldly enough to care if the literary community respects your work?"

First, let me say I don't know that this genre deserves any more respect than romance or westerns or horror or children's literature. Everyone deserves to read great books. I said that before, but let me expand upon the point.

Back when Spencer W. Kimball gave his address urging members to take up the arts,[2] he said that he "envisioned a day when Mormon artists would take a lead in every field of the arts." I really believe he meant it. I don't think he was saying we should settle for a few highly placed writers in the field of science fiction. I believe he meant we should have comic screenwriters working on television—have you noticed how pervasively vile it has become?—and children's writers leading the industry in picture books, and romance novelists teaching the world what true love really is, and video game writers creating something better than another shooter game. The Lord wants us to write for every age group, in nearly every genre, and for every medium. Everyone deserves great literature. I don't think this is just me talking; I think this is the Lord's view on the matter.

And if I could share one thing I've learned about writing, it's this: forget about respect. Most of the world is made up of nonreaders. Only one in fifty people on the street will read a science fiction book this year. So forget about fame. Forget about being lauded by legions of fans.

More importantly, forget about seeking the praise of men. Lehi taught that the one defining characteristic of those who belong to the church of the devil is that they seek the praise of the world and crave the flattery of men. I believe that to the extent any Mormon artist seeks the praise of the world, he will begin to mimic the art of the world, and anything in his work that is good and beautiful and better than what the world has to offer will therefore be diminished.

I see this happen time and again. At times it's almost funny. I went to the Sundance Film Festival one year and walked into the writers' café. Everyone there was dressed the same: black turtlenecks, black pants, black bomber jackets, funky goatees, and little silver stud earrings. I took one look at them, and my heart sank. "Look at all these people," I thought, "trying to be creative while dressed exactly the same!"

Whenever you try to be part of the in-crowd, you immediately begin writing out of fear. You begin mimicking others in order to win their praise. But remember that the prophet didn't say, "I want all of you people to go out and mimic the world." He said, "I envision the day when Mormon artists are leaders in every field of the arts."

We're to become leaders. I believe that so long as we struggle to learn the true principles behind good storytelling, the Lord will guide us. As in any endeavor, it isn't enough to simply pray about it. We need to study what has been done in the past, maybe even take the danged college classes, and then prayerfully approach our work.

So I don't write for the critics. I don't write for the literati. I think I would be perfectly happy if I never won another award. Instead, I write for my audience. That is enough.

Some Mormon readers have seen your magic system in the *Runelords* series as a commentary or critique on our current economic system from a gospel, law-of-consecration perspective. Do you agree with this interpretation?

Absolutely! The central themes of the novels deal with economics and morality.

In the books, men are able to take "endowments" of attributes from others. These attributes include brawn, wit, grace, stamina, and so on. Those who take endowments are called Runelords, while those who give up their abilities are called Dedicates.

When a Runelord takes an endowment, he grows in attributes, while the giver is diminished. Thus, Runelords can become stronger and stronger, wiser and wiser, almost godlike—while those who give up their attributes are diminished. For example, those who give up their wit become fools, while those who give up brawn become weak as kittens, and so on.

When a Runelord takes an endowment, he takes it for life—until either he or his dedicate is killed. If the lord dies first, the endowment returns to the dedicate. If the dedicate dies first, the lord loses the use of that attribute.

Given the fact that dedicates are weak and sickly, given the costs involved in taking endowments, and given the fact that a lord will lose his powers if his dedicates die, it becomes incumbent upon the Runelord to care for his dedicates.

That's the basic concept behind the magic system. In many ways, it is similar to our economic system. Employers search for employees based upon their qualifications. For a day laborer, the main qualification needed might roughly be called brawn, while for an accountant the main qualification might roughly be called wit.

We enter into an unwritten contract under which the employee promises to work for his employer continuously so that he and his family might be supported. Greedy men are then in a position to take advantage of their employees. The goal from a business perspective is to get as much work from an employee as possible while paying the least amount in wages. Under such a system, employers may become rich—so rich that men like Bill Gates lead lives far more elegant than any emperor of ages past—while everyone around them becomes diminished in the process.

That's part of what *Runelords* is about, and if I were to keep it at that level, as a simple vilification of capitalism, it would be no deeper than Orwell's *Animal Farm*.

Orwell, of course, wrote about communism, but somehow it's easier to criticize another person's beliefs than our own. We live with capitalism. Many Latter-day Saints believe that, like the U.S. constitution, it is a system inspired by God. But it's not. Working for another man, dedicating your life in order to enrich him, is nothing at all like dedicating yourself to building the kingdom of God. It's nothing like living a life in which every hour of service is offered in an effort to seek the eternal welfare of others. Capitalism robs every one of us. I've heard rich men say that the greatest blessing of being wealthy was that it gave them time to study the scriptures, to ponder and pray more. Yet most poor people don't recognize that their greatest curse is that they don't have time for those things. I suspect that if we as a people moved closer to the Lord, if we all had the proper time to devote to our families and our community and to the maintenance of our spiritual lives, most of the problems in our society would melt away. But we're so close to capitalism, we've lived with this abomination so long, that we're blinded to the suffering it brings.

So, in the novel I explore questions like, "Why do men perpetuate this system, both as employers and employees?" and "How can a person who is good but who is born into a corrupt society manage to live within the system without becoming part of the problem?"

Now, this all might sound a bit preachy, but it's not. In my own mind, I'm legitimately trying to figure out under what circumstances it is ethical to hire someone to work for you full time, to make someone dependent upon you as a means of support, to take the best part of him and subvert it to your own purposes.

The answer is that I suspect that regardless of how well meaning you are, the practice is at its heart unethical. By subverting a man to your own ends, even as a benevolent employer, you immediately place him in a situation that limits his ability to grow spiritually. How can an employee who is working for me twelve hours a day to meet a deadline possibly take proper care of his family? How can he continue to study the scriptures or continue on his mission of developing his godly potential?

To me it seems like a valuable thing to write about, though few of my readers consciously understand what I'm getting at. Still, I've received dozens of letters from non-member fans who point out that my hero, Gaborn, is a decent person who is trying to live within a corrupt society. They talk about it as if they discovered it themselves—and that delights me! It delights me because the message gets across without my having to hammer people on the head.

How strongly does your sense of the evils of buying another's labor affect you when you need to hire someone?

I typically hire people for short periods to do a specific job. I try to allow them to set their own schedule and usually pay them more than they ask, giving a bonus at the end of the contract. It seems to me to be the only ethical way to resolve the question.

Most of us don't live in an economy where we can work for ourselves. Is it possible to hire people's labor at a price that allows them to take care of their lives and require no more time from them than, say, agrarian labor, which has a long off-season?

This question is not as easy as it sounds. First, I'm convinced that the average man could be self-employed if he wanted to, but too many people are beaten down and lack the faith in themselves to try self-employment.

Second, far too often, instead of attending to our eternal needs we work long hours to build junky cars or CD players or televisions in order to compete with other guys who are building junky cars, CD players, and televisions. Then we waste millions of dollars advertising our wares so that people will be convinced they need our junk. Our time is wasted in mindless materialistic pursuits.

How much time is thus wasted? I think the answer would surprise you. First, imagine we lived in a world where we didn't build inferior products. Add to that a system where the poor didn't labor to enrich the wealthy and the corrupt. How much less work would you have to do? I'm fairly certain that you could more than cut your workday in half. I believe you could cut it by as much as seventy-five percent.

Did you intend the endowment system as an economic metaphor from the beginning, or was it something you discovered as part of the writing and revision process?

I intended it from the beginning. I knew I wanted to write about economics, and I considered a number of possible magic systems and how they might work. After months of deliberation, the idea for the Runelords hit me. Immediately I saw its potential as a metaphor.

How does writing this as a story rather than an essay affect the way you explore your ideas about economics?

An essay might be the best way to explore ideas, but I tell stories in order to elicit an emotional response to those ideas. It's the emotional response I'm after. On one occasion I spoke with Tyler Moulton, an editor at Covenant, who mentioned that psychological studies indicate that real learning may not be able to take place without an emotional stimulus. What we read in essays typically seems rather bland and is easily forgotten. Meanwhile, a story literally transforms you. For example, I received an e-mail from a young lady who felt that after reading my novel she had experienced some break-throughs and finally understood the relationship between free agency, the creation of real properties, and the moral way in which time and properties should be transferred. I have no idea what religion she is, but her hastily jotted fifteen-page essay convinced me that although her thoughts were coming swiftly and were therefore unrefined, she was experiencing a real breakthrough, and she will be a more moral person for it.

Does a story allow you to state your views more strongly, or does embodying your views in characters moderate them?

Both. I can state my views more dramatically, and thus more strongly, in a story. That's part of the reason for storytelling. At the same time, there are moments when a writer needs to back off from the potential of a story. A story can be too powerful for your audience.

What is your typical writing process?

I like to plot my stories. I think first about my audience, what they might like and need in fiction. People seldom really understand why they read what they do, so this can become an involved process. I look for what I call the draws to the work, the often-subtle emotional triggers that authors in that genre are pulling. Once I feel grounded in my audience's hidden needs—and to me that is often the most important point, the motivating factor for writing at all—I will begin plotting a story.

Now, getting grounded might take me only a couple of hours, or it might take weeks, months, or even years. If I'm writing a story similar to one I've written before, one for a known audience, then plotting is easy. But if I'm trying to break into a new market, it might force me to study bestsellers in the genre.

At that point, I may also consider the theme I want to deal with, or I may just be content to let the themes come out as I write. But once I feel grounded, I can sit down and plot. This process can go quickly. It typically takes me about an hour per hundred pages of finished text.

Once I have my outline I can begin writing immediately, but I prefer to let the story gel for three or four months. The outline may change, but typically I arrive at a point after about four months where I must write. When I reach that point, I write straight through, usually twenty to forty manuscript pages per day.

Sometimes I write my novels in thirds—complete a third, do a rewrite until it feels solid, and then move on. But at other times I write it all in a rush.

I typically write three story drafts. I call them story drafts because early on I try not to think too much about language and word choice. I'm far more interested in the larger elements of plot, pacing, characterization, and theme. I may throw out characters, combine characters, or decide the theme requires a whole new beginning to the novel or a whole new end, and then I do whatever is required.

Once I've got the story down, I make two to four more passes where I concentrate primarily on the sentence-by-sentence elements of the tale: the tone, character voices, beefing up descriptive passages, tightening excess wordage, and so on.

As for reader comments, I don't seek them out anymore, so they don't play a part. My readers usually consist of my publishers' editorial staffs.

You've played a lot in your fiction with variations on what it means to be human, from the chimeras of *On My Way to Paradise* to the endowment system of the *Runelords* series. To what degree do you see human behavior as determined by biological and environmental influences? How are those reconciled with free will? How can fiction serve as a tool to explore interactions like these?

At one time I studied medicine with the idea of becoming a genetic engineer. I've heard doctors describe human beings as "a complex set of chemical interactions." In short, there are those who believe we are only biology, that even the societies we have developed are an outgrowth of our biological needs. To a great degree, that's true. So much of how we perceive the world and react to it is biologically motivated.

Then, of course, there are the behaviorists who recognize that much of our behavior is attributed to conditioning. We think and act as we do usually because that is the way we've seen it done before.

But, of course, we have free will. We're not pinballs doomed by gravity and inertia to trickle down a certain slot. Our senses may tell us that a fire is hot and that we should not touch it. Yet I can stick my hand into a flame and burn it to a crisp, if I so desire. I can override my biological impulses. The flesh may be tired, but I can still choose to get off my duff and go home teaching.

I can also override my sociological conditioning. I can decide to eat popcorn for breakfast even though my mother would never have approved. I can choose to pay tithing, even though my parents might never have done the same.

Ultimately, every biological urge and every socially induced behavior can and must bow to free will. It is the single greatest gift God has given us. I believe that we must learn to restrain evil urges and magnify our righteous desires. We must recognize the ills in our own society and overcome them. Our ability to become gods is limited only by our interest in exerting free will in order to remake ourselves in the image of God.

So that's what I think about biology, behaviorism, and agency.

But for a long time I've been fascinated by the possibility of redefining ourselves, by exerting our agency to "fix" our biological weaknesses. I don't think it is a sin to redefine ourselves. When God made Adam, he said he was good; he didn't say he was perfect. We have physical ailments and frailties and room for improvement. For example, doctors are talking about using gene therapy so that we can eradicate genetically transmitted ailments, repair severed spinal columns, or regenerate damaged organs such as the pancreas or liver.

The uses for such therapy are boundless. I suspect that within two hundred years we won't have organizations such as Alcoholics Anonymous. We will simply cure alcoholics by genetically reprogramming them. Even today, I'd bet most people would be willing to undergo such therapy. For example, there are a couple of drugs being tested that, when used in combination, will boost a dog's intelligence by about forty percent. I suspect that when such drugs become available on the market, we will be forming lines to take them. Who wouldn't want to be forty percent smarter?

Well, a hundred years from now, gene therapy may be as common as pills are today. But I'm convinced that some ills aren't categorized and treated properly.

For example, suppose a drug treatment came out on the market that would cure you of excess greed. Would you take it? Would you force it upon those who steal? And what of the consequences? What if you do remove your own greed, so that your only desire is to serve others, to live like some holy man in India, wearing only rags for clothes and eating only rice that other beggars would not touch?

Issues like this fascinate me. What are the consequences of knowing too much, or wanting to work too hard, or even of having a heart empty of fear? If we reengineer ourselves so we can reach such goals, does that mean we have given up free will?

I don't think so. Our biological impulses have long served as shackles to mankind. We're entering an era when even our basic chemistry will bow to free will.

But once we redefine ourselves in biological terms, will we truly be happier? Exploring issues like that is what science fiction storytelling is all about. We can think about our future, about the potential directions and misdirections we might take. And when I tell a story, when you see how such a world might feel, you can learn more thoroughly than if you and I merely sat down and explored an abstract idea.

Many of the activities a writer engages in—for example, participating in conventions, book signings, and interviews—could be classified as self-promotion and marketing. How important a part of an author's work do you think those are? Are there noneconomic benefits from these activities, such as getting in closer touch with your readers?

You know, ultimately self-promotion may be a trap. J.K. Rowling isn't doing national book tours or heading up her own fan club. Instead, she got a big publisher, one with excellent distribution, who put together a fantastic promotional campaign and hired publicists to help stir the pot. In short, they created the rage.

It may seem to outsiders in the industry that the Harry Potter books are a phenomenon, that Rowling has done something that can't be duplicated, but just remember that Scholastic, her American publisher, also happened to be the backer for the Goosebumps series five years ago, the series through which R.L. Stine suddenly accounted for about fifty percent of all sales in the young adult market! Scholastic also happens to be behind Animorphs, the Babysitter's Club, and many other apparent phenomena.

The truth is that if you want to beat Rowling, you have to wait for the furor to die and then go push an equally good product with Scholastic. They seem to be the only publisher on the planet that has the clout to do it. Let them turn you into a superstar.

As for getting in touch with my readers, I just put my website and e-mail addresses in the back of my books now. I may get as many as a dozen pieces of fan mail a day that way, and I'm learning more than ever before just exactly what my readers like and don't like about my work.

In what ways do you think you've developed as a writer during the course of your career? Are there things you can do now that you don't think you could have pulled off successfully when you were first starting to write? What do you do to keep developing as a writer?

Oh my gosh, is that a loaded question. When I first began writing, it was the first day of class in the first grade. The teacher asked me to write my name. I didn't know how, so I asked the girl sitting next to me. She said this is how: N-A-N-C-Y. When I look back at my first book, I feel as if I just wrote N-A-N-C-Y.

Learning how to write is a continual process. There are things I don't know yet, things I won't have time to learn in this life. I rarely read magazines like *Writer's Digest* because the articles for beginning writers tend to rehash ideas I've heard a thousand times. But I do study intensely. Over the past three years I've devoted thousands of hours to delving into audience analysis and studying ways one can imbue a work with epic quality. I've learned a lot about both topics, but you can't find much of what I've learned in textbooks. I have to get it through direct observation and analysis.

What's your view of the fiction writer's role in the building up of Zion? Or, to put it another way, what do you think is the value of fiction both for communities and for individuals?

I'm not a prophet. I don't write scripture. Yet that doesn't free me from the necessity of being a moral writer.

I think that when you as a reader pick up a piece of fiction, to a certain extent you take an intimate journey into another person's mind. For a while at least, when you read my book, you see the world as I see it and think about it as I direct. If I am on a higher spiritual plateau than you are, then this can be uplifting. However, if I'm in a spiritual sewer, you probably really don't want to jump in with me.

One problem we have is that we are all at different levels of spirituality in different areas. For example, you might be a very honest person. You might be a perfect ten when it comes to telling the truth, even hard and ugly truths. At the same time, you might be only a four when it comes to compassion. So when a reader picks up your book, she might look at it and say, "You know, this author seems really cold and distant. This author is on a low spiritual plane," and she'd be perfectly right—in part.

Unfortunately, I'm not a perfect ten on all levels of spirituality. So, at the very least, one of my goals is to be a good host, to tell you a story you will enjoy or hopefully love, and to make the time you spend looking at the world through my eyes worthwhile.

But more important than that, in every story I write, I have characters who must become more decent, more compassionate, and stronger in order to reach their goals. That's not an accident. I suspect that as my readers undergo the protagonists' vicarious spiritual journeys, their hearts will also be changed, and they too will grow.

I would hope my readers would learn to hate the evils I hate—the greed, the violence, the lust and laziness that are so prevalent in our society—and that, just a little bit, my readers will grow.

---

[1] *Suffolk County News*, Sayville, New York, April 22, 1999.
[2] "The Gospel Vision of the Arts," *Ensign,* July 1977.

MARGARET YOUNG

Margaret Young
Novelist

As a writer, Margaret Blair Young moves freely between the literary and popular spheres, publishing both with small, independent journals and presses and large commercial houses. She is perhaps best known for Standing on the Promises, *the trilogy of historical novels about the black Mormon experience that she coauthored with Darius Gray. In addition, Young has published several novels, short story collections, individual short stories, essays, and some poetry. A part-time teacher of creative writing at Brigham Young University, Young has four children and two grandchildren and lives in Provo, Utah. She met her husband, BYU Shakespeare scholar Bruce Young, by taking his literary criticism class. The original version of this interview appeared in* Irreantum, *spring 2000.*

To start off, tell us a little about your earliest published works.

The first story I published in the *New Era* magazine was called "Mrs. Brant." It appeared in June 1979, and my byline was Margaret Blair. The second story they purchased was never published, to my knowledge. That one would've been under the byline of Margaret Blair Fox. Under the Fox name, I published an article about home birth in *Let's Live* magazine, a poem in *Sunstone*—I don't recall the title—and an article called "Artist of the Poor" in *Format: Art and the World*.

House without Walls was my first novel, published in 1991 by Deseret Book. Eugene England characterized it as "home literature"[1]—and it really is, though I'm not ashamed of it. The best story about *House* is that my mother probably bought most of the copies. She distributed them freely, including to a Russian woman, an English teacher, while Mom and Dad were teaching in Russia. This woman read my novel, which spoke to her in some very specific ways, then asked if she could read the Book of Mormon. She and her son, and later her husband, joined the church. When my dad, Robert Blair, was called to preside over the Baltic States mission, this woman's son was called to serve in that same mission.

Salvador was my first novel to win an award, the Utah Arts Council award for novel. Aspen Books published it in 1992, the same year that the University of Idaho Press published my short story collection, *Elegies and Love Songs*. The extent of the university press publicity was their own little catalogs, published on newsprint and sent to various university libraries, resulting in a grand total of 250 sales of my book.

Have you had a sense of breaking new ground in Mormon literature?

We probably need to look back to Virginia Sorensen and Maurine Whipple and Doug Thayer as the head groundbreakers, fine writers who took their culture seriously and wrote about it beautifully. And Levi Peterson is one of my most important mentors.

Mormonism is a bold faith with remarkable claims and a painful past. I am a Mormon who cherishes—or at least tries to charitably confront—some of the pain of my own Mormon history. I believe in the infinite worth of our mortal refining process and in grace. I believe that one of the greatest lessons we will learn in this life is compassion. In some way, all of my work deals with difficult circumstances which—I hope—call the reader to responsibility to comfort those in need of comfort. I hope that call can be extended without invoking clichés or offering easy, too convenient answers.

Give us an overview of the *Standing on the Promises* trilogy.

This project captured my heart—and time—more than any other project in my life. These inspiring, troubling stories have been surprisingly unknown in the church. My coauthor Darius Gray is an African-American who joined the church forty-one years ago, before the priesthood was available to him. Darius was called as the first counselor when the Genesis Group was organized by the First Presidency in 1971 as a support group for African-American Mormons, and he later served as president, reporting to a member of the Seventy.

The trilogy covers the lives of Elijah Abel and Jane James and their families, the three slaves who were in the first company to enter the Salt Lake Valley— Hark Lay, Oscar Crosby, and Green Flake—and Samuel Chambers, a slave who was secretly baptized in 1844 and then joined the Saints in Salt Lake after the Civil War. We also follow Darius's family, beginning with his great-grandfather, who was a slave near Independence, Missouri, at the time of the Saints' expulsion. We use equal parts documentation and imagination. Each chapter has endnotes.

We felt so strongly about this project. For Darius, it was in many ways the culmination of his work in the Genesis Group. It has provided a bridge for many black LDS converts struggling with the harsh words of past church leaders, and it has been well received by Caucasian readers who are already sensitized to race issues in the church, many of them adoptive parents of black or biracial children. It has sold reasonably well but not magnificently, and it has proved an uncomfortable read to some, since it deals with such hard history. The first book of the trilogy sold very well. The second book, which deals with the priesthood restriction and slavery in Utah, did not sell nearly so well. The third book, which covers the civil rights years, did slightly better than the second.

Before working on the trilogy, I used to read several short stories daily and usually a part of a novel. Since 1998, however, most of my reading has been black history or Mormon history. My eyes were opened in so many ways as I focused my research on the race issues in early Mormonism and even in contemporary Mormonism. Much of what I found has been very hard to stomach. There was one time when I was reading statements by former church leaders which were utterly racist, when Darius called me and said, "I just felt impressed that I needed to bear you my testimony. You're reading some hard things, and you need to know that the church is still true. It really does have the keys to God's authority on the earth." It was wonderful to have my guide through this difficult terrain be someone as wise and faithful as Darius.

What was it like writing with someone else? How did you accomplish it? What were the challenges and benefits?

I began writing what I thought would be one novel about black pioneers. I knew that, with my Scandinavian heritage, I didn't really have the background to do this. When I talked about it, I usually added an apology, saying I knew I shouldn't be writing a novel about blacks when I'm so white I can't even tan, but I felt someone needed to write it! Very shortly after I met Darius, I knew he and I were to write this together. The language I was trying for in the book was the language of his childhood; he knew it well. He also knew the history of blacks in the church—and outside of the church—better than anyone I've ever met. And he came with that wonderful genealogy which we could use.

As we worked together, we learned that Darius's contribution was not just linguistic but also logical. I love a good turn of phrase, but he is always looking for the realism of what we're describing. I can create great banter and dialogue between my characters, but he consistently asked me, "Would they actually say this in this circumstance?" and we went from there. We started with some predictable problems of pride, my feeling that I was the writer and he shouldn't interfere with the writing part of it, just help me get the dialect right. But as we worked, we came to respect each other's gifts. He was not shy about making suggestions. And I was not shy about rejecting his suggestions, though I usually didn't because he was usually right.

We really learned to work as a team. Another thing I realized is that it mattered that we were working from two races and two genders. At one point, I thought that when it was done, I'd relinquish marketing to Darius. However, as I spoke to my husband and friends, I came to feel that my whiteness matters too. My presence as coauthor blunts the concerns of anyone thinking the trilogy represents some black guy grinding an axe. And Darius covers the concerns of folks who might accuse me of writing about people I couldn't possibly understand.

You've written, "As a teacher of writing and literature, I find that my students are hungry for good writing, that they feel betrayed by easy resolutions and cheap tears." Will you discuss whether you think such readers are finding more to satisfy them in today's Mormon literature? How can writers reach more readers who perhaps choose not to read Mormon fiction at all because of those easy resolutions and cheap tears?

Before answering that, I should confess that I no longer consider myself a "Mormon writer." I'm still Mormon and still a writer, but I don't see myself publishing with a Mormon house in the future. My personal bookshelves are full of great literature—none of it by Mormons. Darius and I are rewriting the trilogy with hopes of publishing it for a national audience, once Deseret Book returns our rights. We have come upon so much more information than we had when we began the trilogy, and we really want to make the books more accurate and more interesting for any reader, not just a Mormon reader. My other writing projects use Mormonism as a context but aim for a much wider audience than those who frequent Seagull Book. And my main project currently is not a book but a documentary, directed by Alex Nibley and produced by Richard Dutcher, called *Nobody Knows: The Untold Story of Black Mormons*. We have some magnificent, unprecedented footage.

I don't want to sound like a naysayer when I talk about Mormon writers, however. The truth is, we are at a good place in Mormon literature. It's not as good as the place we're heading to, but it's far beyond the world of 1970s romance writer Shirley Sealy. I'm thinking not just about fiction but also playwriting. What a coup for Tim Slover to have *A Joyful Noise* play off Broadway and to be under contract to write more plays! And Eric Samuelsen is a remarkably gifted playwright. In poetry, we have the likes of Susan Howe and Lance Larsen, both published in well-respected journals outside the Mountain West. In fiction, Dean Hughes has shown the depth of his gift in his World War Two series, evidenced by his receiving the Association for Mormon Letters award for the novel in 1997. Marilyn Brown has always had such a talent; I hope her work will get more attention in the future. John Bennion is a fine writer. And Brady Udall is probably our best and has received the national attention he deserves. I'm almost afraid to name names, because there are so many fine authors and I wouldn't want to leave someone out. Those I've named are all active Mormons, as far as I now. There are some less-orthodox Mormons, like Terry Tempest Williams and Phyllis Barber, who have written about our culture and have been very well received outside Utah.

We are doing better. Of course, we still have a lot of sentimental literature, as does much of popular culture, Mormon or non. But we are making tremendous strides. Perhaps our biggest obstacle is that we have a reputation for sugary work replete with clichés, and those who are hungry for meatier fare will tend to presume the whole of Mormon literature can be lumped into a pile of saccharine. Consequently, most of our finest writers will not be looking through Mormon literature to find their mentors but will delve into Pulitzer winners' works.

Tell us about your teaching profession. How does teaching writing and literature affect you as a writer? Is it even possible to teach creative writing?

You bet it's possible to teach creative writing. Much of the process is simply opening up my students to their own voices and their own perceptions, then letting them find their writerly intuition and pursue it. And they do. They really do grow as writers as they read excellent writing—which is essential—and do daily exercises that increase their sensitivity to the world around them. During a poetry unit, I opened each class with two questions: "What poets have you fallen in love with since last class?" and "What have you seen with your poetic eyes?" I got wonderful responses.

I love teaching. I've heard writers say they hate teaching amateurs, because they are inundated with so much lousy writing when the assignments come in. I do not feel that way at all. Rather, I find delightful phrases or insights or images in just about everything my students write. Sure, there are lots of clichés as the kids get started, but we trash those in pretty short order. Most importantly, I get close to my students. As my world expands to include them and their unique experiences, perceptions, and voices, I have that much more fodder for my own writing.

How did you come to writing in general and to Mormon writing? What works of Mormon literature have you personally most enjoyed? What works of general literature?

The Brothers Karamazov was my great initiation. I read it in high school. On one of my trips to Guatemala—which I visited with some frequency with my linguist father, who was studying and teaching Mayan dialects—I took two books besides my scriptures: *Moby-Dick* and Doug Thayer's *Under the Cottonwoods*. One of my non-Mormon friends from high school gave me Don Marshall's *Rummage Sale* for my birthday when I turned eighteen, and I enjoyed it thoroughly. I've already mentioned others of my mentors in Mormon writing.

In general writing, I find my mentors change as my projects change. For years, the author Charles Baxter was one of my favorites, and he started me on several stories in *Love Chains*. Toni Morrison's *Beloved* was perhaps the most influential book I've read because of where it led me.

As far as "coming to writing," I knew for years I wanted to be a writer. The first story I wrote took me a year to finish. I was twenty-one, and it was quite an apprenticeship. I had not realized it was so difficult to write well—I had sold a couple of stories to the *New Era*, but they were not really good stories. Now I have a solid sense of what it takes, and I'm grateful to have the time and energy—and by now a bit of ability—to devote to writing books I care about deeply.

Most fiction is a combination of three elements: what the author has experienced, observed, and imagined. How do those three elements work together for you? How much is autobiographical?

There's the old writer's cliché, "Write about what you know." I have not always obeyed it. When I came to BYU to begin what I anticipated would be my writing career, I "created" stories with mazelike symbols and Mormon themes. I was reading great literature, but all classics. I didn't even know who the contemporary authors were. Professor Bruce Jorgensen made a list for me of about twenty contemporary authors, and I began reading them. Then one night—or actually very early one morning—I began writing something from my own life. No symbols or set-up themes. I had just gone through an excruciating divorce, and I began writing about life with my ex-husband. For several weeks, I would get up at 3:00 A.M. and write that story. Ultimately, I sold it to the *Southern Review*. It was called "Grandpa's Growth" and is also in *Elegies and Love Songs*. That was how I came to understand the "Write about what you know" rule.

So most of my short stories are autobiographical. My novel *Salvador* certainly is. And my play *Dear Stone*—the novel version is called *Heresies of Nature*—though fictionalized, sprang from the life of my husband's sister, Nancy, who died of multiple sclerosis the very day we opened the play. It was an emotional time. Bruce and I had been with Nancy as she died. I called Eric Samuelsen, who had directed *Dear Stone*, and we opened the play as scheduled, dedicating it to Nancy. Bruce had already written the program notes paying tribute to his sister. Of course, the black pioneer trilogy inhabits a world I do not know, which is why it's so essential that I had a coauthor.

Tell us more about your writing habits.

When my babies were little, their naptime was always my writing time, regardless of the condition of the house. I produced a bunch of bad writing during most of those years but learned essential things. I do not demand any conditions for my writing now except time. I don't need to be in a cabin by the ocean or in some Samoan rainforest to get inspired. If I did, I wouldn't have done any writing.

I try to keep the right balance in all the things I'm doing—and I've spoken about that on a number of occasions—but I do find that if I go to the computer near bedtime to do just one or two revisions, several hours will go by without my being aware of the time, and my mind will be so filled with ideas for revisions or plot developments that I won't be able to get to sleep. So Bruce has decided my computer time should be restricted to daytime hours. I usually go along with that.

Because I still have children at home, I do not have the luxury of unlimited writing time, and I find that's good. I tend to leave my writing against my will, but that will pulls me back to it the next day. For the trilogy, I read probably fifty books and kept a file of research notes on my computer, and I continue to research the history. Generally speaking, I have occasionally outlined a plot, but I rarely follow the outline as my characters take on life and decide where they want to go. I usually let them lead me.

Do your books have happy endings? How do you handle flaws in your characters? How do you balance portraying things realistically versus idealistically? What about potentially explicit things like sex and violence?

My books tend to have rather ambiguous endings. I handle flaws in my characters with joy and delight. And I tend much more toward the realistic than the idealistic. There is sex and violence in some of my work. I address this in my opening essay in *Love Chains*. I do not believe in gratuitous sex or violence or in sentimentality.

What has been the general reaction to your story "God on *Donahue*" in *Love Chains*, specifically the reaction to showing God possibly as a character in a pop culture setting?

Some have predictably been offended. I have never considered that the character I created in the hitchhiker was actually God, but he certainly was God in Joseph's imagination, and what Joseph imagined led him to his own epiphany.

Could you comment on the temple as a presence in your fiction? It's in *Salvador, Love Chains, House without Walls* . . .

And it is essential in the trilogy, since the characters—black pioneers all based on real people—desperately wanted temple privileges, which were easily available to white Mormons but not to them. Elijah Abel helped build the Kirtland and Nauvoo temples and was washed and anointed in the Kirtland temple. He helped build the Salt Lake temple too but was denied permission to be sealed there to his wife, though he held the Melchizedek priesthood. This is a sad history for all of us Mormons, but Elijah's answer to the denial should inspire us: He finished his life by serving his third mission for the church. He returned early, very ill, and died two weeks later, on Christmas day. That same day, Jane James walked to President John Taylor's home to begin her own petitions to enter the temple. She continued her petitions until the end of her life.

I certainly see the temple as more symbolic of my faith than a regular Mormon chapel. In the temple, borders come down as we dress alike and speak alike, in some ways. So much of my writing deals with borders we set up between ourselves and others, and the temple is one place that truly teaches us that we are "alike unto God."

You've been involved in the Association for Mormon Letters, *Dialogue*, and other independent intellectual and cultural efforts. What are your thoughts, observations, and hopes related to the place of such efforts in the overall Mormon community?

My hope is for greater unity for all of us Mormons: black and white, male and female, liberal and conservative, intellectual and nonintellectual. And frankly, I hope we do better with outreach to other faith communities. We simply cannot afford to label each other as enemies, as some have done. We cannot afford to nurture our prejudices. We cannot afford to refuse to look at ourselves and our history squarely. Our errors in judgment and our leaders' troublesome past statements are readily available on the Internet, and future generations will find them, as current generations do. I celebrate the ways *Dialogue* and *Sunstone* have really tried lately to explore Mormon thought in nondivisive ways. I am glad to have Levi Peterson editing *Dialogue* and fully support the direction he's taking it.

Have you sent out much for consideration by national agents and publishers? Do you think we'll ever have a Mormon Saul Bellow or Flannery O'Connor, someone winning a Pulitzer or National Book Award for fiction that deals with Mormon themes, settings, and characters?

I've worked with an agent but found that her enthusiasm for my work didn't match the publishers'. She was a New York Jewish woman who learned that Mormon writing doesn't generally invite much of a national audience. Ultimately, she negotiated my contract with Aspen for *Salvador* and got me an advance from the University of Idaho for *Elegies*. More recently, I've marketed my own stuff. But I plan on using my agent in the future.

We've certainly seen some Mormon writers break into the national market, but the cases are rare. Levi Peterson could not sell *The Backslider* nationally, though it's one of the best things any of us Mormon writers has done. Brian Evenson may, in the future, be considered the Mormon Flannery O'Connor because of the grotesqueness of his characters, but his work doesn't have the redemptive qualities of O'Connor's. Brady Udall is doing marvelous work, and he may well be the one to join historian Laurel Thatcher Ulrich as a Mormon Pulitzer Prize winner.

What will it take to get Mormon characters and themes before a national audience? What kinds of stories, characters, plots? People love reading about Asians, Jews, Catholics—why not Mormons more often?

Well, we obviously have had Mormon books and characters before a national audience, but the portrayals have been, almost without exception, biased, often even demonic, as though we are all some version of Mark Hofmann, or sexual deviants, or protectors of sexual deviants. Conversely, we have the problem of home literature that protects more than it reveals and thus would come across as unrealistic and preachy to a national audience.

Richard Dutcher's film *States of Grace* taught us a great lesson as we watched how it was received outside of Utah. Though it is, I believe, the best Mormon film yet made and fully accessible—even moving—to non-Mormons, moviegoers were asked if they were Christians before they bought their tickets and then told that this was a "Mormon" film. Apparently, some evangelical Christians had complained that they had gone to the movie unwarned and then found they were watching Mormon missionaries. Now I'm guessing that if *Under the Banner of Heaven* were made into a movie, it would do very well—and nobody would get interrogated about their religious inclinations before buying a ticket.

We are dealing with a very bad reputation, and it will take some time to get beyond that. Any book that is overtly, faithfully Mormon will face the same challenges Dutcher's movie faced, and, frankly, it probably wouldn't find a national publisher in the first place. I would love to be proved wrong, and I'm hopeful that someday I will be. I hope that someday my books—the ones I haven't yet written—will be read as good literature, not good Mormon literature. I hope that good art coming from Mormons will eventually be met with open minds rather than directions to Recovery from Mormonism. But we must play our part too. We Mormons must transcend our self-protectiveness and do what good writers do: communicate truth through well-crafted language and believable characters who confront uncensored obstacles and don't always find happy endings.

I don't see a Mormon press publishing a genuinely great novel—not with the concerns Mormon presses have, given the audiences they cater to. But I do see fine writers coming from our culture and setting foot on the world stage, adding our distinctive voices to the dynamic symphony the best literature creates.

---

[1] In the 1880s, Orson F. Whitney called for a fine and virtuous "home literature" among the Latter-day Saints, characterized by moralistic, faith-promoting, and didactic literature.